FEB 2 1 2001

Experimental Lives:
Women and Literature, 1900–1945

TWAYNE'S WOMEN AND LITERATURE SERIES

Kinley E. Roby, General Editor

Experimental Lives:

Women and Literature, 1900–1945

MARY LOEFFELHOLZ

Twayne Publishers • New York
Maxwell Macmillan Canada • Toronto
Maxwell Macmillan International • New York Oxford Singapore Sydney

Twayne Publishers	Maxwell Macmillan Canada, Inc.
Macmillan Publishing Company	1200 Eglinton Avenue East
866 Third Avenue	Suite 200
New York, New York 10022	Don Mills, Ontario M3C 3N1

Macmillan Publishing Company is part of the Maxwell Communication Group of Companies.

LIBRARY OF CONGRESS CATALOGING-IN-PUBLICATION DATA

Loeffelholz, Mary, 1958–
     Experimental lives : women and literature, 1900–1945 / Mary Loeffelholz.
         p.   cm. — (Twayne's women and literature series)
     Includes bibliographical references (p.   ) and index.
     ISBN 0-8057-8976-6 (hc) : $22.95. — ISBN 0-8057-8977-4 (pb) : $13.95
     1. Women and literature—Great Britain—History—20th century.
     2. Women and literature—United States—History—20th century.
     3. American literature—Women authors—History and criticism.
     4. English literature—Women authors—History and criticism.
     5. American literature—20th century—History and criticism.
     6. English literature—20th century—History and criticism.
     I. Title.   II. Series.
     PR116.L64   1992   92-5265
     820.9′9287—dc20   CIP

The paper used in this publication meets the minimum requirements
of American National Standard for Information Sciences—Permanence
of Paper for Printed Library Materials. ANSI Z3948-1984. ∞™

10   9   8   7   6   5   4   3   2   1

PRINTED IN THE UNITED STATES OF AMERICA

Contents

CONTENTS

General Editor's Note

The Twayne's Women and Literature Series seeks to provide a critical history of British and American women writers from the Anglo-Saxon age to the modern era and to present women as the subject as well as the creators of literature and to say something about how these dual roles have helped to shape our societies. It is often a record of struggle by women to write, to be published, and to find a sympathetic audience for their work. Each of the volumes examines the cultural influences at work shaping women's roles during a particular period and the attendant consequences for them as women and writers. The Series also presents a chronological account of women's efforts to find and develop their own voices in environments frequently hostile to their being heard at all.

Foreword

One of the great tasks facing this generation of scholars is the construction of women's literary history. Mary Loeffelholz's study of American and British women writers of the first half of the twentieth century is a major contribution to this cultural work.

Such work is not just a necessary compensatory revision of biased literary histories, flawed because they ignore or minimize women's contributions. It also is important because it inherently challenges prevailing sexist ideologies that continue to position women in subservient roles. For knowledge is power. As women learn about the richnesses and complexities of their own cultural history, their political identity *as women* is strengthened. Their sense of themselves and of their possibilities expands.

In reviewing Loeffelholz's survey one is struck by the enormous variety and prodigious originality of women's literary production during this period. From the brilliant creation of the interior monologue by Dorothy Richardson and Virginia Woolf to the complex interweavings of race, class, and gender in Zora Neale Hurston's *Their Eyes Were Watching God*—belatedly recognized as an American classic—to Agnes Smedley's anguished reconstruction of rural poverty in *Daughter of Earth*, the inspired character of the writing of this period is unmistakable. It is a women's literary renaissance.

Indeed, the creative outpouring in this period was so intense one is prompted to speculate why. While undoubtedly the women writers were affected by the same historical currents as the male modernists, there were other factors, I believe, that were critical for the women. One of these, surprisingly (given the mistaken tendency to write off the nineteenth-century women's movement as a failure), was the suffrage movement. Despite its limited success as a revolutionary transformation, the women's rights movement did manage to raise serious questions about gender identity, such that the old certainties about what a woman was or what her proper role or behavior should be had been fractured by the early twentieth century. Indeed, major theoretical justifications for maintaining women's traditional role of passive subservience—a kind of backlash—were reintroduced in the late nineteenth century in the form of Social Darwinism (Darwin himself argued that women were intellectually inferior in *The Descent of Man* [1871]) and the various "sexologies" of the time, such as Richard von Krafft-Ebing's *Psychopathia Sexualis*. These ideological reformulations were enormously influential and contributed to the devalorization of the feminine that occurred in the pre–World War I era.

Nevertheless, the old certainties could not be reconstituted. As Virginia Woolf announced in "Mr. Bennett and Mrs. Brown" (1924), "in or about December 1910, human character changed." "The mirror was broken," she reiterated in *To the Lighthouse*. "The world broke in two in 1922 or thereabout" was how Willa Cather put it. A kind of ideological earthquake had indeed occurred and its seismic patterns reverberate in the works of these women writers.

One can go so far, I believe, as to say that a profound "anxiety of identity" distinguishes the women writers of this period from preceding generations of women writers. It is perhaps this anxiety, about their identity as women in connection with their identity as writers, that subtends the other uncertainties about boundaries seen in their work. For much of the energy in modernism stems from its critique of conventional forms—particularly in art, but also in life. Indeed, the boundary between life and art was itself called into question. But it appears, however, that for the women writers, the primary boundary being challenged was that defining conventional gender identities.

Thus, for example, conventional plots are seen as inadequate, conventional stylistic devices are replaced, even conventional ideas of genre, of what constitutes literature, and of aesthetics are rejected. "What I have written," Agnes Smedley proclaimed, "is not a work of beauty."

At times the energies of these women took the form of rebellion against their literary predecessors. For some, this meant killing the "angel in the house," as Virginia Woolf put it. This comment is usually interpreted to mean that a writer must put aside the subservient selflessness expected of women in a patriarchal society. However, killing the angel also can mean killing the mother, rebelling against one's female antecedents. Many in this generation of writers—probably because of its uncertainties about gender identity—were in rebellion against their actual or literary mothers. Edith Wharton, for example, said she wrote *Ethan Frome* in order to counter what she saw as the "rose-coloured" version of New England presented in the works of her "predecessors," Mary E. Wilkins Freeman and Sarah Orne Jewett. There are no mythic analogues for daughter rebellion in Western mythology; the closest we have is Persephone's disaffiliation from Demeter, but her behavior is so passive—she is really a victim of abduction by Hades in the original myth—that she provides at best an ambiguous model of a daughter-rebel. Yet it may be that there is a pattern in women's literary traditions somewhat parallel to what Harold Bloom has called the "anxiety of influence" in men's traditions, of the son rebelling (anxiously) against powerful paternal predecessors. This is an area that deserves further exploration by feminist scholars.

I offer these sketchy comments only to point to the kind of issue yet to be fully explored in women's literature. Comprehensive studies such as this by Mary Loeffelholz stimulate such speculation and thus invite further research. They also help us as general readers and as teachers to chart the terrain, and as scholars to hold our bearings as we continue the enormous, exciting labor of feminist critical revision.

Josephine Donovan
UNIVERSITY OF MAINE

CHAPTER
1

Introduction

Historical Issues

The immense changes in women's status in Western societies of the twentieth century are often indexed with reference to a single achievement: the granting of the vote to women, the goal on which most late-nineteenth-century women's rights organizations had come to set their primary energies. The years immediately after World War I saw women achieve the elective franchise in both England and the United States. Inspired or shamed partly by women's war service in both countries, the British Parliament, the U.S. Congress, and the state legislatures of the United States finally ratified women's right to vote. In the United States, the Nineteenth Amendment finally passed a two-thirds majority of the state legislatures and became law in 1920. In England, suffrage rights were granted to women over 30 in 1918, and extended to all women over 21 in 1928. Other countries also granted citizenship rights to women in this period; women won the franchise in Canada, Germany, and the Soviet Union after World War I, in France and Italy after World War II.

There are other important markers of women's advances in these years, however. Women's gains in the sphere of political and juridical rights were matched by their increasingly meaningful access to education, especially higher education. In the United States, several of the premier women's colleges—institutions like Mount Holyoke, Smith, Vassar, and Wellesley—had been established in the late nineteenth century. The state land-grant universities founded across the country after the Civil War admitted women, although frequently to different programs than men. A few women made inroads in previously all-male elite institutions: M. Carey Thomas (who would become the president of Bryn Mawr) at Cornell, for example, and Gertrude Stein at Johns Hopkins. Some black women in the United States attended mostly white colleges; when Bryn Mawr rejected Jessie Redmon Fauset on grounds of her race, she went on to take her degree in classics at Cornell. More found their way to black colleges, both coeducational schools and those, like Spelman College in Atlanta, founded specifically for black women; by 1930, Paula Giddings observes, "four out of every ten graduates from black colleges were women and their numbers were increasing."[1] Women began organizing colleges at Oxford and Cambridge in England in the second half of the nineteenth century, and received their first degrees at Oxford in 1920—partly, as with the elective franchise, in reward for women's war service.

These gains took place, however, amid vigorous debate over the purpose and legitimacy of women's higher education. Proponents argued that women deserved a higher education every bit as rigorous as that accorded to men, on grounds of individual fulfillment, service to humankind, and (rather a more doubtful argument) improvement in their capacity to be good wives and mothers. Opponents countered that women were innately different from men, and destined to fill quite different roles; therefore, a traditional male-defined education would actually unfit women for their traditional roles as wives and mothers.

Opponents of women's education had, from their perspective, some legitimate reasons for anxiety. The "New Women"—as people began to call "single, highly educated, economically autonomous" young women college graduates around the end of the nineteenth century—indeed "constituted a revolutionary demographic and political phenomenon."[2] Some demographic evidence suggests that higher education did in fact— in one way or another—"unfit" women "for marriage and motherhood; the experience of power both as individuals and as a group, the experience of winning, the experience of assuming a dominant role, changed them irrevocably."[3] On both sides of the Atlantic, the first waves of women to attend the elite women's colleges married at much lower rates than did the rest of the female population. "Eschewing marriage," the college-educated New Woman instead "fought for professional visibility, espoused innovative, often radical, economic and social reforms, and wielded real political power" (Smith-Rosenberg, 245).

The debate over women's education had not been settled by the first or second decades of the twentieth century. But this much was sure: many women, black and white, from many parts of the class scale, were determined to secure a college-level education. While the elite women's colleges obviously catered to a privileged minority, they made some efforts to reach other sorts of students with scholarship and work-study programs, and state colleges and universities were somewhat more accessible. Women who graduated from college could hope to make professional careers, although barriers to their entry into the traditional masculine professions were still steep. Some medical schools opened their doors to women; some women became professors in colleges and universities, with the women's colleges and women-oriented programs (such as home economics) in mixed schools offering the most employment opportunities; the law was more difficult for women to enter. For the most part, however, "rather than entering the established masculine professions, women in the nineteenth and early twentieth century participated in the development of a new set of professions—secondary school teaching, social work, nursing, and library work."[4] Coded as feminine, these new professions took in many college graduates. Young white middle-class women were also funneled into clerical work, increasingly typed as feminine—and turned into dead-end positions—in the early twentieth century, work that required education but scarcely drew on college graduates' full capacities.

Educated black women entered a labor market segregated by race as well as gender. In some areas, like "the dental, legal, medical, and nursing professions," black women could find a niche by serving their own communities, although often for lower fees than white practitioners could expect to earn. Civil service positions were sometimes accessible to black women, sometimes not, depending on the attitudes of a particular administration. Yet retail and corporate jobs, the expanding consumer and bureaucratic capitalist sectors of the American economy, were more often than not closed to black women (Giddings, 147). Far more likely than white women to be employed outside the home (in 1900, "22.7% of black married women were in the labor force, as compared to only 3.2% of whites" [Matthaei, 133]), black women were clustered in the low-paying fields of agriculture and domestic service.

Radical differences among women in terms of economic status and access to education, of course, were not new in the early twentieth century, but these differences did take on new forms with the opening of formal higher education and some professions to women. Many women did make efforts to work with other women across the boundaries of race and class. Working-class women in the trades and industry, many from immigrant families, began to unionize in greater numbers in the first two decades of the century, and mounted large strikes for better working conditions and higher pay; some privileged women seconded their efforts and marched in their demonstrations. Working-class black women and their allies sought to build alliances with mostly white women's organizations like the YWCA, which in 1920 "went on record as advocating collective bargaining, the rights of workers, and economic justice" (Giddings, 155). Yet too often these alliances were short-lived; the rhetoric and sympathy drawing women to one another could not overcome other basic differences of allegiance and conflicts of interest.

For some observers, both at the time and later, the achievement of formal citizenship rights along with access (in theory) to professional and other kinds of work for women in the 1920s signaled "the end of feminism." From here on, many contemporary observers suggested, women could advance along paths already opened to them; they could achieve their goals as individuals, no longer needing to work together as a self-conscious political group. Women had now only to adjust their own ambitions to their new opportunities, to decide their own future courses, and work out in their own lives, with their own partners, some combination of women's old domestic duties with women's new vocations in the public world. Where there were practical difficulties, the magic new technologies—electricity, preserved foods, household appliances—would lift women's old domestic drudgery off their backs, and free them to pursue work outside the home.[5] The New Woman, some thought, could and would grow up to become everywoman, or at least many women.

Present-day historians, looking back on the 1920s, have often agreed that the decade indeed saw the end of what is sometimes called the "first wave" of American and British feminism. But they do not necessarily see the following decades as a sustained triumph for women. They point to the dissolution of the large suffrage organizations and the absence of issues uniting women on a national level in both countries from roughly 1920 to the late 1960s, when an international "second wave" of feminism began to emerge. In certain respects, these historians argue, women lost the momentum of the first decades of the century in the 1930s and 1940s. American women's participation in higher education and some professions, for instance, actually peaked in the decade between 1910 and 1920, and fell off in the 1940s and 1950s.[6]

Historian Nancy Cott has recently challenged the "end of feminism" thesis, however. Feminism could not have ended in 1920, Cott argues, because strictly speaking it had not even been born yet. She points out that the word *feminism* itself entered the English language and began to be widely used only after 1910: "Only a rare quirk prior to 1910, usage of *feminism* became frequent by 1913 and almost unremarkable a few years later" (Cott, 13). The old nineteenth-century women's rights organizations had not used the word; Elizabeth Cady Stanton and Susan B. Anthony did not describe themselves as feminists. If the 1920s indeed saw the demise of the earlier women's rights movement, these years also, Cott argues, saw the rise of something new, designated by the new tag, "feminism."

The new feminists—men among them—tended to think of themselves as more modern and radical than activists in the older "Woman movement," as it was called. Beyond women's suffrage, they wanted "freedom for all forms of women's active expression, elimination of all structural and psychological handicaps to women's economic independence, an end to the double standard of sexual morality, release from constraining sexual stereotypes, and opportunity to shine in every civic and professional opportunity" (Cott, 15). More explicitly than the nineteenth-century activists, the new feminists exalted individual fulfillment for women as human beings. Where some in the earlier movement made claims for women's special virtues, "feminists offered no sure definition of who woman was; rather, they sought to end the classification *woman*. They posited a paradoxical group idea of individuality," acting as a group in order to abolish women's special disadvantages as a group (Cott, 8). Without one central political goal (as suffrage had earlier been), without one single definition of *woman*, the activities of the new feminism, Cott argues, were correspondingly more diffuse and variegated than those of the old Woman movement.

Whatever their specific interpretations of the shifts in women's consciousness in the 1920s, feminist historians agree that the triumph of the women's suffrage movement and the opening of colleges and professions to women left plenty of unfinished business, both for relatively privileged women and for others. It was not so easy, after all, for women to demand or receive treatment as individuals. White professional women found both subtle and not-so-subtle discrimination blocking their advancement. Since the woman's struggle had presumably been won, however, many of them hesitated to blame discrimination for their difficulties; they blamed themselves instead, as individuals, for not sufficiently internalizing the standards of the male professional world (Cott, 226–35). Black women, facing institutionalized racism as well as institutionalized sexism, may well have been less inclined to imagine that their failures were only individual, more willing to see feminism as an ongoing necessity. Yet, as Elise MacDougal wrote about black women's activism in 1925, black women's "feminist efforts are directed chiefly toward the realization of the equality of the races, the sex struggle assuming a subordinate place" (cited in Giddings, 183).

Subordinate or unacknowledged, however, the "sex struggle" over paid work went on. In both professional and nonprofessional occupations, job segregation by sex—the assumption that certain kinds of work belong only to men, others only to women—persisted then as it persists today, overriding individual preferences or abilities. Jobs typed as "feminine" paid less. Efforts to unionize women's work ran up against resistance from male-dominated unions and division among women workers themselves. Some white women resisted and feared competition from black women, just as white male workers feared competition from women workers, who might undercut their wages. Some women wanted wages and jobs identical to men's; others argued that women's hours should be shorter, their working conditions less hazardous, because of women's special roles and physiology.

It was above all this crucial question—the relationship between women's domestic roles, especially as mothers, and paid work—that the triumph of the nineteenth-century women's rights movement left unresolved. The earlier New Woman accepted, even gloried in, her unmarried state; younger women were determined to forge alternatives. As a Smith College student editorialized in 1919, "we cannot believe it is fixed in the nature of things that a woman must choose between a home and her work, when a man may have both. There must be a way out and it is the problem of our generation to find the way" (cited in Cott, 181). Combining dominant models of middle-class motherhood with paid employment turned out to be difficult indeed. Men, as a rule, did not care to assume more housework and child care, nor did they desire economically independent wives. The collective housekeeping arrangements advocated by feminist thinkers like Charlotte Perkins Gilman and Ethel Puffer Howe failed to materialize on any large scale, either in the Western capitalist democracies or in the Soviet Union after the revolution of 1917, where they were to have been an integral part of Marxism's answer to "the Woman question." While more married white women did enter the U.S. labor force throughout the first half of the twentieth century, joining the large numbers of married black women who had long done paid work outside their homes, public opinion in England and the United States remained strongly against the employment of mothers with young children. Individual ambition, striving, and independence in the public world were all very well for men, and increasingly so for unmarried women; but competitive individualism and motherly self-sacrifice did not seem to mix.

The choices between work and love for women in the first half of the twentieth century were complicated for other reasons, as well. Around the turn of the century, new ideas about women's sexuality and new ideals for marriage began entering popular discourse. The work of Sigmund Freud in Austria, the founder of psychoanalysis, and of Havelock Ellis in England, one of the founders of the new academic discipline of "sexology," began to shape distinctly modern notions of sexuality. According to Freud and Ellis, sexuality was a natural and not necessarily evil human instinct that society systematically repressed. Viewing conventional religious and moral sanctions on sexuality with skepticism, Freud and Ellis both questioned whether repression ultimately served human happiness. While Freud, at least, did not believe that repression could be wholly done away with in human life, most popularized versions of his theories "presented the sexual impulse as an insistent force demanding expression."[7] According to Freud and Ellis, women and even children, not just grown men, were sexual creatures. Challenging Victorian ideals of women's sexual "passionlessness," the new psychologies of sex asserted that women desired and needed sexual fulfillment.

The impact of these new ideas, coupled with other social changes, on actual women's lives was mixed. For some women, the freedom to acknowledge and explore sexual desires, within and sometimes outside of marriage, was utterly exhilarating or quietly satisfying. Social scientists began surveying women about their sexuality—itself a development that speaks volumes—and found out that many women desired and found sexual satisfaction in marriage. For young unmarried men and women, an emerging youth culture spread from the urban working classes out to the middle-class suburbs, helped by the introduction of the automobile, which "marked the end of the 'gentleman caller' who sat in the parlor," and by the availability of work outside the home or family farm. "Increasing economic independence led to less parental supervision over premarital behavior, at the same time that work allowed the young to continue to meet away from home" (D'Emilio and Freedman, 240).

Nowhere are changing attitudes toward women's sexuality better marked than in the early-twentieth-century birth-control movement.

Families in America and England had attempted to limit births well before the twentieth century, a trend that moved faster among professional than working-class couples, and that accelerated around the beginning of the century. In the United States, over the course of the nineteenth century, "the average number of children per (white) woman fell by half, from 7.04 in 1800 to 3.56 in 1900" (Matthaei, 169). In Great Britain, "an average working-class family had 5.11 children in the 1890s; an average professional family, 2.80. By the 1920s, the working-class family was down to 3.05 children; the professional family, to 1.69."[8] These steep declines began in the absence of major advances in contraceptive technology, and so must be attributed in large measure to conscious decisions on the part of women and cooperating men to limit family size by the means available—chiefly abortion, abstinence, withdrawal, pessaries (ancestor of the diaphragm) and condoms.[9]

Public discourse about sexuality and contraception in the late nineteenth century, however, had not always kept pace with practice. The Comstock Act of 1873 attempted to outlaw the distribution of contraceptives and contraceptive information through the U.S. mail. From another political angle, nineteenth-century middle-class feminists advocated "voluntary motherhood" for women, reasoning that if the vocation of motherhood was so sacred, it ought to be entered upon only with full choice and deliberation by women. "Voluntary motherhood" placed less emphasis on contraception than on women's right to refuse male sexual advances, "which they perceived to be riddled with danger, contamination (through prostitution), and the perpetual double standard" (Petchesky, 44).

The twentieth-century birth-control movement overturned the basic assumption of the "voluntary motherhood" campaign that sexuality was intrinsically dangerous to, and undesired by, respectable women: "To advocate fertility control for women through access to contraceptive devices rather than through abstinence implied an unequivocal acceptance of female sexual expression. It weakened the link between sexual activity and procreation, altered the meaning of the marriage bond, and opened the way for more extensive premarital sexual behavior among women" (D'Emilio and Freedman, 233). If most nineteenth-century feminists had attempted to eliminate the sexual double standard by bringing men around to women's standards of sexual purity, many twentieth-century feminists and sex radicals (both men and women) sought instead to give women the same freedom of sexual choice as men.

8

Less radically, the idea of "companionate marriage" gained currency in the early twentieth century. In contrast to the nineteenth-century model of "separate spheres" for women and men, private and public, supposedly fulfilling the quite different natures of the two genders, companionate marriage emphasized similarities and shared ground between husband and wife. In the family envisioned by the ideology of separate spheres, a husband-breadwinner fought for the family tooth and nail in the jungle of the public sphere, while his wife created a pure and loving "haven in a heartless world" for children—and the exhausted father—at home. The ideology of companionate marriage assumed that women might not be sequestered in the home all their lives, that educated women, with some experience of their own in the public sphere, could talk to men on their own terms, as equal companions rather than as members of a different species. For separate-sphere ideology, home was the sacred abode of Mother; companionate marriage foregrounded instead the value of heterosexual intimacy between husband and wife.

In practice, however, the ideals of companionate marriage ran up against the unresolved problem of combining careers with motherhood—as well as other, deep-seated forms of prejudice and desire. Who decided which of two equal companions would assume responsibility for looking after the children, or for minding the house that, all labor-saving appliances notwithstanding, refused to mind itself? Valuing heterosexual intimacy between equals did not settle problems rooted in the gendered division of labor. And both men and women could be ambivalent about the new fashions (especially of the 1920s) and romantic ideals that valued—to a point—common characteristics among the two genders. Where did a spunky, bright, boyishly desirable female companion end, and a competitive, mannish, overbearing New Woman begin?

New fashions of romance, sexuality, and marriage, along with new ideas of female psychology, did not eliminate timeworn vocabularies of derogation reserved for women who usurped male prerogatives. Indeed, Freudian psychology added new scientific authority to those old saws, asserting that women who competed with men in traditionally male spheres of aspiration were driven by "penis envy," the inability to accept their biological destiny as women. If the new psychologists of sex attributed sexual drives to women, they also prescribed where and how those drives were to be fulfilled: in relationships with men, ideally culminating in the birth of male children—which compensated women, Freud thought, for their "missing" penis. "For women, psychology, like so many

9

other progressive intellectual movements before it, reiterated in new language the oldest and most limiting strictures about their lives" (Anderson and Zinsser, 217).

For women not committed to heterosexual relationships, the ideas of the new sexologists and changing ideals of women's sexuality posed even harsher dilemmas. In the nineteenth-century era of separate spheres, unmarried middle-class women could fit, if sometimes as subordinate figures, into the female-centered, middle-class world of hearth and home—"the female world of love and ritual," as one historian has called it. [10] Whether married or unmarried, women could enjoy strong and physically affectionate bonds with one another. Later in the nineteenth and early twentieth century, women took their bonds outside the home, re-creating in the new women's colleges and settlement houses (missions run by wealthier women in poor urban neighborhoods) the emotional ties of the private sphere (D'Emilio and Freedman, 190–91). Since women were thought to be fundamentally different from men, by nature and social experience, it made sense for women to feel closer to other women. Since middle-class women, by contrast with men, were thought to have little sexual drive, their physical affection with one another was not socially suspect, nor scrutinized and categorized in either/or terms as sexual or nonsexual, even when two women openly made their lives together.

As the quasi-Freudian belief in sexuality as an irresistible natural force gained wider currency, however, women who were not clearly heterosexually active became objects of suspicion in new ways. If a woman did not have "normal outlets" for her sexual instincts, it could mean one of two things: either she was repressing her sexuality, and thus (in popular Freudian belief) on her way to embittered neurosis, or she belonged to a class of people newly labeled by the sexologists: a "female invert," a "homosexual woman" (terms that began coming into use in the 1880s), a lesbian. For some women, these new forms of stigmatization were devastating. Respected in their communities, living in honored relationships with other women, they had not expected to be told—especially by other women—that their lives were stunted or out of date as feminist models. For other women, however, growing public discussion of homosexuality and "female inverts," even in a pejorative medical context, conferred a sense of sexual identity and potential community. The difficulties then lay in casting off pejorative evaluations of lesbian sexuality, finding other like-minded women, and living safely in a heterosexist society. These were no small challenges. Some women did, however, find their way into the growing urban homosexual subcultures. Such subcultures ranged from the "furnished-room districts of large cities . . . where working women might form relationships with one another" (D'Emilio and Freedman, 227), to the famous lesbian literary salons of Paris, where Natalie Barney, Radclyffe Hall, and other expatriates from England and the United States wrote, postured, and loved.

Black women in the United States also experienced the new ideologies of sexuality in complicated ways. Unlike middle-class white women, they had never been cast by dominant white culture as asexual or passionless. Under slavery, black women were assumed to be available sexual objects to their masters regardless of their own wishes, an assumption whites often rationalized in terms of black women's supposed innate hypersexuality (in contrast to their "own" women's chastity). The same assumption of hypersexuality was extended to black men, with horrifying consequences: lynch mobs punished assertive black men for alleged sexual crimes against white women, in a wave of violence that crested in the early twentieth century and did not begin to abate somewhat until the mid-1930s (Giddings, 206).

Black women and men asserted control over their own sexual and family lives, in the wake of this history, in different ways. Many seized the opportunity to marry legally after the end of the Civil War, and hoped to emulate the model of a male breadwinner protecting a female housekeeper and mother; as one male ex-slave told his former master, "I am going to feed and clothe them [my family] and I can do it on bare rock."[11] To many blacks hoping to secure middle-class status, sexual respectability along white middle-class lines seemed of key importance to economic stability and racial progress.

Yet such status and respectability, given the enduring racist barriers to black men's upward mobility, often remained elusive. A strong counter-tradition in twentieth-century black American culture centered around the figure of the blues woman. "These black women," historian Barbara Omolade recounts, "lived lives of explicit sexuality and erotic excitement with both men and women. As they broke away from the traditional paternal restraints within the black community, they were castigated for seeming to reflect the truth of the white man's views of black women as whorish and loose." Even so, they "model[ed] for southern rural black women a city life full of flashy clothes, fast cars, and access to sophisticated men."[12]

Whatever their own choices, black women knew firsthand their own vulnerability and the vulnerability of black men to white sexual panic. Black antilynching movements, spearheaded by women like Ida Wells-Barnett and Nannie Helen Burroughs, gathered momentum from the 1880s through the early decades of the twentieth century, gradually picking up allies among some Southern white women who rejected the supposed protection offered them by white male violence (Gidding, 206–10). Along with or ahead of Freud, these reformers advanced what amounted to a trenchant analysis of the evil social consequences of repressing sexuality and projecting its supposed contaminations onto others. Unlike the popularizers of Freudian psychology, however, black women reformers could not be content to regard sexuality as a strictly natural or strictly private matter, something to be released safely in the bedroom between a man and a woman. Their history brought them face to face with the realization that sexuality was not a private, natural, inevitable force, but a vehicle of power and domination, a burning area of public conflict between blacks and whites, men and women.

The social changes of the first half of the twentieth century were bracketed by world wars: World War I, fought mainly on and around the European continent from 1914 to 1918, and World War II, truly a global struggle from 1939 to 1945. The world wars helped shape changes in women's sexuality, in women's employment patterns, in women's education, but they have mostly been studied as crucibles of male experience and the male literary imagination. The horrors of trench warfare; young men's loss of faith in Victorian platitudes of duty and honor; the physical and emotional wounds of the "Lost Generation" after World War I; the voluntary enlistment of idealistic left-wing young men from England and the United States in the Spanish Civil War; the mechanized, swift destruction of World War II, were explored and relived by male authors in innumerable works of poetry and fiction that challenged the adequacy of nineteenth-century literary forms to twentieth-century experience. The encounter between men and modernized war is by now a staple theme of twentieth-century literary history. But what does that history have to say to and about women?

Scholars of women's history and literature have begun to assemble information about, and interpretations of, women's place in and between the world wars. Their new research has not only illuminated women's lives, but cast new light upon the way we look at men's experiences in the world wars. War, write the editors of a recent volume, "must be understood as a *gendering* activity, one that ritually marks the gender of all members of a society, whether or not they are combatants"; it strongly brands men as men, women as women.[13]

The actual ways in which the world wars marked citizens with gender, however, were complex and contradictory. In certain respects, the twentieth century's total wars destabilized traditional gender roles. British women drove ambulances in World War I and served in medical corps near the front lines. At home, some of them took over places previously reserved for men; when Somerville College for women at Oxford University was converted into a war hospital, the women undergraduates who were moved to the ancient men's college of Oriel enjoyed firsthand the pomp and privilege that men of their class took as their due. As manpower shortages in both wars became acute, government and industry in Britain and the United States mounted recruiting campaigns that drew substantial numbers of women, some of them married with young children, into the labor force, defying long-standing prejudice against the employment of mothers. In World War II, Great Britain went so far as to register and draft single women into the work force and women's military corps. Some women in both countries entered jobs in heavy industry, were unionized for the first time in their lives, and made better money than they had ever seen before—although still not the same wages as male workers. In the United States, wartime exigencies enabled some black women to escape from agricultural work and domestic service into factory work at higher wages, thus challenging job segregation by race as well as gender. U.S. government propaganda from World War II has supplied us with the standard image of these women: "Rosie the Riveter," her hair tied up in a bandanna, a pack of cigarettes rolled into a short sleeve of her work shirt. Sexual customs loosened further, for gay men and lesbians to some degree along with heterosexuals, as both young women and men found themselves in unfamiliar places, cut off from community supervision, and uncertain of their futures (D'Emilio and Freedman, 260–61).

If the world wars shook loose some constraints of traditional gender roles, however, they reinforced others. All wars tend, first and foremost, to segregate men and women into separate spheres of experience: women to mind the home front, men to the battle front as protectors of the home front. With the exception of Russian women, who saw active combat in regular military units, and of some women who fought as guerrillas in the resistance movements of occupied countries, women were (and for the most part still are) debarred from combat. True, the advent of mechanized total war in the twentieth century made the distinction between home and battle front tenuous at times; as early as World War I, "the symbolic value of the homefront as an inviolate zone had been eroded by the advent of Zeppelins, aerial bombing, guerrilla combat, and extended occupation" (*BL*, 5–6). Nevertheless, governments, concerned with the morale of soldiers and civilians alike, did their best to prop up the ideals of home and family—the "normalcy" to which soldiers could hope to return. If Rosie the Riveter took over a man's job, it was with the understanding that she did it to help the boys at the front; that she longed to become altogether feminine again at home, in the bosom of her family; and that the job belonged to the man when the fighting was over. Government and industry worked together after the wars—with a combination of propaganda, advertising, and outright dismissal of women workers—in reestablishing the "normal" division of labor, with a male breadwinner protectively supporting a female housewife-consumer.

The very heavy-handedness of state propaganda and policy making about gender during and after the world wars, however, betrayed the effort it takes to establish and reestablish social arrangements that are supposedly "natural." As Margaret and Patrice Higonnet put it, "war crystallizes contradictions between ideology and actual experience,"[14] between tradition and propaganda on the one hand, and the concrete needs of individuals on the other. The "realities of the two world wars contradicted the myth that war compels men to go forth and fight in order to protect their women, who remain passive and secure at home with the children" (*BL*, 1). These realities demonstrated that the sexual division of labor is not dictated by nature, that women can do "men's work," that things as we know them could change.

Given war's complex and contradictory "gendering activities," individual women's experiences in and attitudes toward war varied tremendously in the twentieth century. The gender ideology that assigned women to the home front and men to the battle front put women in awkward positions. As guardians of domestic order and peace, they were supposed to be naturally more gentle and pacific than men, devoid of aggressive instincts (as the new Freudian language might put it). Yet they were expected at the same time to support war efforts patriotically, in their special womanly roles. World War I propaganda "linked women's patriotic duty to motherhood: legions of nationalistic mothers were pictured bravely sending the boys off to war. The Second World War eroticized images of femininity, producing not only Mrs. Miniver but romantic and kittenish sexual partners and Hollywood pinups," the images of movie stars that hung in soldiers' lockers and decorated fighter planes. "No matter how she is manifest, though, this goddess always contrasts with, even while supporting, Mars" (BL, 2; Mars is the Roman god of war).

For feminist women and women of left-leaning politics, these images of patriotism produced special conflicts. Most women's rights organizations tabled their demands during World War I; British suffragists, for instance, abandoned demonstrations and acts of civil disobedience "for the duration." When patriotism was linked to women's traditional roles in one way or another—as mother, as desirable yet pure sexual object— questioning those roles could be tantamount to questioning patriotism. On the other hand, a woman choosing to be a pacifist could sometimes be excused—and dismissed—for displaying a merely feminine aversion to violence. Criticizing men's privileges was more difficult for women conscious of the terrible price masculinity could exact of men. Some young women enjoyed their expanded domestic freedoms during men's absence, their new jobs and their presence in the universities, with a bad conscience. Others joined the ambulance and nursing corps, or the women's auxiliary corps of the services—to work off their guilt at being "protected," or to participate somehow in the great masculine adventure. Women were prominent in international pacifist organizations; at the same time, some British women handed out white feathers, a sign of cowardice, to male passersby who were not in uniform.

Women writers of the time shared these contradictions. Virginia Woolf's pacifism was staunch and unwavering, and she never failed to connect it to her feminist critique of male privilege and of social hierarchy generally. For every Virginia Woolf, however, there may have been an Edith Wharton, who roundly condemned President Woodrow Wilson for dragging his heels on bringing the United States into World War I. Women's situations in, and attitudes toward, the world wars were undoubtedly shaped by their gender—but also by differing class allegiances, political and religious affiliations, racial and ethnic identities. War strongly genders women as women, men as men, but the meanings of woman and man nevertheless are not everywhere the same in war. It is clear, however, that criticism must come to terms with the relationships between women writers and the world wars, as it has for so long explored war's effects on men.

Issues in Literary Scholarship

Literary historians usually label the dominant literary movement of the years 1900–1945 "modernism." Modernism, most would agree, has a fundamentally adversarial character: its practitioners set themselves against what they took to be the middle-class pieties of nineteenth-century life and art. They celebrated the artist's freedom to defy conventional expectations of what made a beautiful painting, a finished novel, a moving poem, even a grammatical sentence. They saw the artist as the master of his own medium (be it words, paint, or music), and emphasized the artist's freedom with the medium itself over his representation of an external, agreed-upon social reality. In painting, Matisse and Picasso worked with flat areas of paint, or with the multiple perspectives of cubism, rather than with fixed, three-dimensional realistic perspective. In literature, T. S. Eliot wrote *The Waste Land* (1922) as a collage of quotations and parody, without a fixed, unifying authorial perspective. Breaking up the stable perspectives of nineteenth-century art, modernists both responded to an increasingly fragmented external world and asserted their own autonomous power over that world. They often saw themselves as part of an avant-garde, waging war on "the sensibilities of the conventional reader" and "undertak[ing] to create ever-new artistic forms and styles and to introduce hitherto neglected, and sometimes forbidden, subject-matters."[15] For American writers particularly, rebellion against conventional sensibilities often took the form of expatriatism, leaving the United States behind for other cultures thought to be less hidebound and more receptive to the arts.

If this is modernism—it is at least the image many modernists had of themselves, and the dominant idea of modernism in present-day literary history—what place did women writers have in it? My use of the masculine pronoun to describe the prototypical modernist artist in the preceding paragraph was no accident. A growing number of feminist literary critics are calling attention to the subtle and sometimes not-so-subtle misogyny of modernist theory and practice. The quasi-military image of the artist as a kind of guerrilla warrior against conventionality, for one thing, seems inimical to women. Moreover, the middle-class culture against which modernism rebelled was often identified with women: women as a guardians of domesticity, as producers and consumers of sentimental popular culture.[16] Filippo Marinetti's famous "Futurist Manifesto" of 1909 (an important modernist document) put the connection between modernist militarism and misogyny bluntly enough: "We are out to glorify war: / The only health-giver of the world! . . . Ideas that kill! / Contempt for women!"[17]

Sandra Gilbert and Susan Gubar, among the most influential new feminist critics of modernism, see literary warfare between men and women as the central, energizing conflict of modernism. They argue that male modernists, threatened by women's very real encroachment upon spheres of learning and power hitherto reserved for men, responded with mingled anxiety and aggression. Witnesses to "the astonishing rise of both critically and commercially successful women of letters throughout the middle and late nineteenth century in England and America" (Gilbert and Gubar, 141), the male modernists often asserted their own writerly identities through attacks on literary women and on the sort of writing—lovesick, popular, sentimental—for which women writers were stereotypically held responsible (125–62).

Given the extent to which modernism vented its rebellious energies on figures of women (whether real or imagined), women writers who identified with modernism, Gilbert and Gubar suggest, were in an ambivalent position. Modernism helped women writers rebel against their mothers' roles: in one of her most famous essays, Virginia Woolf wrote that she had had to kill "the Angel in the House," the figure of the ideal Victorian mother in her own mind, before she could become a novelist herself.[18] Not only did many women modernists reject their mothers' ways of living for themselves, some of them also—along with modernist men—criticized earlier women writers for their supposed conventionality, their evasion of sexuality, their sentimentality.[19] Being a modernist meant rejecting the culture of the Victorian mother and her values; yet many women could not be wholly comfortable with such a rejection. If Woolf wrote of killing off the mother in herself, she also wrote that "we think back through our mothers, if we are women."[20] In modernism's climate of sexual warfare, Gilbert and Gubar argue, women writers were torn between admiration for and rejection of their literary foremothers (165–224).

Gilbert and Gubar are surely right to identify hostility between men and women as a major theme of literary modernism, and to trace this hostility to sweeping (but unfinished) changes in gender roles. Their approach, however, has its limitations. For one, Gilbert and Gubar's thematic approach to modernist literature for the most part fails to engage modernism's genuine formal departures from nineteenth-century literary and artistic conventions.[21] What difference does it make, for example, when a woman poet writes in free, disconnected, allusive lines rather than in traditional forms? When she abandons conventional syntax and grammatical expectations? When she writes a novel without an authoritative third-person narrator, and without a definite beginning, middle, and end?

Toril Moi, among other feminist critics of modernism, has argued that modernism's formal innovations allowed modernist writers to challenge definitions of gender identity as well as definitions of the novel. She sees in Virginia Woolf's modernism "what we might now call a 'deconstructive' form of writing, one that engages with and thereby exposes the duplicitous nature of discourse."[22] The fragmentations and lack of centralized authority that characterize so much modernist writing, in other words, question the notion that human beings have fixed natures, male and female, fixed ideal destinies, and fixed relationships to one another. Modernism's formal practices have the power to call into question aspects of everyday power relationships that we think of as given, self-evident, "natural."

Moi's interest in the potentially feminist implications of modernist form, then, usefully supplements Gilbert and Gubar's thematic analysis of modernism's war between the sexes. Moi shares with Gilbert and Gubar, however, the tendency to see modernism as a movement oriented around one fixed dichotomy. For Gilbert and Gubar, that dichotomy is the tense stand-off between the sexes; for Moi, it is the seemingly absolute distinction between modernist "deconstructive" forms and the older forms of "bourgeois realism" (as summed up best in classic nineteenth-century English novels) committed to the wholeness and solidity of individual identity.

Cary Nelson's recent work on modern American poetry presents an alternative to both of these dichotomous versions of modernism.[23] Like Gilbert and Gubar, Nelson sees modernist literature as embedded in social circumstances; he takes issue with the notion that great literature by definition rises above the contaminations of everyday life and historical specificity. Even more so than Gilbert and Gubar or Moi, Nelson concerns himself with many writers (both women and men) who are not usually included in the modernist canon of the few "great writers" who turn up time and time again in syllabi and anthologies. He argues that we—starting with the literary-critical academy—have forgotten the "almost inconceivable variety of poetry at work in the culture" of early-twentieth-century America (Nelson, 75). And our forgetfulness shows a distinct pattern: "no texts are merely erased from our memory in a neutral and nonideological fashion" (52). Textbook versions of modernism, Nelson finds, actively repress the work of writers in whose texts political commitments and historical contexts clearly occupy the foreground. And they have actively minimized the political engagements of writers who are canonized, cordoning off (for example) Edna St. Vincent Millay's romantic lyrics from her left-wing political poems, or (on another end of the political spectrum) Ezra Pound's fascism from his poetry in the *Cantos*.

While Nelson, like Gilbert and Gubar, documents modernist writers' engagement with history and politics, he insists that neither the politics nor the literature of modernism can be reduced to *one* narrative, *one* conflict that explains everything. If struggles over the social meaning and organization of gender were important for many modernist writers, so too, Nelson reminds us, were class conflict and struggles for racial justice. While crediting Gilbert and Gubar with "mount[ing] an important challenge to the traditional suppression of gender issues in academic scholarship on modern poetry," Nelson objects that their "position on male and female writers is far too dichotomous and essentialist" (252n5). Gilbert and Gubar, in other words, look at the immense variety of modern literature and see only two meaningful groups, men and women, locked in conflict over the single issue of gender; they tend to judge all women's writing as doing one thing, all men's writing as doing another.

Nelson joins many other recent scholars of modernism, especially those exploring the place of black American writing in modernism, in reminding us that the actual social and literary landscapes of these years were more complicated than a simple gender dichotomy can suggest. He urges us to beware of any attempt to organize the variety of modern literature around a single theme, conflict, or metaphor. Gender warfare between women and men, although an important theme in modern literature, is not the only story. Women writers did not move in lockstep as a unit; they had different literary aims, different class, race, and ethnic identities. Edith Wharton's identity crisis as a writer and a wealthy member of New York's social "four hundred" was not identical to Anzia Yezierska's struggle to write her way out of the Jewish immigrant ghetto on New York's Lower East Side, or to Angelina Weld Grimké's ambivalent position on the borders of the Harlem Renaissance. Being a modern woman, writing as a woman, meant different things to differently positioned women—and the same goes for modern men.

Like Toril Moi, Nelson celebrates modernism's radical experiments with form, the power of modernist disruptions and juxtapositions to put everyday life into question. Unlike Moi, however, who identifies traditional realistic form in fiction with an oppressively fixed bourgeois ideology of human identity, Nelson does not dismiss traditional forms out of hand. Looking at the variety of poetry produced in the years 1910–45, Nelson finds "that traditional forms continued to do vital cultural work throughout this period. Far from being preeminently genteel, poetry in traditional forms was a frequent vehicle for sharply focused social commentary" (23).

Traditional forms, in other words, could and did entertain radical visions, could and did pose radical questions about life. Nor did readers, writers, and editors always see traditional forms and modernist experimentation as mutually exclusive. In early-twentieth-century journals of American protest poetry, Nelson finds traditional and experimental forms "coexisting" in "a dialogue rather than a competition to be won" (25). The same, I think, is true of modern literature at large, fiction as well as poetry. While the more radically experimental forms of modernism undoubtedly do challenge readers to redefine their sense of the real, the ordinary, and the everyday, it does not always follow that formally conservative works enact uniformly conservative visions of life.

My goal in this study is to combine some of the virtues of the new critical approaches to modernism into a comprehensive general introduction to women and literature in the years 1900–1945. Along with Gilbert and Gubar, I hope to convey the degree to which literature participated in the early twentieth century's pitched battles around definitions of masculinity and femininity. Like Toril Moi, I will explore the relationship between challenges to traditional literary forms and challenges to traditional ideas about women's and men's identities. Following Cary Nelson's example, I hope to suggest something of the sheer variety of women's literary production in these years, the extent of women writers' differing concerns, the diversity of the forms and genres in which they chose to write. Benefiting from the new scholarship on women in the Harlem Renaissance, I will ask how our ideas about modernism as a whole might change if we saw Harlem as a modernist center on a par with Paris or London. While some of the writers presented here strike me as more interesting than others, I do not want to rank them solely on the basis of a fixed conception of modernism. Their differences, as Cary Nelson argues, should meet in the form of a dialogue rather than a competition.

CHAPTER
2

The Women of Imagism:
H. D., Amy Lowell, and
Marianne Moore

In the January 1913 issue of Harriet Monroe's *Poetry: A Magazine of Verse*, three poems—"Priapus," "Epigram (after the Greek)," and "Hermes of the Way"—appeared under a name new to readers of poetry: "H. D., Imagiste." The initials belonged to Hilda Doolittle (1886–1961), a young American woman then living in London. The new identity under which she appeared had been crafted by her friend (and onetime fiancé) Ezra Pound, then a rising young American poet also living in London; responding to Harriet Monroe's request for contributions, Pound helped edit and then sent off Doolittle's poems. His gesture was very much in character, for Pound enjoyed assisting (and sometimes bossing around) other young poets. This gesture, however, paid off more handsomely than most, launching a movement along with a poet. "H. D." was the name under which Doolittle would publish for the rest of her life; "imagism" gathered other poets to its banner, and became—for a few years anyway—a key word by which to identify what was new in twentieth-century poetry.

After introducing H. D. as the first imagist, Pound and others in their group published articles in *Poetry* that tried to explain what the label meant. Pound issued three central tenets of the movement: "1. Direct treatment of the 'thing' whether subjective or objective. 2. To use absolutely no word that does not contribute to the representation. 3. As regarding rhythm: to compose in the sequence of the musical phrase, not the metronome." Imagism set itself against what its practitioners thought of as the excesses of nineteenth-century poetry—its flabby poetic diction and windy subjectivity—exalting by contrast a poetry of concentration, free-verse forms, and objectivity. An image, according to Pound, "presents an intellectual and emotional complex in an instant of time"; the subjectivity that found its way into imagist poetry, in Pound's theory, was a subjectivity united with—or displaced onto—the more objective presentation of an image. The young British poet-critic T. E. Hulme, whom Pound much admired, set the tone for imagism by calling for a "hard," "dry" poetry as a tonic for soggy nineteenth-century emotionalism.[1]

There is a certain irony in H. D.'s identification as the first "imagiste," for the imagist aesthetic, like many modernist ideologies, was in some ways hostile not only to its nineteenth-century artistic precursors, but also to values traditionally defined as "feminine." If imagism—at least in the eyes of its male expounders—was hard, dry, and objective, where did it leave women, who were culturally expected to be soft and emotional?

The strictures of imagism, her editor Louis Martz suggests, may have "provided H. D. with a discipline" through which to channel "her violently responsive nature."[2] But many present-day readers agree that H. D.'s poetry overran definitions of imagism almost from the first, and H. D. herself denied that the label fit her poetry after World War I.[3] While many of the poems she published in the years 1913–17 are indeed sparing of adjectives and conventional poetic diction ("Oread," "Garden," and "Sea Violet" are among the most famous imagist poems by any author), others are both longer and more fulsome in terms of poetic diction; they do not confine themselves to "an instant of time," but tell by implication stories of some complexity, often stories taken from Greek mythology. Sometimes neglected in the past by readers who wanted to read all of H. D.'s early work through narrow definitions of imagism, these poems have more recently been read with great interest by feminist literary critics who see in them a retelling of mythology from a feminine, perhaps even a feminist, point of view.

In "Pursuit," for instance, the speaker follows the traces left behind by another woman—perhaps a nymph, or a goddess—who was herself in flight from a pursuer. The poem recalls the myth of Apollo and Daphne, in which the god of poetry chases the nymph until she turns herself into a laurel bush, rather than be raped by him. (The hyacinth in "Pursuit" reminds us of another of Apollo's loves, the boy Hyacinth, whom Apollo accidentally killed.) "You were swift, swift!" the speaker says of the fleeing woman—but not swift enough. At the end, she wonders, did the woman "stammer with short breath and gasp: / *wood-daemons grant life— / give life—I am almost lost*"? For she "can find no trace of you / in the larch-cones and the underbrush"; it is as if someone had lifted her off the earth. The speaker empathizes with the threatened woman, not with the male god. If H. D., too, like Apollo, in some sense "pursues" the nymph, she does so in order to reconstitute the nymph's experience and recenter the myth upon her rather than Apollo.

H. D. follows a similar strategy in "Eurydice." In the Greek myth, Eurydice was the wife of Orpheus, a poet so gifted that he could cause stones and trees to move. One day Eurydice stepped on a snake and died. Determined to recover her, Orpheus went down to the underworld and sang for its rulers, Hades and Persephone; they consented to let Eurydice return, provided that he not look back at her on the way up. He did, of course, and Eurydice faded back into Hades. In H. D.'s poem, Eurydice voices her own disappointment, anger, and loss. She speaks to Orpheus, asking him whether he looked back at her merely to see "the light of your own face, / the fire of your own presence?" Perhaps the male poet has used her only as a mirror; if so, this has cost Eurydice all hope of life. Could I have "breathed into myself / the very golden crocuses" just one more time, she says, "I could have dared the loss"; instead, "everything is lost." As the poem goes on, however, Eurydice finds new sources of strength. "My hell is no worse than yours," she tells Orpheus, and even in hell "I have the fervour of myself for a presence / and my own spirit for light"; she ceases depending on him for existence and voice. Revising Greek myths in which the male human or the male god, Orpheus or Apollo, is the poet and women are silent ancillary figures, H. D. finds ways of making the ancient stories speak in women's voices.

The years during and immediately after World War I were poetically productive but personally stressful for H. D. She published frequently in the important modernist periodicals and was for a time assistant editor of the *Egoist*; her collections of poetry appeared at a steady pace: *Sea Garden* in 1916, *Hymen* in 1921, *Heliodora* in 1924. She had married Richard Aldington, a British poet in the imagist circle, in 1913; she became pregnant, but miscarried in 1915, and was told not to risk another pregnancy under wartime conditions in London. Aldington soon involved himself with other women, and H. D. became increasingly preoccupied with the novelist D. H. Lawrence, another member of their literary circle. Given to bouts of what the critic Rachel Blau DuPlessis has called "romantic thralldom," H. D. "was especially vulnerable to the power of the 'heros fatal,' a man whom she saw as her spiritual similar, an artist, a healer, a psychic."[4] She was conscious of her vulnerabilities, and may have tried to write them out in poems like "Eurydice," but could not break the cycle completely. Lawrence was all-too-suited for this role in H. D.'s script of thralldom, but was already married and reluctant to be drawn in completely. (H. D.'s autobiographical novel *Bid Me to Live* tells her part of the story, with Lawrence appearing under the name of Rico.) In 1918 H. D. retreated from London into the Cornwall countryside, from preoccupation with Lawrence into an affair with another friend, Cecil Gray. This affair, although brief in itself, would change her life: it gave her a child and saw the beginning of her lifelong friendship with a woman companion and author in her own right, Bryher.

Born Annie Winifred Ellerman, the daughter of wealthy British parents, Bryher had discovered H. D.'s work through the volume *Des Imagistes*, compiled by Pound in 1913. She began a correspondence with the American poet Amy Lowell, who was then popularizing imagist verse in the United States; learning that H. D. was living in England, Bryher determined to meet her. At a low point in her own confidence, pregnant with Cecil Gray's child, H. D. found Bryher's support very nearly lifesaving. When H. D. contracted influenza, Bryher helped nurse her through the illness and the birth of her daughter, Frances Perdita, on 31 March 1919. From that point forward, H. D. and Bryher traveled together, lived for some periods together, and were of central emotional importance to each other—despite the complicated web of other relationships, including Bryher's 1921 marriage to writer and publisher Robert McAlmon, in which the two women were involved.

Aware that their feelings exceeded early-twentieth-century heterosexual norms of women's friendships, H. D. and Bryher consulted the famous sexologist Havelock Ellis for insight into their own sexual natures. Bryher, whose feelings (marriage and all) seem to have been less ambivalent than H. D.'s, flirted with the then-current scientific theory that she was a congenital "invert," a male soul born by some accident into a female body. H. D. seems to have found herself less easily classifiable in such terms. Seeking a vocabulary in which to express and understand what we might now label as her bisexuality, H. D. explored and translated the diverse human relationships taken for granted in ancient Greek poems and myths during the 1920s; eventually she would take her questions about her own identity—along with a new problem, a persistent writer's block—to the founder of psychoanalysis himself, Sigmund Freud.

H. D. dedicated *Hymen* in 1921 to Bryher and Perdita, friend and daughter. Taken together, the title and dedications spell out the complexity of H. D.'s emotional world in these years: Hymen is the god of marriage, but the relationships celebrated in the dedications were outside the boundaries of conventional marriage. The title poem, an extended wedding-masque, takes place in a ceremonial world inhabited almost entirely by women. A male figure enters the scene toward the end: not the human bridegroom himself, but the god of love, an abstract idea—"*a flame, an exaggerated symbol*"—as H. D.'s stage instructions indicate; his song is then sung by a chorus of young boys. The women's world, ceremonially segregated from that of men, is both sensual and dignified, but the heroic symbolism of masculinity still pulls on the poet's imagination. The following poem, "Demeter," speaks in the voice of the mother-goddess, who tells us, "I am greatest and least." A monumental figure with fingers "wrought of iron / to wrest from the earth / secrets," she still remembers herself as a young mother girding her daughter's head with slender hands, and, recalling her daughter's kidnapping by Hades, god of the underworld, her parting words cry that his "kiss was less passionate!" than hers, the mother's.

In these poems and in those of H. D.'s next two volumes, *Heliodora* (the title plays on her name) and *Red Roses for Bronze*, heterosexual romance does not have clear priority over other relationships in passion; love is not so orderly, nor are gender roles so completely fixed, despite their acknowledged power. The paradoxical combination of powerful social roles (like that of the male hero) with lack of absolute certainty and fixity yields both turmoil and the possibility of insight toward change. Ringing variations on one of the surviving fragments of the ancient Greek lyric poet Sappho (whose poems tell of her love for both women and men), H. D. concludes that "to sing love, / love must first shatter us" ("Fragment Forty"). Poems like "Toward the Piraeus" and "Fragment Sixty-eight" (another interpretation of Sappho) explore the complexity of variously gendered love-triangles: their voyeuristic agonies, their twists of identification with the rival. In "Myrtle-Bough," an unusual and difficult variation on the triangle motif, H. D. reimagines the relationship between Haromodius and Aristogiton, famous Greek warriors and lovers who died fighting for each other and against tyranny. Identifying for a moment with the ethos of the heroic male lovers, the speaker asks them to "let me be a brother / to your need, / shoulder to steel-clad shoulder";

she seeks, however, to disarm them of their heroic armor, to return them to the bodies the armor covers and to other, more complicated, versions of love. Poised between different kinds and genders of love, ambivalent about entertaining human love at all, H. D. sums up her predicament in words taken once again from Sappho's poetry: "*I know not what to do / my mind is divided*" ("Fragment Thirty-six"). This self-division, however close it may bring her to paralysis, was nevertheless the force generating H. D.'s poems (along with her autobiographical prose experiments *Palimpsest* and *Hedylus*) in these years.

As the 1930s advanced, however, H. D. found herself less and less able to write her self-divisions, even with the aid of Greek and mythic masks through which to speak her own conflicts. At the urging of Bryher, who had been in psychoanalysis since 1928, H. D. began to look for an appropriate analyst. After abortive attempts at beginning therapy with analysts in London, H. D. in 1933 went to Vienna for the first of her sessions with Freud. This relationship, unlike that with the earlier therapists, immediately warmed on both sides. Freud admired H. D. and took her work seriously; H. D. found Freud's greatness equal to his reputation.

H. D. left literary record of her experience with Freud in her prose memoir *Tribute to Freud* (published in 1956), as well as in a poem entitled "The Master," left in typescript at her death because she chose not to publish in her lifetime. It is clear from the unpublished poem that H. D. brought to psychoanalysis, among other issues, the question of her own sexual identity. "I had two loves separate," she writes, "and told the old man / to explain / the impossible" ("The Master," part 2). The answer Freud and Freudian thought gave her was doubtless complicated, perhaps even self-contradictory. Freud believed on the one hand that all human beings were in some way bisexual at birth, not already programmed to respond in a fixed way to the opposite gender. On the other hand, he argued—on many if not all occasions—that anatomy ultimately did lay down a normative heterosexual destiny for women, against which bisexuality or lesbian sexuality were inadequate protests.[5] H. D. fought with Freud's ideas on this and other topics: "I was angry with the old man / with his talk of the man-strength" ("The Master," part 4). Yet, when asked "to explain / the impossible," she wrote, "he did." Whatever Freud himself said about anatomy and destiny in the course of H. D.'s analysis, H. D. seems to have taken from their encounter the more androgynous vision of a woman who "needs no man, / herself / is that dart and pulse of the male" ("The Master," part 5).

H. D. may have found psychoanalysis with Freud satisfying, for all its conflicts, because of Freud's emphasis on the importance of early relations in psychic development, especially the relation with the mother. Freud urged H. D. to try writing without the aid of the Greek masks for a time, out of her own memory; he "stimulated her to explore her feelings about her mother, to forge a strong bond of identification with her mother, and to connect her personal experience with the universal mother-symbols of myth" (Friedman, 137). Despite his dismissive comments on femininity elsewhere, Freud insisted on the importance of this primary relationship and its successive echoes in H. D.'s life, including her relationship with Bryher.

H. D.'s analysis with Freud ended in 1935 as the Nazi threat grew. Its effects on her poetic creativity were not evident for a time. In the years immediately following, she wrote, but did not publish, two prose memoirs, *Bid Me to Live* and *The Gift* (eventually published in 1960 and 1982 respectively). When she finally returned to poetry with an outpouring of new work, different in kind from and more ambitious than anything she had previously done, it was not prompted directly by the experience with Freud; World War II was the catalyst. The blitz that laid waste to London inspired H. D. to three new, long, poetic works about the world destroyed and remade: *The Walls Do Not Fall* (1944), *Tribute to the Angels* (1945), and *The Flowering of the Rod* (written, but not published, in 1946). In H. D.'s plan, the three works were to be part of one long poem. When all three were finally issued together as *Trilogy* (1973), what may be H. D.'s most important work was finally complete.

Trilogy abandons the Greek purism of H. D.'s earlier masks for a heady syncretism of mythologies and esoteric lore: Egyptian gods, Christian scripture, and alchemy join the familiar Greek pantheon. Decisively breaking with the straitjacket of imagism, *Trilogy* recovers for H. D.'s poetry some of the Christian traditions of her upbringing, the symbolism of her own Moravian childhood. After all, Freud had reminded her, was she not born in Bethlehem, Pennsylvania? Mythic meaning was not confined to ancient Greece, but embedded in the poet's contemporary world as well, even if—perhaps especially if—that world lay in pieces all around her. Musing on the bombed houses of London, H. D. grieved that "the shrine lies open to the sky"; nevertheless, "as the fallen roof / leaves the sealed room / open to the air," the poet could newly "wonder / what saved us? what for?" (*Walls*, 1). Piecing together meaning from fragments of London, fragments of myth, H. D. hailed her own rebirth as a poet with the return of peace in Europe.

The Walls Do Not Fall makes a case for the poet's importance in a world where the sword seems mightier than the pen. Imagining herself, like the prophet Jonah, temporarily imprisoned in the whale's belly (*Walls*, 4). H. D. derides those for whom "poets are useless" (*Walls*, 8). On the contrary, she says, society owes "protection for the scribe" who understands the secret meanings "stored / in man's very speech" (*Walls*, 8), for without the word, the sword could not exist (*Walls*, 11).

Each part of *Trilogy* features a central mystic vision; in *The Walls Do Not Fall*, the poet shares a vision in which "Ra, Osiris, Amen appeared" to her (*Walls*, 16). Linking these Egyptian gods with the "Christos-image" (*Walls*, 18), H. D. names this constellation of images, "the One, Amen, All-father" (*Walls*, 24) to whom all religions pray. Punning on the name of Osiris, she suggests that "Osiris equates O-sir-is or O-Sire-is" (*Walls*, 40). The poet, the scribe, can decode the meaning—Father—embedded in the god's seemingly foreign name.

Despite the vision of the father-god, *The Walls Do Not Fall* closes in a world still at war and uncertain of its survival. By himself, H. D. suggests, the father-god is not all-powerful. *Tribute to the Angels*, the second section of *Trilogy*, adds to this a vision of a mother-goddess. Knowing that the Hebrew etymology of the name Mary is "bitter" or "bitter waters," H. D. conjures with the words: "*marah*, / a word bitterer still, *mar*"; making the words "fuse and join / and change and alter," the poet watches them turn from "mer, mere, mère, mater, Maia, Mary"—and finally, "Mother" (*Tribute*, 8).

The mother figure seems more charged and ambivalent for H. D. than the father-god. She is, over and over again, "bitter." The poet asks her hard questions: "what is this mother-father / to tear at our entrails? / what is this unsatisfied duality / which you can not satisfy?" (*Tribute*, 9). H. D. is at pains to distinguish her vision of the mother from the debased, clichéd, over-familiar images found in every "cathedral, museum, cloister" (*Tribute*, 29), insisting that her vision brings with her not "the tome of the ancient wisdom" but "the blank pages / of the unwritten volume of the new" (*Tribute*, 38). She seems to argue that the mother figure is necessary for rebirth, for at the end of *Tribute to the Angels*, unlike *The Walls Do Not Fall*, resurrection is at hand: "*we pause to give / thanks that we rise again from death and live.*"

The Flowering of the Rod concludes *Trilogy* with a vision of the child added to the father and mother figures of the earlier parts of the poem. Kaspar, one of the three Wise Men, is visited by Mary (both Mary Magdalene, the prostitute-saint, and the Virgin Mary), who grants him a vision of the Christ child. *Trilogy* thus incorporates a version of the Christian holy family, but this vision also had personal meanings for H. D.: "Father, Mother, and Child are the family constellation buried in the unconscious and retrieved for H. D. through psychoanalysis" (Friedman, 78). H. D.'s experience of analysis with Freud, in other words, may have made her both more familiar with her own family history and more confident in exploring mythological images of the family. H. D. acknowledged that her methods in *Trilogy* might not please all readers, especially readers for whom Christianity was not just another version of an age-old myth, or who questioned whether any genuinely new poetry could come of synthesizing old myths. "This search for historical parallels," she confessed, "has been done to death before, / will be done again" (*Walls*, 38). But she gambled on the relevance of her poetic faith for a world sick of war. In *Trilogy* and other works after 1945, especially her long poem *Helen in Egypt* (1961), she tried again—as she had after World War I— to draw the imagination of her readers away from the figure of the heroic male warrior, to convince the warriors themselves to lay down their arms. In the beginning, she maintained, was the Word, not the sword.

Amy Lowell (1874–1925) was less a skilled poet in imagist terms than she was imagism's best public champion, at least in the United States. Born to one of New England's wealthiest and most illustrious families, Lowell came relatively late to a sense of her own vocation. Her father's death in 1900 left her in possession of the family estate, Sevenels (in Brookline, Massachusetts) and a generous income (like Bryher, Lowell would be able to support other poets' work financially). In 1902 she began writing serious poetry; in 1910 the *Atlantic Monthly* published "A Fixed Idea," a conventional sonnet about a claustrophobic love affair, spoken from the (traditionally) male point of view of the partner who feels oppressed by the weight of his beloved "at rest / Heavy upon my life." By 1912, she felt ready to issue her first collection, A *Dome of Many-Colored Glass*. There is much in this first book—including the title, taken from Percy Bysshe Shelley's elegy for Keats, "Adonais"—to link Lowell's poetry back to the nineteenth-century masters she admired; there is rather little to suggest that Lowell would soon ally herself with more radical movements in twentieth-century poetry. The year 1912 also saw another significant beginning for Lowell: she befriended an actress, Ada Dwyer Russell, who became her lifelong companion.

Reading H. D.'s first imagist poems in 1913 gave Lowell both new impetus in her career and a cause to embrace. Deciding that she too was an imagist, Lowell set off to London to meet Pound, fortified with a note of introduction from Harriet Monroe, the editor of *Poetry*. On a second trip, in 1914, she met others in the imagist circle, including H. D., and laid plans for a volume designed to introduce the new movement on a wider scale in the United States: this collection, *Some Imagist Poets*, first appeared in 1915, and Lowell issued a second and third collection under the same title in the next two years. Pound resented Lowell's appropriation (so to speak) of his invention, and began calling the movement "Amygism"; Lowell retaliated with "Astigmatism" (published in *Sword Blades and Poppy Seed*, 1914), a satire on a poet who sets out one day with his walking stick—one of Pound's favorite props—and strikes the heads off all the flowers he sees because they happen not to be roses, the only flowers he admires. Lowell sealed her identification with imagism in the United States with a 1915 lecture tour promoting the new poetry, and in 1917 published a book of critical essays derived from her lectures, *Tendencies in Modern American Poetry*.

Lowell's own poetic output in these years was varied and prolific, if not always of memorable quality. She experimented with free forms, but never wholly abandoned conventional forms. She tried her hand at long ballad-style narrative poems ("The Great Adventure of Max Breuck," "The Cremona Violin") and at free-form "polyphonic prose," or prose poetry (*Can Grande's Castle*). "Reaping" and "Off the Turnpike" are dramatic monologues written in New England dialect, in imitation of and challenge to Lowell's friend Robert Frost. More successful by far is her dramatic monologue "Patterns," spoken by an eighteenth-century woman who receives news of her fiancé's death in battle. The poem comments not only on the futile repetitions of war (Flanders, where the fiancé dies, was a bloody battlefield of World War I as well as of earlier conflicts, but also on the social patterns of courtship and sexual restraint that confine the speaker's life.

Pictures of the Floating World (1919) is Lowell's most lyrical, most nearly imagist, and perhaps most successful single volume. Featuring a number of adaptations of Japanese and Chinese poetry (for which Pound had earlier set a fashion), *Pictures* also includes love lyrics reflecting Lowell's life with Ada Russell: "Mise en Scene," "Venus Transiens," "Madonna of the Evening Flowers." In these poems, as Gillian Hanscombe and Virginia Smyers point out, "the beloved is associated with gardens and flowers," with traditional feminine imagery,[6] while the speaker often takes on the traditionally masculine role of observing and finding metaphors for the beloved.

In the 1920s Lowell added to her own poetic work and her campaigns on behalf of other writers a major new critical project, her biography of John Keats. The strain told on her. Already in precarious health (she was terribly overweight all her adult life), Lowell suffered a stroke in 1925 and died a day later, with Ada Russell at her side. As Lowell's literary executor, Russell brought out her remaining poems posthumously; but many modernist women writers, including H. D. and Bryher, knew they had lost a friend and an energetic American champion with Lowell's death.

In 1921 Bryher and H. D. together brought out, through London's Egoist Press, a collection of poems by Marianne Moore (1887–1972). Moore and H. D. had been classmates at Bryn Mawr College in Pennsylvania (H. D. left without completing a degree; Moore took her B.A. in 1909), but they did not know each other at school. H. D. and Bryher had come to know Moore instead through the poems she began publishing in *Poetry* and the *Egoist*—the most important journals of imagism and the new poetry—in 1915. Moore met with Bryher and H. D. when they visited New York in 1920 and continued to correspond with both women, who were determined both to promote Moore's work and to bring her to the flourishing American literary colony in London (with Bryher's ever-ready financial help). Moore refused, however, to take the bait, remaining in the New York City apartment she shared with her mother; when H. D. and Bryher brought out her 1921 *Poems*, they did so without Moore's authorization or assistance.[7]

One of the most important facts of Moore's relationship to imagism, as the story of her relationship with H. D. and Bryher suggests, may be that she kept some distance between it and her own work. Like Wallace Stevens and William Carlos Williams, members of her literary circle in Greenwich Village, she made her life's work on American soil and with an eclectic mix of materials, rather than the classically pure Greek models favored by her more distant friend H. D. (at least in the earlier part of H. D.'s career). Many of her poems do share certain imagist characteristics: they avoid nineteenth-century conventions of poetic diction and poetic form, and seem full of things described with precision rather than abstract lyric emotion. But she did not write consistently in the imagists' free verse, often composing her poems in syllabic stanzas with subtle, understressed rhyme schemes. (Syllabic meter counts syllables rather than accentual feet: see, for instance, the 1-3-9-6-8 rhymed stanzas of "The Fish.")[8] More important, as T. S. Eliot noted in his 1923 review of *Poems*, her poems were too complex and rapid in their association of images to quite meet imagist expectations.[9]

Moore's characteristic strategies, in fact, challenge any simple interpretation of Ezra Pound's imagist dictum calling for "direct treatment" of things in themselves. What, after all, are things in themselves? In Moore's poems, no thing is or can be isolated in itself. Things always gather to themselves webs of association, and they never come to us shorn of the meanings they have already acquired. Moore's persistent habit of quoting other writers' words in her poems underlines and celebrates the way the human mind perceives things through a network of prior associations. Looking at something as apparently simple as a snail's shell, for instance, Moore is reminded of an ancient philosopher's dictum: "If 'compression is the first grace of style,' / you have it" ("To a Snail"). Another short poem about a more elaborate object, "No Swan So Fine," also begins with a quotation, this time from a contemporary news magazine—"No water so still as the dead fountains of Versailles"—before moving into a description of a "Louis Fifteenth / candelabrum-tree." Moore's own notes to the *Complete Poems* (like T. S. Eliot's famous notes to *The Waste Land*) courteously direct her readers to some, but by no means all, of the sources of her quotations. The poet herself would almost certainly not have expected her readers to recognize all her borrowings. Knowing the source of every quotation in Moore's poems is probably impossible and surely less important than understanding what her practice of quotation says about the workings of the mind that brings such heterogeneous materials together in the very act of perception.

The mind itself, critics of Moore have often argued, is the subject of her poems: the mind regarding its sense-objects and itself, the curious mind, the mind attentive to the multiple languages we negotiate in everyday life. A much-anthologized short poem, "The Mind Is an Enchanting Thing" (first published in 1943) overtly takes the mind as its subject. An "Enchanting Thing," the mind is also, Moore stresses, "an enchanted thing." Taken together, the two parallel adjectives suggest that the mind is both active and passive: enchanting in its own ceaseless activity of association and questioning, enchanted like the eye rapt in gazing at the world, "the glaze on a / katydid-wing / subdivided by sun / till the nettings are legion." In the poem's metaphors, the mind becomes what it looks on and what it acts like. Moore's comparison of "the mind / feeling its way as though blind" to the kiwi bird that "walks along with its eyes on the ground" was apparently suggested to her by a mundane source:

her typescript of the poem bears her sketch of the bird off a can of Kiwi brand boot polish.[10] To Moore's capacious curiousity, a tin of shoe polish yields as much material to the imagination as "Gieseking [a famous pianist] playing Scarlatti;" the meanings of the everyday world, no less than the special meanings of art, are legion. Moore's vision of the mind does not particularly respect hierarchies of low art versus high art, commercial language versus aesthetic language.[11] It does, however, respect cheerfulness and flexibility as high ethical and aesthetic values. The mind "takes apart / dejection," eschews rigidity, and creates beauty out of its own lack of final certainty.

Moore's poetic techniques might at first glance seem best suited to small subjects; like the imagists, she is often associated with lyric poems of tightly constrained observation. Yet a poem like "The Mind Is an Enchanting Thing" questions hierarchical rankings of subject by size: is the mind a small subject, or a large one? There can be no simple answer. And while many of Moore's published poems are relatively short, "An Octopus" (first published in 1924) takes on a large subject: Mt. Rainier, in Washington state, which Moore had visited with her mother and brother in 1922. Moore knew that mountains, of course, were favorite poetic haunts of the nineteenth-century romantic poets. William Wordsworth's crossing of the Alps and ascent of Wales's Mount Snowden provided him with the climax and conclusion of his autobiographical epic, *The Prelude*. Percy Bysshe Shelley, of the next generation of Romantic poets, chimed in with his shorter lyric, "Mont Blanc." In choosing the mountain as a poetic subject, Moore took on one of the central icons of romanticism and reworked it in her own modernist idiom (a challenge that her friend William Carlos Williams would later take up as well, in book 2 of his long poem *Paterson*). No one would mistake Moore's mountain for Wordsworth's or Shelley's. At the same time, it has a grandeur all its own, and as a piece of American nature writing, "An Octopus" can stand in company with Henry David Thoreau's exploration of his pond in *Walden*.

Like Thoreau, Moore has a passion for detail and exactitude, and finds precision no obstacle to enchantment. No denizen of the mountain is too small for her notice; on the "octopus of ice" (the shape the mountain's glaciers assume, as mapped from the air) the small and the large are of equal importance. "'Picking periwinkles from the cracks' / or killing prey with the concentric crushing rigor of the python," the octopus, like Moore's eye and voice, is omnivorous. Incorporating quotations from guidebooks, National Park regulations, and naturalists' descriptions of the mountain, Moore's poem makes no claim to be the first or last word on the place. She avoids the (culturally masculine) stance of the American Adam who wishes to be first on the scene of a virgin world. "Big Snow Mountain is the home of a diversity of creatures"—including human ones; there are always already other presences here. If the mountain is not the vision of a solitary I/eye, the poem has no overt "I" at all. The speaker does, however, address a "you"—perhaps herself, perhaps anyone else who undertakes to see the mountain as she has.

Once again, the subject of "An Octopus" is as much the habit of the observing mind as it is the mountain itself; once again—as the title's metaphor makes clear—things never exist in themselves, in isolation, for Moore's imagination. An octopus is always reaching out to connect, like the mind that dares see an octopus in the arms of a glacier. An extended passage in the middle of the poem implicitly contrasts Moore's own attitude toward her subject with the mindset of the Greeks who, she says,

> liked smoothness, distrusting what was back
> of what could not be clearly seen,
> resolving with benevolent conclusiveness,
> "complexities which still will be complexities
> as long as the world lasts;" . . .

Perhaps this passage ventures an oblique reply to modernists like H. D. who still, in 1924, prized Greek texts and wrote through their masks. While Moore's poem honors their striving for clarity, it ends without Greek conclusiveness. One of the "symmetrically pointed" arms of the glacier is "cut by the avalanche," seen "launched like a waterfall." The poem ends dramatically on a freeze-frame of action rending symmetry, stasis in motion: a complexity that Moore may fix for an instant in time, but that she chooses otherwise not to reduce.

During the years of World War II, Moore, like H. D., tried to find ways of writing poetry from the sidelines. Instead of embarking on longer forms, however, in the vein of H. D.'s epic *Trilogy*, Moore actually curtailed her style: "Her work of the forties affirms not only poetic unity and closure but also concision." These poems also saw "a marked and lasting return of the poetic speaker's 'I,'" absent from poems of the 1920s like "An Octopus."[12] Her greatest achievement in this vein, perhaps one of the great war poems of the century, was arguably "In Distrust of Merits" (first published in 1943). Undertaking the risk of direct moral statement, employing more traditional religious emblems (the star of David, the halo) rather than Moore's usual heterogeneous mix of associations, the poem's elaborate syllabic form conveys at once urgency, the hesitance of reflection, and dignity. A middle-aged woman in 1943, Moore turns what might have been her disqualifications for writing a poem about war—her distance from combat, her gender—into the very subject of her poem, questioning her own moral status as observer of the conflict. "I must / fight till I have conquered in myself what / causes war, but I would not believe it." Her disbelief in her own involvement is what the poem tries to conquer. A brilliant internal rhyme links "I must," in the final stanza, with "dust" and "rust"; moral responsibility evaded will only let the heart sink into the corruption of hatred.

For many readers, Moore's poetry after the war falls off from the quality of the earlier years. Margot Holley notes the death of Moore's mother in 1947, and speculates that it "was a staggering loss—not just of her mother but even more of her closest friend, her sternest critic, and the voice that had stirred and joined her own in some of her finest poems" (Holley, 133–34). Honors came to Moore in plenty during these years: the Pulitzer Prize and a National Book Award in 1951 for *Collected Poems*, the coveted Bollingen Prize in 1953, and many others. Like Robert Frost, she became a recognized public persona, a poet to invite to ceremonies dedicating buildings or even opening the baseball season. Yet her poems resist hardening into the shape of a conventional monument to civil or poetic pieties. More so perhaps than any of the other women associated with imagism, Moore fashioned a poetic style of self-critical thought; and as self-effacing as this style was in some respects, as critical as Moore was of the egoism of "I," no careful reader would ever be likely to mistake her poetry for anyone else's.

CHAPTER
3

Women Poets to World War II

H. D., Amy Lowell, and Marianne Moore form a group within twentieth-century women's poetry because of their common association with imagism—however unjust that label may be to their eventually diverse achievements. The poets discussed in this chapter are more difficult to classify. Some affiliated themselves with movements in which few other women were represented; others did not travel under the banner of any particular group. The British poets Alice Meynell, Charlotte Mew, and Edith Sitwell lived and worked for the most part in London. Mina Loy, born in London, spent the last 30 years of her life in the United States after sojourns in many of the European capitals of modernist innovation. Sara Teasdale, Edna St. Vincent Millay, and Louise Bogan were Americans who made their careers primarily in the literary centers of the eastern United States; Gwendolyn Brooks emerged in the early 1940s as a voice from the black community of Chicago's South Side. Elinor Wylie, also an American, spent creative years abroad in England. Their lives and works ranged from traditional to iconoclastic—often representing a combination of both.

The life and work of Alice Meynell (1847–1922) bridged the transition between Victorian England and the twentieth century. Her first volume of poetry, *Preludes*, appeared in 1875. She married the journalist Wilfred Meynell in 1877 and bore him seven children. Meynell became a devout Catholic as an adult, and in form and inspiration many of her poems resemble the lyrics of Christina Rossetti, nineteenth-century England's greatest religious poet.

"Modern Mother" illustrates Meynell's position between the two eras, Victorian and modern. Written in the uneasy consciousness that mothers were no longer unanimously viewed as the founts of goodness and light (by the turn of the century psychologists were beginning to blame mothers for all sorts of unhappiness in their children), the poem presents a self-doubting mother who looks for "not so much / Thanks as forgiveness" from her child.[1] Trying to recover this Victorian icon for the modern age, Meynell points out that "childish eyes, these new, these bright / Intelligible stars" still rest upon the mother's "misgiving breast."[2]

Meynell's religious inclinations in no way sequestered her from the active social issues of her own time. In her later years Meynell came to support the cause of women's suffrage with energy; she made speeches, wrote, and marched on behalf of the cause, although she would never be comfortable sharing a platform with the more "militant" members of the movement, who advocated civil disobedience.[3] The outbreak of World War I, during which one of her sons went to prison as a conscientious objector, also prompted Meynell to write several poems in which her religious convictions and her feminism helped shape her attitude toward the war.

However modern their subjects, Meynell's poems always lean back to older times. "Saint Catherine of Siena" tells a story of the saint bringing comfort to an imprisoned man, but uses that story to make an unexpected point for women's suffrage: "Will the man of modern years," she asks, "—Stern on the Vote—withhold from thee, / Thou prop, thou cross, erect, in tears, / Catherine, the service of his knee?" (*Poems*, 42–43). The ideological burden of the poem is rather mixed: do women deserve worship on bended knee, or the vote? Meynell seems to suggest they deserve both, but she also knows that historically men have been quite willing to tender women the one without the other.

Meynell's war poems also bear mixed messages. Her son Francis, a conscientious objector, helped publish them, and they have been read as both feminist and pacifist.[4] In their entirety, however, they are not so clear. In "Summer in England, 1914," Meynell does lament the slaughter of "a thousand shattered men, / One wet corruption," which she charges to "man's unpardonable race." Yet she still clings to hope in the ultimate meaning of the sacrifice, which she understands in Christian terms: "The soldier dying dies upon a kiss, / The very kiss of Christ" (*Poems*, 69–70). "In Honour of America, 1917," celebrates America's entry into the war (*Poems*, 94); "To Conscripts" exhorts draftees to become free through submission: "Accept your victory from that unsought, / That heavenly, paradox" (*Poems*, 97).

Other poems raise the troubling question of women's relationship to this wartime discourse of sacrifice. In "A Father of Women," a daughter demands of her father (both an earthly father, and God) "For my delicate mind a casque, / A breastplate for my heart, courage to die" (*Poems*, 78). The poem concludes by inviting "Fathers of women" to "Approve, accept, know" their own daughters as heroines, "Now that your sons are dust." More concretely, "Nurse Edith Cavell" tells the story of a nurse dying in the line of duty: "that day she met the Immortal Dead" (*Poems*, 80).

Meynell's Christianity and her feminism combined to urge not pacifism exactly, but rather women's right to share in the meaning and dignity of wartime sacrifice as she understood it. That meaning, of course, was even then being called into question by younger writers, both male and female; their scorn for Victorian ideals of courage and duty would shape a postwar literary landscape in which Meynell's work would come to seem of an earlier world indeed.

Charlotte Mew (1869–1927) read and admired Alice Meynell's poetry as a schoolgirl.[5] But Mew did not publish her own first collection of poetry, *The Farmer's Bride*, until 1916, and her work belongs to a generation after Meynell's. Her major technical achievement, as James Smith notes, lies in the refinement of "a rhyming free verse"; combined with her preference for dramatic monologues, Mew's technique at best combines the fluid pacing of speech with the gravity and closure of rhyme.[6]

Mew won the admiration of Ezra Pound, among others, for "The Fete." One of her most ambitious dramatic monologues, "The Fete" is spoken by a 17-year-old boy. Given leave to go to the fair with his schoolmates, he falls in love with a circus performer. His eye encompasses everything tawdry about the fair, while his desire idealizes the woman in heroic terms; he glories in the change and dreads it at the same time. "There is something new in the old heavenly air of Spring— / The smell of beasts, the smell of dust—*The Enchanted Thing!*"[7] At the same time, however, the advent of desire writes itself over his memories and perceptions, leaving disorder in its wake:

> All my life long I shall see moonlight on the fern
> And the black trunks of trees. Only the hair

Of any woman can belong to God.
The stalks are cruelly broken where we trod,
  There had been violets there,
  I shall not care
As I used to do when I see the bracken burn.
         (*Poems*, 32)

Mew herself had reason to regard desire with ambivalence; morally conventional, all her life long she fell in love with women who did not reciprocate her feelings. (The novelist May Sinclair, who helped publish Mew's poetry, was among the most important of these relationships.) How much of Mew's own feelings were displaced into her romantic monologues is for anyone to guess. "Ne Me Tangito"—apparently Mew's mistake for *nolle me tangere* (do not touch me), the actual Latin words of the Biblical quotation she takes as the poem's epigraph (Fitzgerald, 138)—may, however, be one of Mew's more direct poems about Sinclair.

The "you" addressed in "Ne Me Tangito" has rejected the speaker's touch. The poem's epigraph from Luke (about the sinning woman who touched Jesus) implies that the speaker is a sinful woman, perhaps, but not deserving of rejection. "Odd, *You* should fear the touch, / The first that I was ever ready to let go," she begins; instead of reciprocating, the other person has responded to her with "ugly doubt," seeing in her touch "the shade of something vile." The speaker retaliates by telling a vivid, disturbing dream in which the beloved turns into a child at her breast (*Poems*, 56).

"The Fete," "Ne Me Tangito," and many other of Mew's poems delicately explore tangled erotic situations; they have the courage of fantasy. Unlike her friend Sinclair, she seems not to have sought out the newly fashionable scientific theories of psychology and sexuality, but it is hard to see how her poetry would have been the better for it if she had. Dreamy, evocative, a blend of traditional forms with modernist free verse, Mew's poetry occupies a small but very distinctive place in early-twentieth-century poetry.

Unlike Mew, Mina Loy (1882–1966) would struggle with questions of women's sexuality in consciously modernist terms. Born in London, she did much of her life's work in expatriate artist's colonies: Paris (where she knew Gertrude Stein and Djuna Barnes), Florence, and New York's Greenwich Village.

In Florence, around 1913–14, she met and had an affair with Filippo Marinetti, the leader of Italian futurism (the aggressively modern, macho, machine-age artistic movement). She embraced the movement eagerly, even writing her own "Aphorisms on Futurism."[8] But Marinetti, true to his own militarist doctrines, was finally more interested in World War I than in Loy; in the face of her own personal "utter defeat in the sex war," Loy had to work out her own thoughts on the conjunction of feminism and modernism.[9]

Loy exhorted herself and other women to "Leave off looking to men to find out what you are *not*. Seek within yourselves to find out what you *are*." This did not for Loy mean renouncing men or heterosexuality altogether. It did mean, she thought, that "Woman must destroy in herself the desire to be loved" and "the manmade bogey of virtue," the obsession with women's virginity (Hanscombe and Smyers, 116–17).

Her poems, which she began publishing in 1914, are experimental collages: free-form, modern, oblique but risky in their imagery. Her "Love Songs: 1915–1917" celebrate "Love—the preeminent litterateur" (*Baedeker*, 107). While fearing that "Evolution   fall foul of / Sexual equality," the speaker survives her own melting "Into abysmal pigeon-holes / Passion has bored / In warmth." "Some few of us," she says—a few modern women who dare sexual experience?—"Grow to the level of cool plains / Cutting our foothold / With steel eyes" (*Baedeker*, 102): futurism's machine-man reenvisioned as woman.

In her major long poem, "Anglo-Mongrels and the Rose" (written 1923–25), Loy's "intricate debunkings of English upper-class culture" in Cary Nelson's words, "link the impoverished ideals of empire" with a constricted, self-enclosed sexuality (Nelson, 73). Where a conservative poet like T. S. Eliot frowned on what he saw as the sexual excesses and confusion of 1920s London in *The Waste Land*, Loy mocked "the Anglo-Saxon phenomenon / of Virginity delightfully / on its own   defensive!" (*Baedeker*, 125).

Loy published only a few new poems after the 1920s, turning much of her energy instead toward painting and decorative arts. She left Europe permanently in 1936, settling first in New York and then in Colorado, where she continued her artistic work until her death.

Edith Sitwell (1887–1964) was the eldest of three children who all made important literary careers for themselves. She became best known for her poetry, but like her younger brothers, Osbert and Sacheverell, she also wrote novels and memoirs. And like Marianne Moore, Sitwell did distinguished editorial work for modernist writing. Along with her brothers, she sponsored and edited a yearly anthology, *Wheels*, from 1916 to 1921; *Wheels* published Edith's work, but also that of writers like Nancy Cunard, Aldous Huxley, and Wilfrid Owen. [10]

In "Some Notes on My Own Poetry," her introduction to her 1949 collection *The Canticle of the Rose*, Sitwell located her own poetic genealogy in a combination of English tradition and international modernism, naming the English Renaissance poets Sir Philip Sidney and Thomas Campion as her precursors in discussions of poetry and the modernist architect Le Corbusier as her guide to the new sounds of "the heightened speed of our time." [11] Her poems bear out this double ancestry. Many of them are written in traditional rhymed forms, others in free forms that mimic the rhythm of popular dances or song. Many of them draw on fairy tale or mythic subjects, but usually in fractured, dreamlike ways that defy traditional narrative.

"Green Geese," for example (first published in 1923), is written in rhymed couplets and seems based upon a traditional kind of fairy-tale metamorphosis. "The trees were hissing like green geese," the poem begins. They are trying to tell that "great Queen Claude" is dead, and "buried . . . deep in the potting shed" (CR, 12–13). By implication, Queen Claude is dead of foul play, since queens are unlikely to be buried in potting sheds. She has metamorphosed into the plants and spices of the shed, where "her sandalwood body leans upright"; she struggles to make the living hear her voice, but finally seems to acquiesce in her fate. Rather than narrate the implied events directly, Sitwell invests the story in the sensual details of the life from which the queen's ghost is receding.

Sitwell's most sensational achievement of the 1920s was *Facade*, a cycle of poems accompanied by the music of the young and gifted composer William Walton. (Sitwell's collaboration with Walton anticipated the working relationship Gertrude Stein would develop with Virgil Thomson in the 1930s.) In *Facade's* first public performance, on 12 June 1923, Sitwell recited her own poems from behind a curtain, her back turned to the audience, with the aid of an elaborate megaphone. The event furnished both admirers and detractors (probably greater in number) of the Sitwells with ammunition. [12]

The individual poems of *Facade* are very much of their time, striking the notes of the 1920s. "The Drum" seems to recollect World War I in the guise of a grotesque, childish nightmare: "What is the march we hear groan / As the hoofed sound of a drum marched on / With a pang like darkness, with a clang / Blacker than an orang-outang?" (CR, 28). "Polka" imitates the lively, stomping rhythms of the dance, and playfully pictures Robinson Crusoe looking on in a twenties nightclub, finding "fresh isles in a Negress' smiles— / The poxy doxy dear" (CR, 51). "Hornpipe" (CR, 62) mocks the great nineteenth-century age of British Empire, imagining Tennyson and Queen Victoria looking on disapprovingly as Venus rises from the waves of Britannia was said to rule ("Rule, Britannia" is still the British national anthem).

In 1924 Sitwell read T. S. Eliot's *The Waste Land*. According to Victoria Glendinning, "Eliot's poem, which she came to tentatively and late, was to affect what she herself was to be writing in the next five years— though she denied Eliot's influence" (Glendinning, 100). Eliot's presence is certainly marked in her long poem "Gold Coast Customs," first published in 1929, which one critic called "Edith Sitwell's *Waste Land*, footnotes and all."[13]

The poem casts contemporary London in the guise of the "Gold Coast" of Africa, where (according to Sitwell's anthropological headnote) "the death of any rich or important person was followed by several days of national ceremonies, during which the utmost license prevailed, and slaves and poor persons were killed that the bones of the deceased might be washed with human blood" (CR, 133). Sitwell's use or misuse of anthropology unfortunately carries with it racist associations; she repeatedly symbolizes London's corruption in "The Negro" who "rolls / His red eyeballs, / Prostrates himself" (CR, 140). Her prophetic denunciation of "the rat-eaten bones / Of a fashionable god that lived not / Ever, but still has bones to rot" (CR, 141) owes a great deal to Eliot's "rats' alley / Where the dead men lost their bones" (*The Waste Land*, 3.115–16).

"Gold Coast Customs" ends with a call for an apocalypse in which "the rich man's gold and the rich man's wheat / Will grow in the street, that the starved may eat" (CR, 149). Sitwell implies that it will take "blood and fire," however, to bring this about. She later wrote, with the advantage of hindsight, that the poem was "about the state that led up to the second World War" (CR, xxxi).

"Gold Coast Customs" was the last poetry Sitwell wrote for many years. Although she wrote fiction and nonfictional prose, Sitwell—like H. D.— was silent as a poet in the 1930s. And like H. D., she began writing poetry again under the stress of World War II.

"My time of experiments was done," Sitwell said (CR, xxxiii). Her wartime poetry was written in a long, prophetic line, apparently influenced by Walt Whitman's example. In her "Eurydice" (worth comparing to H. D.'s earlier poem of the same title), the poet sees "Fires on the hearth! Fires in the heavens! Fires in the hearts of Men!" But like H. D. and Marianne Moore (if less eloquently than H. D.'s *Trilogy* or Moore's "In Distrust of Merit"), she still asserts that "All the weight of Death in all the world / Yet does not equal Love" (*CR*, 163).

Sitwell's fame survived World War II. In 1948, she and her brother Osbert visited the United States. New Directions, the important modernist press, issued *A Celebration for Edith Sitwell* (with essays by William Butler Yeats and Gertrude Stein, among others) to mark the occasion.[14] In 1954 she was named a Dame Commander of the British Empire.

Sara Teasdale (1884–1933) was one of America's most popular poets during the early twentieth century, working entirely in traditional forms. Literary histories focused on the formal experiments of modernism have understandably tended to pass her by. Nevertheless, her poems, while traditional in form, questioned some of the roles traditionally allotted to women in poetry, especially love poetry. Carol B. Schoen argues that Teasdale's poems about women like the famous actress Eleonora Duse and the ancient Greek poet Sappho "considered significant themes of the right [of women] to achievement and power."[15]

Schoen points out that for Teasdale, as for many other late-nineteenth- and early-twentieth-century readers, Sappho "served as the archetypal woman artist" (Schoen, 43). Teasdale's "To Cleis" and her long dramatic monologue "Sappho" raise the troubling question of whether a poet and a mother can reside in the same woman. "To Cleis" ponders whether Cleis, Sappho's daughter, could "bear her burning eyes."[16] In "Sappho," the poet gives thanks to Aphrodite (the goddess of love) for having made her "life too sweet / To hold the added sweetness of a song" (*CP*, 92); content in her daughter, she is no longer a poet. Teasdale suggests either that a woman cannot be a mother and a poet at the same time, or that if she can, we—outsiders—can never know about it; that intimacy will never be committed to writing.

Other kinds of women's love, however, can be sung in Teasdale's lyrics. "Driftwood" elaborates a small but lovely metaphor for the effect of love upon the woman's song. Her "forefathers," the speaker says, gave her "My spirit's shaken flame," but her lovers "gave the flame its changeful / And iridescent fires," as a driftwood log burns with more brilliant colors—a "jewelled blaze"—because of its immersion in sea and salt (*CP*, 117). The coloring of erotic experience, in this poem, is radiant rather than staining or polluting for the female speaker.

44

Teasdale took other women's poetry seriously enough to edit an anthology, *The Answering Voice: One Hundred Love Lyrics by Women*, that featured contemporary as well as earlier women poets.[17] In her foreword to the anthology's 1928 edition, she noted the new independence of women's love poetry and ascribed it to women's growing economic autonomy in the world at large (Schoen, 159). She realized, too, that women's poetry could no longer be well represented in a volume dedicated only to love poetry (Schoen, 158), but went ahead anyway. Teasdale recognized and hailed—albeit with some reservations—a new, modernist future for women's poetry, but chose to pause on the threshold of that future in her own work.

The name of Elinor Wylie (1885–1928) is often coupled with that of Sara Teasdale: both were popular poets, both worked in traditional forms. Judith Farr notes that Teasdale thought Wylie enough of a rival to spare some private mockery for her.[18] More so than Teasdale, however, "Wylie led a life of histrionic aspect, and in her meticulous attention to her appearance and surroundings, she tried . . . to lend her life artistic dimension" (Farr, 17).

The traditional problem of the relationship between art and life, and particularly between artifice and the female body,[19] lies at the heart of Wylie's work and makes it harsher and stranger, in some respects, than Teasdale's. The relationship is most explicit in her novel, *The Venetian Glass Nephew* (1925), in which a woman chooses to become a china doll for the sake of her husband, a man made of glass. Life becomes art, but always at a price.

In the short lyric "Valentine," the speaker imagines serving up her own heart, an apple fallen from a tree, "With spice and salt, / In a carven silver cup."[20] She chooses "the comforting power of aesthetic objects, her private universe," over "the natural and hostile world" of time and decay (Farr, 82). Withdrawn from the natural world, needing no sustenance from it, protected from other human beings, she keeps the heart "sweet / By some strange art"; and before death, she will consume it: "Wild honey I shall eat / When I eat my heart."

In another poem, the speaker imagines her dead skeleton turned into an art object—"delicate and slim, / With stars for eyes" and "bones . . . light / As filagree of pearl"—to inspire passion or terror in men (*CP*, 82). By becoming an art object, the speaker becomes beautiful but invulnerable, able to survey men's reactions from the double distance of art and death.

Wylie admired the work of William Butler Yeats, who also wrote of the poet's metamorphosis into an art object in poems like "Sailing to Byzantium," and her admiration was returned (Farr, 66). But her central literary passion was for Percy Bysshe Shelley. Wylie, whose own life was matter for scandal after she left her first husband and their son, identified both with Shelley's idealism and with his vilification at the hands of moralists (Farr, 113–26).

She wrote in a late sonnet to Shelley that "Your path is printed on the atmosphere / Forever as a flame against the smoke / Of obscure vision" (CP, 156). As with most of what poets write in praise of other poets, this must be read as Wylie's hope for herself as well: that her own fame would outlast scandal, if only (as she could not help knowing) on a smaller scale.

Like Elinor Wylie, Edna St. Vincent Millay (1892–1950) was a fine crafter of traditional poetic forms, including the sonnet. She won national attention early in her career for her meditative poem "Renascence," published in the anthology *The Lyric Year*. One of the admirers of her work, Caroline Dow, helped Millay apply for a scholarship to Vassar. The elite women's college and Millay were a productive match in many ways. Millay excelled at some of her classes and made friends to whom she was passionately devoted; she would later eulogize one of them in her "Memorial to D. C." a short sequence of effective lyrics.[21] While at Vassar, Millay wrote and acted in college plays, in addition to working on her lyric poetry.

The year of her graduation, 1917, also saw the publication of her first volume of poetry: *Renascence and Other Poems*. In addition to the title poem, an inspirational monologue of faith lost and recovered, the book featured conventional short ballads of love, nature, and loss.

In the fall of 1917, Millay moved to New York. She soon met the artistic regulars of Greenwich Village and began acting with the Provincetown Players—the talented playwrights' theater for which Millay herself, Susan Glaspell, Floyd Dell, and Eugene O'Neill at one time or another wrote plays. Millay had several love affairs with members of the Village scene before marrying Eugen Boissevain in 1923. In this lively atmosphere, her poetry began to grow sharper and wittier; she also became more concerned with politics. She published a good deal in the next few years: *A Few Figs from Thistles* (1920; revised and enlarged, 1921, 1922), *Second April* (1921), *The Harp-Weaver and Other Poems* (1923), and a verse play, *Aria da Capo* (1920).[22]

A *Few Figs from Thistles* became one of Millay's most popular collections, and set the tone of the youth-loving 1920s for which she has chiefly been remembered. "First Fig" will be familiar to many readers: "My candle burns at both ends; / It will not last the night; / But ah, my foes, and oh, my friends— / It gives a lovely light!" (*CL*, 127). The two lovers of "Recuerdo" go "back and forth all night on the ferry," finally giving "all our money but our subway fares" to the old woman selling newspapers in the morning (*CL*, 128). "Midnight Oil" boasts that "The years that Time takes off my life, / He'll take from the other end!" (*CL*, 144).

Slight as some of these poems are, they flippantly challenge traditional ideas of women—and women's lyric poetry—as lovelorn and passive. Moreover, they often do not draw distinctions between love and work; the speaker seems to imply her right to merge the two. For whom or what is the speaker burning her midnight oil—for an individual man, for her own poetry? For Millay herself in these years the answer would quite often have been both.

Millay was one of many American writers of the 1920s who became concerned with the country's increasingly repressive political climate. She and other writers took an active part in the protests around the trial and eventual execution of Nicola Sacco and Bartolomeo Vanzetti, charged with murder and robbery. Italians and anarchists, Sacco and Vanzetti were tried at the hands of a Massachusetts judge, Webster Thayer, who was openly prejudiced against their case. Last-minute appeals and picketing of the Massachusetts State House, at which Millay was arrested, failed to halt their execution.

Millay responded with bitter poems—"Justice Denied in Massachusetts," "Hangman's Oak"—published in *The Buck in the Snow* (1928). She wrote in "Anguish" that she was no longer satisfied, "As in my youth," with "the flask of song, and the good bread / Of beauty richer than truth"; instead, "The anguish of the world is on my tongue" (*CL*, 229).

Millay's politicized work never wholly crowded out quieter lyrics. *The Buck in the Snow* juxtaposes poems like "Anguish" with "Winter Night," reminiscent of Robert Frost's New England poetry, which celebrates a fruitful alternation between physical work and reflective thought. The hours of day, "gone in hewing and felling," give way to the evening of "question and reply, / And the fire reflected in the thinking eye" (*CL*, 245). "Winter Night" presents a more sober, disciplined version of love and work than the earlier "Midnight Oil," in keeping both with Millay's more settled life and with her evolving convictions in the late 1920s.

Her 1937 verse drama, *Conversation at Midnight*, attempted a thoroughgoing exploration of the political spectrum of the 1930s. Norman accurately points out that *Conversation* is not "a play in the usual sense; it is a dialogue among seven men of differing backgrounds and beliefs who meet for an evening of conversation and drinking—literally, for a symposium," like the philosophical drinking parties of Plato's dialogues.[23] They range from the conservative and wealthy Merton, to Carl, poet and communist. Of them all, Ricardo, the gathering's host, and John, painter and liberal, are probably the closest representatives of Millay's own thoughts.

The men speak in the shadow of impending war—"Two wars in a generation," Ricardo gloomily forecasts, will utterly "debase / Those whom it does not destroy."[24] Carl regards all wars as capitalist ventures (36); Pygmalion, "the salt of the earth," confesses that "there's lots of men that love a fight; and war—don't you see—it takes them out of their rut." Besides, "It's good for a man now and then to get away from his wife" (38). It is left to John and Ricardo to present a "liberal" alternative. "It is difficult to dramatize the liberal attitude," Ricardo confesses; "We weave / No pattern of uniformed men in the shape of our emblem; we sing no lusty song; we have no battle-cry" (112). Still, John insists, they have a role: we are "the insistent leaven / That leavens the reluctant whole" (113).

Conversation at Midnight is indeed "liberal" in the sense that it puts faith in dialogue, the "free" exchange of voices, to regulate differences. Of course the dialogue is only free within limits, since Millay is the sole author behind it. But she does give Carl, the communist poet, some effective lines of rejoinder to her work's own liberal faith in dialogue (111). And the kind of conversation she dramatized so abstractly would be very shortly enacted in real life, as the United States debated what role it would play in World War II.

Conversation at Midnight, true to its format, ends without a definite resolution among its points of view. As the war advanced, however, Millay threw her poetry openly behind military commitment and against U.S. isolationism, in some ways revising her own 1920s distrust of militarism. In the wake of Germany's annexation of Czechoslovakia, she wrote a sonnet on the Western allies' lack of response: "We save our skins a craven hour or two" (*CL*, 369). The Nazis' destruction of a Czechoslovakian village a few years later prompted her to a long ballad-style poem, *The Murder of Lidice* (1942).

Her contemporary critics were not kind to Millay's late political poetry, and more recent readers have generally followed their example. Still, as we have seen, her wartime dilemma was real both for herself and for other women. Feminist values were often associated with antimilitarism, as in Millay's own work of the 1920s. Feminists could hardly acquiesce in the rise of Nazism; yet how could women speak in favor of war without merely becoming cheerleaders to the hearty masculine war-fever of a character like Millay's own Pygmalion?

The very fact that *Conversation* takes place solely between male characters points to women's alienation from mainstream dialogue about the war. If H. D. and Edith Sitwell recovered their poetic voices during World War II, they did not, unlike Millay, publicly attempt to influence its advent or its course. Virginia Woolf, in *Three Guineas* (1938), would urge women to embrace their alienation from mainstream, male-dominated political discourse. For better or worse, Millay chose another path. The poetry of her final years can be compared and contrasted with that of more programmatically leftist poets like Genevieve Taggard and Muriel Rukeyser, whose work will be taken up in a later chapter.

Louise Bogan (1897–1970) was born just long enough after the generation of Teasdale, Wylie, and Millay to see them as important influences on her own poetic work. She survived them longer still, and became one of the earliest and best critics to look back and assess women's place in modern poetry. Bogan's own attitude toward being, and being labeled, a woman poet was complex; her changing evaluations of her poetic foremothers and peers chart the rise and fall of experimental modernism from the 1910s into the 1950s.

Early in her career, Bogan experimented with poems written in modernist free verse, like "Betrothed" (first published in 1917).[25] She also knew and admired, however, the work of women poets writing in traditional lyric forms: "In the poems of Christina Rossetti, Alice Meynell, Lizette Woodworth Reese, and Sara Teasdale, she found vigorous syntax in short forms and high, controlled feeling" (Frank, 33). And when she encountered William Butler Yeats's lyrics, with their combination of high ambition and romance with plain language, Bogan was more than ever convinced of the power of form. "From the early 1920s she took [Yeats] as her standard, measuring everything she wrote against the purity and power of his forms" (Frank, 48).

Bogan's first collection, *Body of This Death*, appeared in 1923. Although it included "Betrothed," the volume's most impressive poems were written in brief rhymed forms. "Medusa," for instance, is composed in quatrains, with the second and fourth lines rhyming. Only one stanza diverges from the pattern, incorporating a fifth line—but it does so memorably: the extra line comes with the speaker's recollection of seeing the Medusa herself, "The still bald eyes, the serpents on the forehead / Formed in the air."[26] This sight disrupts the poem's form, yet confirms it. As in the myth, seeing the Medusa turns the speaker and his or her world to stone, frozen in time.

Read one way, "Medusa" can be seen as a poem about the ambivalent power of art to freeze life, an idea returned to in "Statue and Birds" (BE, 14). Surrounded by birds and vines in a garden, a statue stands "with hands flung out in alarm / Or remonstrances." Everything around it moves and lives, but the statue's "inquietudes of the sap and of the blood are spent." But are they? The poem's last two lines reveal the statue's gender—"her heel is lifted"—and her wish to move from her pose; yet "the whistle of the birds / Fails" when it meets her stony breast.

Like Elinor Wylie, Bogan was fascinated with the problem of a woman taking herself as an object of art: an object immune to death and time, but also thereby frozen to feeling and change. In "The Alchemist" (BE, 15), one of Bogan's finest lyrics, the speaker tells of submitting her own life to the crucible of art. "I burned my life, that I might find / A passion wholly of the mind"; the act of purification founders, however, on the stubborn persistence of "unmysterious flesh." To succeed wholly in turning oneself into art might be either to die, or to regret the bargain and the metamorphosis, like the statue in the garden who would move off her pedestal.

Writing as a young woman, Bogan tentatively envisioned a Yeatsian old age for herself in which fleshly love would not altogether die into art—an alternative to the immortally youthful female statue. In "The Crows," an older woman, "a stem long hardened, / A weed that no scythe mows," may still feel desire, if only to the mocking music of the crows that fly indifferently over barren as well as fertile fields (BE, 17). As she grew older, however, Bogan remained divided between the claims of form and feeling.

This fundamental self-division helped shape Bogan's ambivalent attitude toward other women poets of the time. In 1939 she shrewdly warned Edna St. Vincent Millay against the dangers of the role of "unofficial feminine laureate," conjuring her instead to "withdraw . . . her own personality from her productions."[27] She praised Marianne Moore in 1944 for showing more warmth in her poetry without lapsing into "that self-pity which often attacks women writers when they let down their guard" (SC, 253). In 1947, on the other hand, Bogan relaxed her emphasis on women's need to guard their emotions to emphasize the great and, she thought, now overlooked "importance of keeping the emotional channels of a literature open," and praised earlier women poets like Teasdale, Millay, and Wylie for having "restored genuine and frank feeling to a literary situation which had become genteel, artificial, and dry" (SC, 341).

Where feeling and form were kept in balance, Bogan thought, women had immense gifts in lyric poetry. Bogan became increasingly hostile, however, to other sorts of poetic ambition in women. Her attitude toward Edith Sitwell from 1925 to 1954 cooled from qualified admiration for her verbal brilliance to dismissal of her "prophetic" and "sybilline" ambitions (SC, 21–27). Bogan abhorred Millay's and other writers' turn toward political subjects in longer poetic forms in the 1930s and 1940s. Generous and acute in assessing the contributions of women like Emily Dickinson and Elinor Wylie to American poetry, Bogan also helped shape a literary history forgetful of other forms of women's poetry. Only recently have literary scholars begun to place the accomplishments of women in lyric poetry in the context of other ambitions, other achievements as well.

Gwendolyn Brooks (b. 1917) grew up in the large black community of Chicago's South Side. At the nexus of railroad lines from all over the United States, Chicago in the early twentieth century was the destiny of choice for many black men and women leaving the rural South for the hope of better-paying jobs in Chicago stockyards, railroad yards, and industry. Those hopes were not always realized, at least not immediately; Brooks's father, on settling in Chicago, found that "he had to accept various odd jobs to sustain his family," and the Depression hit black families hard.[28] Yet young Gwendolyn grew up in relative security. "My father provided me with a desk," she would later write in her memoirs, "a desk with many little compartments, with long drawers at the bottom, and a removable glass-protected shelf at the top, for books." Among those books, "to look down at me whenever I sat at the desk, was Paul Laurence Dunbar," one of the important early black writers of the Harlem Renaissance: "'You,' my mother had early announced, 'are going to be the *lady* Paul Laurence Dunbar.'"[29]

Brooks grew up to join a thriving Chicago literary scene: "1941 through 1949," she recalled, "was a party era. . . . My husband and I knew writers, knew painters, knew pianists and dancers and actresses, knew photographers galore" (*Report*, 68). In 1941 she joined in the poetry workshop organized at the Southside Community Art Center by Inez Stark Boulton, a former reader for the famous modernist magazine *Poetry* (*A Life*, 2). Growing more confident in her own writing, Brooks began publishing in magazines, and in 1943 won the Midwestern Writers' Conference poetry award; Harper and Brothers shortly afterward accepted her first collection of poems, *A Street in Bronzeville* (1945).

The poems of *A Street in Bronzeville* are not easy to classify according to Louise Bogan's conventional distinction between poems of personal feeling and poems of craft and form. Many of them are written as dramatic monologues, sometimes spoken from a plural voice of the street: "Patent leather" mocks a man "With pretty patent-leather hair" from the point of view of "Us other guys," envious of his success with "That cool chick down on Calumet" (a street in Chicago). [30] They take on risky emotional subjects—in "The Mother," a speaker addresses the ghosts of her "dim killed children" (*Bronzeville*, 3)—without being overtly and specifically confessional. In the words of Hortense J. Spillers, one of Brooks's best critics, "Brooks's poetry . . . is not weighed down by egoistic debris, nor is her world one of private symbolisms alone, or even foremost; rather, she presents a range of temperaments and situations" through different narrative voices. [31]

Technically, as Brooks's readers from 1945 to the present have observed, the poems in *Bronzeville* range adroitly between rhymed, closed forms and off-rhymed, looser-line forms. "The Sundays of Satin-Legs Smith," for instance, evokes blank verse, sometimes even heroic couplets ("He awakes, unwinds, elaborately: a cat / Tawny reluctant, royal. He is fat / And fine this morning" [*Bronzeville*, 24]), without settling into fixed form. As Houston A. Baker, Jr., notes, "Brooks employs polysyllabics and forces words into striking combinations" while still "preserv[ing] colloquial rhythms." [32]

"Gay Chaps at the Bar," the concluding sequence of poems in *A Street in Bronzeville* (46–57), showcases Brooks's gift for combining modernist off-forms with colloquial language and contemporary subjects. Written, according to Brooks's dedication, as a "souvenir for Staff Sergeant Raymond Brooks [her brother] and every other soldier," "Gay Chaps at the Bar" is a series of sonnets on the experience of soldiers in World War II. The sequence's opening and concluding poems, "Gay Chaps at the Bar" and "The Progress," are spoken by "we," the anonymous soldiers. Other poems, like "Love Note I: Surely" voice the perspective of the soldier alone, concerned for his life and those he left behind. Still others speak from a generic, detached narrator's position, sometimes ironically: "God Works in a Mysterious Way," for instance, both uses and mocks an old-fashioned poetic diction in its picture of "an eye that all its age had drawn its / Beam from a Book" (54). In "The White Troops Had Their Orders but the Negroes Looked Like Men," a similarly impersonal narrator reports the reactions of white soldiers at black troops entering the U.S. Army (one of President Roosevelt's major policy initiatives during World War II). Wartime exigencies, she finds, "taxed / Time and the temper to remember those / Congenital iniquities that cause / Disfavor of the darkness" (52): for the duration, for some soldiers, suspending racism was simpler. The narrator encompasses both the white soldiers' racism and their half-willing suspension of it, with irony—perhaps, also, with some understated sympathy.

Brooks's career after A *Street in Bronzeville* would continue her first volume's dialogues between formalism and colloquial language, between white Western literary traditions and black oral traditions, between narrative distance and social engagement. Her second volume, *Annie Allen* (1949), won the Pulitzer Prize in 1950; its centerpiece, "The Anniad," reworks the titles of classical Western epics (the *Aeneid* and the *Illiad*) into the "mock-heroic journey of a particular female soul," a young black woman.[33] In the 1960s, Brooks turned away from Western written tradition and toward the black aesthetic movement, to which she contributed not only as a poet but as an editor and essayist—a double role that recalls the editorial contributions of earlier modernist women poets like Marianne Moore and Edith Sitwell. Like Edna St. Vincent Millay and Elinor Wylie, Brooks succeeded brilliantly in the sonnet form; more successfully than Millay, however, Brooks has found other forms in which to address war, injustice, and issues of cultural pride, forms that do not hand the dialogue over to the men who have mastered it all along.

CHAPTER 4

British Fiction and Consciousness: Dorothy Richardson and Virginia Woolf

The early years of the twentieth century saw a concerted attempt by many authors of fiction to challenge the inherited conventions of nineteenth-century realism. *Realism*, one must remember, is a word of many meanings in literary criticism, philosophy, and everyday parlance. It is sometimes used in a very general sense, sometimes in more specific ways; it refers to literary movements that took place at slightly different times and meant slightly different things in different countries. For the purposes of this chapter, realism is a way of writing novels that entered English literary history in the mid-nineteenth century. In classic English nine-teenth-century realism, novels were expected to have an authoritative third-person narrator, who would tell readers what was happening in the minds of his or her central characters and would also supply lavish de-scriptions of the physical details of the worlds in which those characters made their way. The narrator might also supply moral or ironic com-mentary on the story being told, from the vantage point of his or her special knowledge, assuring readers that the novel's world was both real and comprehensible.

As one aspect of their comprehensibility, realist novels were expected to have beginnings, middles, and ends; something definite had to happen, something that counted as a story. The story of a young hero might, for example, begin with his unhappy childhood and end with his establishment in a career and a happy marriage that symbolically put that childhood to rights. The story of a heroine might be similar, save for women's rather more limited career choices; in George Eliot's *Middlemarch* (1860), Dorothea Brooke makes a career of her first, disappointing marriage to a male scholar, whose death eventually releases her to a happy ending in another marriage. Not all nineteenth-century realist novels, of course, had happy endings: Maggie Tulliver, another of Eliot's heroines, expiates her rebellious childhood by drowning rather than marrying at the end of *The Mill on the Floss*. But happy or unhappy, realist novels did come to expected forms of closure under the powerful guidance of their narrators, and did for the most part offer externally detailed accounts of worlds their readers accepted as "real."

In the early twentieth century, all these attributes of nineteenth-century realism came under attack. Virginia Woolf's famous essay "Modern Fiction," written in 1919, neatly summed up an argument whose main battle lines had been drawn for several years. Woolf paid her respects to earlier generations of novelists: "Our quarrel," she said, "is not with the classics," but with those of her contemporaries who were repeating outworn formulas of realism.[1] In writers like H. G. Wells and Arnold Bennett, Woolf argued, "the enormous labour of proving the solidity, the likeness to life, of the story is not merely labour thrown away but labour misplaced to the extent of obscuring and blotting out the light of the conception." Life was lost in the amassing of realistic detail, and the writer was forced "by some powerful and unscrupulous tyrant who has him in thrall to provide a plot," to obey the conventions of realist closure within the prescribed 32 chapters of a respectable Victorian novel (CR, 153).

Nineteenth-century realism, Woolf charged in effect, is no longer real. In the real life of consciousness, "an ordinary mind on an ordinary day . . . receives a myriad impressions—trivial, fantastic, evanescent, or engraved with the sharpness of steel." This life does not order itself in the shape of a linear plot with its predictable highlights and emphases: "Life is not a series of gig lamps symmetrically arranged; but a luminous halo, a semi-transparent envelope surrounding us from the beginning of consciousness to the end" (CR, 154). Let the modern novel, Woolf argued, "trace the pattern" of those impressions in consciousness rather than retrace the conventions of realism; let us redefine reality as consciousness itself, not the objects of the external world.

Like most manifestos issued by writers, Woolf's is both informative and open to question at the same time. While the turn toward consciousness in twentieth-century fiction is a movement of major importance, it is important to remember that it does not mark an absolute break with nineteenth-century realism. Late-nineteenth-century novelists like Henry James and George Meredith, to seize only two examples, gave a great deal of space to sheerly mental reflection on the part of their characters: James's *The Portrait of a Lady* and Meredith's *The Egoist* both feature famous chapters of decision in which their heroines do nothing but think (about marriage or approaching marriage). Reflecting back in 1938 on the emergence of the new fiction of consciousness, Dorothy Richardson herself cast James in "the role of pathfinder," despite his allegiance to "nearly all the orthodoxies" in social matters. [2] What at least some twentieth-century writers did differently, however, was to turn consciousness into the driving agent of the story, and represent it without the stabilizing third-person omniscient narrators of James and Meredith.

But just what does it mean to "represent" consciousness? Can a novel directly "trace the pattern" of impressions on consciousness, as Woolf implies, without any literary conventions getting in the way? Whatever the pattern of neurons firing at any given moment in the human brain may look like, that pattern surely does not make its way directly onto the literary page. In order for consciousness to be represented on the page, it must be put into recognizable forms of language. Perhaps, as some philosophers argue, everything that we could call "consciousness" already has, in some way, a linguistic form; in any event, nothing can enter literature without taking on linguistic form. Tracing consciousness in literature without *any* conventions getting in the way, therefore, is a kind of impossibility, for where there is language there are conventions.

Yet the conventions of language and literature are not, as Woolf realized, fixed for all time. For many twentieth-century writers, approaching consciousness in literature meant not simply abolishing all literary conventions (which probably cannot be done), but playing with and disrupting old conventions, or setting up obtrusive, antirealist conventions that draw attention to the shaping power of artifice, to the inextricability of language and consciousness. James Joyce's *Ulysses*, for instance, which Woolf singled out for praise in "Modern Fiction," contains one chapter ("Nausicaa") that parodies the style of romantic popular fiction, another ("Oxen of the Sun") that runs through imitations of the entire history of English prose; the book as a whole is structured by a set of parallels to Homeric myth. Clearly, *Ulysses* does not present readers with sheer consciousness stripped of convention, any more—as we shall see—than do the novels of Virginia Woolf. *Ulysses* instead brings a multitude of conventions to bear against the apparent solidity and singleness of realist conventions.

Woolf's manifesto for modern fiction's turn to the reality of consciousness, therefore, needs to be read and understood with qualifications. That does not diminish the importance of this turn, a turn that Woolf, Dorothy Richardson, and many other writers thought particularly important to women writers. For one thing, the turn to consciousness undermined external hierarchies of what constituted an important subject for fiction. "Let us not take it for granted," Woolf wrote, "that life exists more fully in what is commonly thought big than in what is commonly thought small" (CR, 155). If women's lives have usually been debarred from action on a large and public scale, still women have lived in consciousness; therefore, they have, according to Woolf, as much access to human reality as men, and equal claims to importance in fiction. Moreover, the turn to consciousness, by dethroning realistic conventions of plot and closure (what "counts" as a finished story), allowed women writers to dethrone the eighteenth- and nineteenth-century novel's two favorite plots for women: the plot that leads to marriage, and the plot that leads to death.[3] These twin struggles—to ratify the importance of women's lives in consciousness, and to unseat the heroine's marriage/death plot—shaped the careers of both Dorothy Richardson (1873–1957) and Virginia Woolf, the two most famous women writers identified with the modernist novel of consciousness in England.

Although relatively little read today, Dorothy Richardson was at one time ranked with Joyce and Woolf as an inventor of the stream-of-consciousness narrative technique in English literature. Her multivolume life's work, *Pilgrimage* (centered upon her autobiographical protagonist, Miriam Henderson), although scarcely profitable either for Richardson or for her long-suffering publishers, was hailed and attacked on both sides of the Atlantic as a pioneering effort of modernist fiction.[4] Indeed, the very phrase "stream of consciousness" seems to have been introduced into literary criticism in a review of the first volume of *Pilgrimage* by May Sinclair, another British woman novelist, who observed that in Richardson's fiction, "Nothing happens. It is just life going on and on. It is Miriam Henderson's stream of consciousness going on and on. And in neither is there any grossly discernible beginning or middle or end"—only consciousness without conventional realist plotting or closure.[5] More so perhaps than either Joyce or Woolf, Richardson seemed to aspire to represent her heroine's consciousness without intervening artifice. There are exceptions to *Pilgrimage*'s apparent lack of external design; Gloria G. Fromm points out that the novels of volume 2 (*The Tunnel* and *Interim*) "have echoes of a famous classical journey in search of self, Dante's *Divine Comedy*," echoes made explicit when, in *Interim*, Miriam attends a lecture on the Italian poet. Like the *Divine Comedy*'s 33 cantos, *The Tunnel* has 33 chapters.[6] In comparison to Joyce's use of Homeric motifs in *Ulysses*, however, Richardson's use of Dante seems deliberately restricted in scope; and Richardson eschews Joyce's stylistic leaps from chapter to chapter. The quality of Miriam Henderson's consciousness remains at the fore throughout *Pilgrimage* and changes in its main outlines only slowly.

The four volumes of *Pilgrimage*—running well over a thousand pages—cover Miriam Henderson's life from her teens into her midthirties, closely following the pattern of Dorothy Richardson's own experiences from 1890, when her middle-class family fell into financial straits, to 1912, when Richardson herself was at work on *Pointed Roofs*, the first book of *Pilgrimage*. The novel recounts the life of a young, struggling, ambiguously middle-class, turn-of-the-century English woman with zeal and thoroughness. Historical changes that would affect women profoundly surface in unpredictable ways throughout *Pilgrimage*, emerging only as they enter Miriam's consciousness. Richardson's narrative technique thus gives her readers a sense of change as it is actually lived, in all its ambiguity, rather than with the advantage of hindsight's linear and hierarchical ordering of events. In the world of Miriam's consciousness, daring to wear unrestrictive women's clothing for the first time (1:124) marks an epoch in women's emancipation as surely as does the more public historical achievement of women's suffrage.

Young Miriam, like her author, responds to her family's financial crisis by seeking and finding employment in a school abroad; the beginning of *Pointed Roofs*, and of subsequent books, highlights work and independence rather than courtship as the starting place of a woman's story. Like the heroine of Charlotte Brontë's *Villette*—one of the books on young Miriam's shelf (1:23)—Miriam crosses the English Channel to work in an environment dominated by women, both excitingly different and suffocatingly devoid of privacy. There she talks, observes, and remembers, at once part of the community of women and alienated from it. In one telling incident, Miriam distances herself from her schoolmates, wondering at the other girls' wish to lie down on a hot afternoon: "It surprised

and disturbed her. It suggested illness and weakness. She could not remember ever having lain down in the daytime (1:137). Yet a contrary
memory does soon surface: "She remembered with triumph a group of
days of pain two years ago. She had forgotten. . . . Bewilderment and
pain . . . her mother's constant presence . . . everything, the light everywhere, the leaves standing out along the tops of hedgerows as she drove
with her mother, telling her of pain and she alone in the midst of it . . .
for always . . . pride, long moments of deep pride" (1:137; ellipses Richardson's). Remembering her first menstruation (a reality of life usually
denied the heroines of nineteenth-century realist fiction), Miriam alters
her earlier sense of distance from the other schoolgirls. Richardson's
narrative technique in passages like these registers her heroine's consciousness as multilayered, partly hidden or repressed, ambivalent and
contradictory. Her rendition of mental process in many respects parallels
the contemporary ideas of Freudian psychoanalysis, which were making
their way into British intellectual life during the years Richardson worked
on *Pilgrimage*.[7]

Pilgrimage goes on to follow Miriam through teaching jobs in England, the death of her mother, her move to London, and her early love
affairs. Richardson modeled Hypo Wilson, the most important of Miriam's lovers, on her own relationship with the British realist novelist
H. G. Wells. Their awkward affair epitomizes Miriam's consistent belief
that women and men are fundamentally different, mutually uncompre-
hending: she earlier complains of "the hard brutal laughing complacent
atmosphere of men's minds" (1:443). Wilson/Wells's rationalism and worship of science runs directly against Miriam's preference for intuition, and
confirms her realization (despite her ambivalence about women's weak-
nesses) that she "wouldn't have a man's—*consciousness* for anything"
(2:149). Miriam's exclamation neatly intimates Richardson's aim in the
whole of *Pilgrimage*: to find a literary form suited to a woman's
consciousness.

Gloria Fromm suggests that in the final, incomplete book of *Pilgrimage (March Moonlight)* Richardson "was straining to reach the year 1913,
when *Pointed Roofs* was finished" (370). This suggests that Richardson
intended *Pilgrimage* to reach fruition as a full-fledged *Kunstlerroman*, a
story of how an artist discovers and embraces her or his vocation, like
Joyce's A *Portrait of the Artist as a Young Man*. In *Dimple Hill*, the last
completed book of *Pilgrimage*, Miriam moves to the country, looking for
a quiet place in which to attempt serious writing. So, too, had Richardson worked on the opening of *Pilgrimage* in Sussex. Yet something seems

to hold Richardson back from closing the circle between her heroine and herself; *Pilgrimage* never did conclude with its heroine sitting down to write her own life, her pilgrimage, and perhaps never could come to so definite a conclusion. If, as Fromm argues, Richardson by the end had "come to think of herself and of *Pilgrimage* as one and the same" (371), there may have been an unsolved problem for her in so close an identi-fication between art and life: if the end of *Pilgrimage* were to allow Mir-iam to become her author, would that be the end for character and author both? *Pilgrimage* avoids this closure, as it avoids other realist conventions of closure, and leaves Richardson's readers with the sense of having ap-proached, if never quite arrived at, the point of art's dissolution into life.

The daughter of aggressively conventional, middle-class parents, Rich-ardson was hardly destined by birth to literary circles; all the more re-markable, then, was her stubborn courage in coming to her vocation. For Virginia Woolf (1882–1941), matters were very different. Born Ade-line Virginia Stephen, daughter of Leslie Stephen, a formidable Victo-rian man of letters, and Julia Duckworth Stephen, also of an intellectual and artistic family, Woolf was related to and raised in the heart of literary London. Her father recognized her literary talents when Virginia was barely in her teens, and came to expect that she would follow in his footsteps as a writer. Yet her familial heritage was anything but an un-complicated blessing for Woolf; coming to terms with it and with her vocation demanded courage probably equal in degree to Richardson's, if perhaps different in kind.

Most writers' lives are of interest to their readers, but Woolf's has been especially so for many reasons: biographers have explored not only her distinguished circle of family and friends, and her own literary produc-tivity, but also Woolf's periodic mental breakdowns and eventual suicide. The challenge, for biographers and readers, lies in trying to understand the relationships between all these facets of Woolf's life and work. To begin with, the Stephen family was large and emotionally complex, comprising children from Julia Stephen's previous marriage as well as Virginia's two brothers, Thoby and Adrian, and her sister, Vanessa. The children, boys and girls, were at first rather haphazardly educated at home by their parents. Later the boys would be sent off, at some financial sacrifice, to the best of schools and to Cambridge University. Realizing that this was not to be for her, Virginia began to glimpse the outlines of male privilege and women's relative deprivation, even in upper-middle-class families.

Leslie Stephen was by most accounts a demanding, sometimes charming, sometimes irascible father and husband; Julia, a beautiful, generous, but also overextended and perhaps emotionally unavailable mother. She died of influenza when Virginia was 13, and Virginia's first breakdown followed close on this family crisis. Whatever precisely triggered Virginia's illness, it is clear that the Stephen household at this time was a desolate place for all its inhabitants, even an exploitative place for the daughters of the house. In his grief, Leslie Stephen leaned heavily on Stella Duckworth, his stepdaughter by Julia's first marriage. After Stella left to marry, the emotional and practical burdens of the household fell on Virginia's older sister, Vanessa; Virginia observed her father's sometimes irrational demands, his assumption that women owed him altruistic service, with anger and distaste.[8]

And there was more. While the exact timing of some episodes was unclear in Woolf's later memory, she recalled and wrote of being sexually abused by her half-brothers, Gerald and George Duckworth. It began with Gerald, in her recollection, before her mother's death, when she was about six years old; it continued with George (who also extended his unwelcome attentions to Vanessa) well into her adolescence. According to Louise De Salvo, this experience was crucial for Woolf's later life and work, and must radically modify other biographers' rosier pictures of a close-knit, brilliant Victorian family. It was not an isolated aberration, De Salvo argues, but part of a pattern of male privilege: if Leslie Stephen assumed that emotional and practical service from his daughters was his by right, Gerald and George extended that assumption of masculine prerogative to sexual availability.[9]

De Salvo sees Woolf's crises throughout her life as the resurfacing of this early violation. Most of Woolf's biographers have noted instead that the timing of her breakdowns tended to coincide with the completion of her books, and ascribed them in part to anxiety over sending her work out into the world.[10] (On some level, of course, these explanations may not be mutually exclusive.) If her early experience within the Stephen family sensitized her to power and its abuses, Woolf enlarged this sensitivity into systematic criticism of social institutions as well as individual behavior; she understood, as Berenice Carroll has argued, that "personal relations are the mirror of the social system, and its crucible."[11] She came to make wide-ranging connections between different forms of power and exploitation, seeing imperialism and male dominance, for instance, as related patterns of oppression; she struggled to find narrative forms through which such connections could be represented and understood.

Leslie Stephen died in 1904, finally breaking up the Victorian household. The Stephen children moved into a more bohemian district of London, Bloomsbury, by which name their intellectual circle would soon come to be known. Virginia's career as a published writer began with unsigned reviews later that same year, and by 1907 she was at work on her first novel, then titled "Melymbrosia." It was several years in the writing. Virginia married Leonard Woolf (a Cambridge man and member of the Bloomsbury circle) in 1912; the novel, now retitled *The Voyage Out*, appeared in 1915 with a dedication to "L. W."

Both *The Voyage Out* and Woolf's second novel, *Night and Day* (1919), are conservative works by comparison with the novels that would follow. Yet both novels press against the limitations of realism's traditional plots for women. *The Voyage Out* (despite its dedication to Woolf's husband) obliquely criticizes the traditional marriage plot by killing off its young protagonist, Rachel Vinrace, after she has accepted Terence Hewett's proposal. Rachel escapes England and begins to expand her own horizons, but the voyage is to be one-way only; and English imperial power, English literature, English ways of life are felt even in the novel's exotic South American setting. Rachel's fatal fever comes on as her fiancé reads Milton's *Comus* aloud to her, and she slips away to the tune of other snatches of English poetry.[12] The juxtaposition implies, perhaps, that both marriage and canonized, male-authored English poetry contain something deadly to young women.

Night and Day brings its marriage plots to happier resolutions: two pairs of engaged lovers switch and discard partners, overcome the weight of their different backgrounds and parental objections, and agree to live happily ever after in slightly less conventional versions of marriage. Complex and stylized, overseen by an authoritative, ironic narrator, the novel's elaborate love-ballet suggests that marriage at best is a comically arbitrary form for human passion. Moreover, the stylized happy ending leaves out a member of one of the original pairs, Mary Datchet, who takes her energies into feminist political work. Looking up at her windows, the engaged lovers see "the illuminated blinds, an expression to them both of something impersonal and serene in the spirit of the woman within, working out her plans far into the night."[13] While the narrator earlier looks at Datchet's actual work with some skepticism, the novel still insists on her significance. The marriage plot does not achieve full closure for everyone: it leaves out something important, something that even the engaged couples are drawn to, a sense of alternative possibility.

It was *Jacob's Room*, in 1922, that fully established Woolf's reputation as an experimental novelist; Woolf's friend and fellow novelist E. M. Forster told her that *Jacob's Room* had "clean cut away" the excess realist baggage of *Night and Day*.[14] What this excision leaves behind, however, is something both more and less than the stream-of-consciousness technique as practiced by Dorothy Richardson. Unlike Richardson's *Pilgrimage*, *Jacob's Room* does not focus on the consciousness of a single protagonist, and it does feature an intrusive narrator. At the center of the novel is Jacob Flanders, an unexceptional middle-class young man whom the novel follows through childhood, youth, and young adulthood; he goes to his death in World War I. Yet the novel seldom gives us entry into Jacob's consciousness, as one might expect; for the most part, Jacob is seen through the consciousness of others around him, often minor characters who enter and exit the novel in a single scene. Many readers of the novel have been baffled by this technique and have judged it a failure by traditional criteria, complaining that the novel is not unified and that readers cannot identify with Jacob.[15] Woolf's technique is too deliberate, however, to be accidental. To her mind, "the damned egotistical self" marred Richardson's and Joyce's experiments with the stream of consciousness.[16] *Jacob's Room* instead displaces the selfhood of its central character; its technique mounts "an interrogation of the notion of individuality."[17] As Alex Zwerdling argues, to understand *Jacob's Room* we need "to think about Woolf's technique in relation to purpose," and we need to understand the novel's purpose in relation to the historical context of its writing.[18]

The millions of young men like Jacob who died in World War I (Jacob's last name, Flanders, is the name of an infamously bloody battle in the war) were the subjects of much eulogizing literature as Woolf was writing *Jacob's Room*; the meaning or absurdity of the war itself was an agonizing topic for British writers and intellectuals. As a feminist and a pacifist, Woolf regarded this whole enterprise with distrust. How, then, to write a novel of development about such a young man without collapsing into romanticized eulogy?

By not centering on Jacob's own consciousness, Zwerdling notes, *Jacob's Room* maintains some "ironic distance from Jacob and his contemporaries" (Zwerdling, 73); we empathize with his childhood terrors and explorations, but also witness his easy assumption of class and gender privilege. Visiting the Parthenon—an inevitable stop on a well-off young man's Grand Tour of Europe—Jacob objects to the real women travelers who unwittingly obstruct his view of the Parthenon's sculpted women:

"'It is those damned women,' said Jacob, without any trace of bitterness, but rather with sadness and disappointment that what might have been should never be."[19] Jacob's comfortable nostalgia at what "might have been" anticipates all the later laments for his decimated generation of young men, but the narrator immediately counters with an ironic parenthesis: "This violent disillusionment is generally to be expected in young men in the prime of life, sound of wind and limb, who will soon become fathers of families and directors of banks" (*JR*, 151). As Woolf and her readers well know, however, her ironic narrator is in one respect wrong; whatever his general sense of entitlement, Jacob will not live to take his patriarchal place as father or director.

"This double awareness of the sharpness of grief and its absurdity," Zwerdling argues, "gives Woolf's satiric elegy its special edge and accounts for the novel's rapid shifts in tone" (Zwerdling, 82). *Jacob's Room* grieves, but without abandoning a critical perspective on the life of such young men. It mourns Jacob without pretending to grasp his essence, for Jacob as glimpsed in the consciousness of others cannot possibly exhaust his reality: "what remains is mostly a matter of guess work. Yet over him we hang vibrating" (*JR*, 73). Irony and uncertainty are not to be denied, but do not preclude genuine feeling. "Such is the manner of our seeing," insists the narrator; "Such the conditions of our love" (*JR*, 72).

Like *Jacob's Room*, *Mrs. Dalloway* (1925) continues both Woolf's explorations in the novel of consciousness and her concern with the historical aftermath of World War I. The action of *Mrs. Dalloway* occupies a single day in London; its main characters are Clarissa Dalloway, an upper-class woman married to a politician (both of whom made a brief appearance earlier in Woolf's *The Voyage Out*), and Septimus Smith, a lower-middle-class clerk, war veteran, and victim of shell shock. The novel spends much of its time in their consciousness, but also represents the thoughts of other, minor characters: Clarissa's daughter Elizabeth; her former suitor, Peter Walsh; Elizabeth's tutor, Doris Kilman. Clarissa and Septimus live their separate days, which end with Septimus committing suicide and Clarissa giving a party. They never meet in the flesh, although Clarissa learns of Septimus's suicide from his doctor, who attends her party. The challenge—for Clarissa herself and for readers of *Mrs. Dalloway*—lies in trying to understand the relationship between these parallel worlds, the establishment and its margins; in trying, that is, to undo the limitations of what Woolf called "the damned egotistical self," bound by the circumference of one consciousness.

Reflecting on the suicide of the young man she never met, Clarissa Dalloway runs through a range of emotions, from anger at the intrusion of death into her party to identification with his gesture. "A thing there was that mattered; a thing, wreathed about with chatter, defaced, obscured in her own life, let drop every day in corruption, lies, chatter. This he had preserved. Death was defiance. Death was an attempt to communicate," she muses, eventually deciding that "She felt somehow very like him—the young man who had killed himself."[20] Like him in what respect? How do we, and Woolf, finally judge Mrs. Dalloway?

For some critics, Clarissa Dalloway's life (especially as summed up in her party) is hollow beyond redemption. According to Emily Jensen, Clarissa "recognizes that she has committed her own kind of suicide: she has in fact committed one of the most common of suicides for women, that respectable destruction of the self in the interest of the other."[21] For other readers, however, Clarissa is more sympathetic. Zwerdling points out that our access to Clarissa's consciousness directly engages our sympathies for her as they are not engaged for Jacob Flanders (Zwerdling, 137). Moreover, Clarissa's own moments of empathy with people distanced from her by class, gender, and the vicissitudes of time "suggest that Clarissa's soul is far from dead, that she can resurrect the intense emotions of youth despite the pressure of a society determined to deny them quarter" (Zwerdling, 142). For Rachel Bowlby, part of what makes *Mrs. Dalloway* so "innovative" as a novel is "that the heroine is the woman of fifty," Clarissa, rather than "her eighteen-year-old daughter on the brink of courtship" (Bowlby, 87). In terms of the traditional marriage plot of nineteenth-century realist novels, Clarissa's potential as a heroine would have been exhausted years ago, her identity forever frozen as "Mrs. Dalloway." Representing her heroine as socially circumscribed, to be sure, but not as hopelessly frozen, Woolf ventures on new ground in both the novel and women's lives.

Another older woman stands at the center of Woolf's next novel, *To the Lighthouse* (1927): Mrs. Ramsay, wife and mother, who gives a dinner party in part 1 ("The Window"), dies in a parenthesis in part 2 ("Time Passes"), and is memorialized by the novel's survivors in part 3 ("The Lighthouse"). The novel is framed by two actions: the voyage to the lighthouse, planned in part 1 but not completed until part 3, and a painting of Mrs. Ramsay that her younger, unmarried friend Lily Briscoe is trying to complete. Mrs. Ramsay poses for Lily in the window of part 1; the painting remains unfinished during the 10 years in which "Time Passes"; Lily summons up Mrs. Ramsay in memory and finishes her painting in part 3. Lily is not the only consciousness through which the novel is narrated, but she becomes increasingly dominant in the book's conclusion. *To the Lighthouse* paints a portrait of a late Victorian mother and family, then, partly from the point of view of a woman who feels lucky to have escaped those institutions—but who also, like Woolf herself, loves and mourns what she has escaped.

To the Lighthouse explores "the sexual polarization of Victorian family life" (Zwerdling, 185), its consignment of women and men to different kinds of work and modes of thought. Woolf presents the Victorian sexual division of labor schematically and symbolically, through repeated metaphors and extended similes that become emblematic in her characters' consciousness. Mr. Ramsay, a philosopher, spends his days on a heroic (sometimes mock-heroic) quest to move, in logical thought, from Q to R.[22] Mr. Ramsay works—his son Andrew tells Lily—on "'Subject and object and the nature of reality.' . . . And when she said Heavens, she had no notion what that meant, 'Think of a kitchen table then,' he told her, 'when you're not there'" (*TTL*, 38). For Mr. Ramsay, "reality" lies not in the sensuous appearance of "lovely evenings" but in their reduction to "angular essences" in thought (*TTL*, 38). But not even Mr. Ramsay can live for long in the realm of angular essences. Descending from his abstracting mental labors, he looks to his wife for emotional rejuvenation; his son James experiences his father's demand as "the beak of brass, the arid scimitar of the male, which smote mercilessly, again and again, demanding sympathy" (*TTL*, 59).

It is Mrs. Ramsay's job to provide sympathy, to "rise in a rosy-flowered fruit tree laid with leaves and dancing boughs" (*TTL*, 60) at her husband's need, as it is her job not to neglect lovely appearances, but to manufacture them: to see (with the help of servants) that the house is clean, the dinner table pleasing, the food delicious. Mr. Ramsay's work, ideally at least, is linear and progressive, moving from Q to R in thought; he hopes he has produced work that will endure, but frets at the thought of being surpassed and forgotten. Mrs. Ramsay's work, by definition, cannot endure: dinners are eaten, parties break up, houses do not stay clean, children grow older. Her time is circular rather than linear and progressive; her work always needs to be done over again.

And yet her work, the novel suggests, is a kind of art. After getting off to a rocky start, Mrs. Ramsay's dinner party coalesces into a kind of artistic image: "Now all the candles were lit up, and the faces on both sides of the table were brought nearer by the candle light, and composed, as they had not been in the twilight, into a party round a table, for the night

67

was now shut off by panes of glass, which, far from giving any accurate view of the outside world, rippled it so strangely that here, inside the room, seemed to be order and dry land; there, outside, a reflection in which things wavered and vanished waterily" (*TTL*, 146–47). The window in which Lily Briscoe earlier framed Mrs. Ramsay for her painting, now reflects and frames the dinner party indoors as Mrs. Ramsay's own artistic creation. This creation is costly for Mrs. Ramsay, and Lily Briscoe refuses to participate wholeheartedly in it, resents her and Mrs. Ramsay's feminine responsibility for helping the male guests shine. The thought of her own painting protects Lily from being caught up in Mrs. Ramsay's projects: "She remembered, all of a sudden as if she had found a treasure, that she had her work" (*TTL*, 128). In her own mind, Lily defends a life and an artistic identity different from Mrs. Ramsay's. Still, the artistic triumph of part 1 is Mrs. Ramsay's: "Of such moments," she thinks at the dinner table, "the thing is made that endures" (*TTL*, 158).

But is Mrs. Ramsay right? Her death in part 2 tests our faith in any such endurance. The most technically innovative section of *To the Lighthouse*, "Time Passes" might be called stream of consciousness without an individual, human consciousness; it seems to render the time of nature or of things or of the dreaming mind rather than conscious human time, whether Mr. Ramsay's linear masculine time or Mrs. Ramsay's time of daily, repeated tasks. The household lays itself down to sleep, and for 10 years lives a nightmare. Human events—Mrs. Ramsay's sudden death, Prue's death in childbirth, Andrew's death in World War I—happen in parentheses, and are deprived of the rituals, conventions, or human responses that would give them meaning. Mrs. Ramsay's death on a stormy night, the narrative suggests, disrupts some fundamental connection between the human mind and nature (*TTL*, 193). World War I widens the breach still further: "to pace the beach was impossible; contemplation was unendurable; the mirror"—a traditional symbol for the correspondence between mind and nature—"was broken" (*TTL*, 202).

"Time Passes" makes a novelistic reply to Mr. Ramsay's philosophical work on "subject and object and the nature of reality." It imagines, to recall Andrew's words to Lily, what a kitchen table is like when you're not there—what a whole house is like when no one remains to take care of it, what a world is like when there is no reciprocity between subject and object. The answer, not anticipated in Mr. Ramsay's philosophical speculations, is that the table grimes with dust, the house decays, things fall apart. Unlike the ideal kitchen table, the "angular essences" of Mr. Ramsay's work, real objects do not stay still, outside of time, while the mind goes from Q to R. Without Mrs. Ramsay's care in sustaining connections between subject and object, the world decays; subject and object are interdependent. In her own way, "Time Passes" shows, Mrs. Ramsay, as much as her husband, worked on "subject and object and the nature of reality," even if her work was not dignified with the name of philosophy.

In part 3, "The Lighthouse," night ends: the novel's surviving characters return to the house to resume life there, and to mourn—each in his or her own way—the absent Mrs. Ramsay. Mr. Ramsay bullies his children, Cam and James, into sailing to the lighthouse on the errand left incomplete 10 years ago; Lily sets up her easel, with the unfinished painting of Mrs. Ramsay, on the lawn. The novel thus comes to two endings, in a way, rather than one, suggesting two different ways of assimilating Mrs. Ramsay's legacy.

Cam and James, in the course of their journey to the lighthouse, symbolically internalize conventionally masculine and feminine roles on their parents' pattern. Initially joined in an unspoken league to resist their father's "tyranny to the death" (*TTL*, 246), along the journey they develop separate relationships with their father. James's hostility, his yearning for his mother, and his vague memories of his father's castrating power ("Something, he remembered, stayed and darkened over him; . . . something arid and sharp descended even there, like a blade, a scimatar" [*TTL*, 276]), struggle with and eventually give way to identification with Mr. Ramsay. James arrives at a masculine lighthouse, "a stark tower on a bare rock. It satisfied him" (*TTL*, 301), and thinks to himself that he and his father "share[ ] that knowledge" (302). Cam, on the other hand, is attracted to her father's masculinity, rather than identifying with it: "For no one attracted her more; his hands were beautiful, and his feet, and his voice, and his words, and his haste, and his temper, and his oddity, and his passion . . ." (*TTL*, 253). She arrives at an island of imagination ("Small as it was, and shaped something like a leaf stood on its end with the gold-sprinkled waters flowing in and about it, it had, she supposed, a place in the universe—even that little island?" [*TTL*, 281]), rather than at James's hard phallic truth, and feels that her father's strength makes her imaginative revery safe (*TTL*, 304). Going "to the lighthouse," for both Cam and James, means arriving at dichotomized adult gender roles; their journey symbolically sketches how such gender roles are reproduced from generation to generation.[23]

Lily Briscoe's painting, however, suggests an alternative ending: Lily loves Mrs. Ramsay without becoming her, without reproducing Mrs. Ramsay's roles in her own life. She moves through stages of mourning in part 3, from numbness and denial of loss (*TTL*, 220), to anger at Mrs. Ramsay's abandonment of her (*TTL*, 223), to memories that acknowledge Mrs. Ramsay as a fellow artist in her own way, "making of the moment something permanent" (*TTL*, 241). She begins to feel the emptiness where Mrs. Ramsay used to sit: "how could one . . . express that emptiness there?" (*TTL*, 265). Finally her grief makes its way out: "'Mrs. Ramsay!' she said aloud, 'Mrs. Ramsay!' The tears ran down her face" (*TTL*, 268).

Acknowledging her grief helps Lily "attack" her painting (*TTL*, 269), and for an instant at least brings Mrs. Ramsay back to life: she "sat there quite simply in the chair, flicked her needles to and fro, knitted her reddish-brown stocking, cast her shadow on the step. There she sat" (*TTL*, 300). Restoring the presence of what has been lost, of course, is one of art's traditional functions. Yet Woolf in the end qualifies this restoration. Lily looks out to sea, imagining that Mr. Ramsay must by now have landed at the lighthouse, then turns to complete her painting: "She looked at the steps; they were empty; she looked at her canvas; it was blurred" (*TTL*, 310). Her intense feeling of Mrs. Ramsay's presence is gone. Nevertheless, "as if she saw it clear for a second, she drew a line there, in the centre. It was done; it was finished"—she can complete the painting without Mrs. Ramsay, and without becoming the kind of woman Mrs. Ramsay was. Lily's last thought is, "I have had my vision": her vision memorializes Mrs. Ramsay and her world, but it is her own.

To the Lighthouse has probably become Woolf's best-known novel, and a favorite with most of her readers. The years immediately following its publication, however, saw no slackening of Woolf's productivity. Soon after *To the Lighthouse* appeared, she conceived *Orlando* (1928), a fantasy-biography of her friend and sometime lover Vita Sackville-West. Woolf's Orlando starts out a young man, born to a noble house in the Elizabethan age; he becomes a poet, changes sex, wins fame as a woman for her poem "The Oak Tree" (as Sackville-West did for her poem *The Land*), and finally fetches up with a husband in the twentieth century, while his/her biographer comically pants and strains to do a biographer's duty by this protean character. *Orlando* is many things at once: a love letter and tribute to Vita, its "playfulness" at the same time "masks a set of quite serious questions about the significance or determinability of sexual difference, as of the nature of history or of a coherent 'life'" (Bowlby, 59). What is femininity, what is masculinity? *Orlando* asks, without finally settling on any one answer.

A few days after *Orlando* was published, Woolf delivered two papers on "Women and Fiction" to audiences from the women's colleges at Cambridge. Revised and expanded, the lectures became *A Room of One's Own* (1929), Woolf's most famous excursion into polemical prose. *A Room of One's Own* examines how women's exclusion from money and education shaped what women had been able to accomplish thus far in English literature. Speaking through a fictional persona, "Mary Beton" (the name comes from the old ballad "Mary Hamilton"), Woolf concludes that "it is necessary to have five hundred a year and a room with a lock on the door if you are to write fiction or poetry," advantages to which relatively few women had access.[24] Yet this "prosaic" conclusion hardly begins to suggest Woolf's accomplishment in *A Room*; more important than this conclusion itself is the fact that Woolf's persona "has tried to lay bare the thoughts and impressions that led her to think this" (*Room*, 109). *A Room of One's Own*, as many critics have noted, is about a process of thought rather than a single conclusion. Wandering from Oxford—where she is excluded from lawns and libraries—to the British Museum in her quest to grapple with the topic of "Women and Fiction," Woolf's narrator acts out Woolf's concern with the effects of material circumstances on thought itself.

Woolf's next novel, *The Waves* (1931), marks her furthest departure from realist conventions. It is told through the soliloquies of six characters, speaking at different stages in their lives, beginning with childhood and ending with death's approach. An omniscient, disembodied narrator marks off sections of the book with descriptions of natural time passing, the sun rising, climbing, at zenith, and falling; these episodes of prose-poetry draw on Woolf's experiments in part 2, "Time Passes," of *To the Lighthouse*. Like *Jacob's Room*, *The Waves* centers around the figure of an absent young man: Percival, who dies not in war but by accident—off overseeing Britain's empire, he is thrown by his horse. Narrated entirely without realist interaction or dialogue between characters, *The Waves* foregrounds the problem of isolated consciousness, "the feeling that even our most intimate relationships are flawed by our limited access to other minds" (Zwerdling, 10–11).

Woolf's final two novels, however, return in different ways to external realities beyond and between individual, isolated minds. Unlike Richardson, Woolf did not challenge nineteenth-century realism by replacing it with *one* form, one kind of narration; the variety of her novels suggests that there is no one form for reality in general or even for the reality of one woman's experiences. *The Years* (1937) is a modernist reworking of the family saga, following the fortunes of the Pargiter family from 1880 to the "Present Day" and ending with a party that recalls the final pages of *Mrs. Dalloway.*[25] If the novel has a central consciousness, it belongs to Eleanor, the eldest daughter, who never marries; again, Woolf challenges the marriage plot of traditional realism, according to which a woman like Eleanor would have no possible story.

Between the Acts (1941), Woolf's last novel, also represents a family, this time in the traditional setting of the English country house. Here the action of the novel is confined to one summer day in 1939 rather than fifty years, but the day itself includes a village pageant representing scenes from all of English history. Woolf's title is often understood as referring to the interval between the world wars; written as Germany's bombers nightly laid waste to London, *Between the Acts* questions ideas of history as progress, indeed questions the very survival of European society (Zwerdling, 302–23; Bowlby, 146–59). Woolf drowned herself in the river Ouse, near her home, before seeing *Between the Acts* published.

Introducing a volume of critical essays on Woolf in 1971, Claire Sprague observed that while Woolf was "often mentioned together with Joyce and Lawrence," she was "neither so highly valued nor so well known as they," and surmised that Woolf was "the victim of an obscuring personal legend created by her contemporaries": the legend of a mildly mad artist removed from real life.[26] Speaking in 1941, E. M. Forster dismissed Woolf's feminism—unmistakably an area in which Woolf did care about real life—as "old-fashioned."[27] Woolf's reputation since 1971, however, has risen dramatically, spurred in part by the recent publication of her diaries, letters, and journalism, and in part by the resurgence of feminism, in light of which Woolf's thought looks prescient rather than old-fashioned. Her formal innovations in the novel have come to be seen as inseparable from her feminist concern for aspects of women's experience traditionally left silent; both alike challenge conventional and male-oriented assumptions about what "real life" is. Now available in its entirety, Woolf's life work stands more and more clearly among the towering literary careers of this century.

CHAPTER
5

British Women Novelists

While Virginia Woolf and Dorothy Richardson are often cited as the central modernist women novelists of Great Britain, other British women wrote prolifically in the novel both before and after Woolf and Richardson defined their breaks with the genre's nineteenth-century past. Some wrote in more traditional realist forms; others extended modernism's explorations of the stream of consciousness and its search for alternatives to realist conventions of plot and closure in the novel.

Of the many British women novelists active from 1900 to 1945, this chapter can discuss only a few: May Sinclair, Radclyffe Hall, Ivy Compton-Burnett, Jean Rhys, Rebecca West, Vita Sackville-West, Elizabeth Bowen, and Rosamund Lehmann. These novelists are curiously neglected in many histories of the twentieth-century British novel, both individually and—perhaps even more significant—as a group. For example: one recent critical survey aimed at students and general readers, Douglas Hewitt's *English Fiction of the Early Modern Period, 1890–1940*, devotes only one full chapter to a woman novelist, Virginia Woolf, and only a few sentences to figures like Compton-Burnett and Bowen in a concluding chapter in the 1930s.[1]

Why this comparative neglect? The answers are complicated, and Hewitt represents only some of them, but his comments are nevertheless suggestive. To begin with, Hewitt dismisses Woolf's modernism as wholly apolitical, a retreat from public issues into what is "private" and "intimate" (128). He contrasts her modernism unfavorably with the belief of more realistic (and also male) novelists like Arnold Bennett and John Galsworthy that "the personality of a man or women is to a considerable extent determined by . . . 'house property,' the external economic, social, and public aspects of their life" (131).

It is not true of Woolf, as I and other critics have already argued, that she believes human personality is not affected by its surroundings. On the contrary, Woolf registers with fascination the way changes in the material organization of everyday life help shape consciousness. The real problem is that for Hewitt, the private or personal is not political. Real politics, he believes, inhere in war, class struggle, and above all, imperialism—not just "imperialism as such but also the implications about class and national identity which are inherent in it" (6). Issues of gender, sexuality, and the family occupy only a parenthetical place in his account of modernity, between loss of religious faith and Freudian ideas, and women are not visible as active shapers of history even here; instead it is "family stability" that has, mysteriously and passively, "weakened" (6).

The accomplishments of Woolf, Richardson, and the group of novelists discussed in this chapter tend to remain invisible to a literary history like Hewitt's, that cannot see relationships between the private and the public, or see women's efforts to reshape those worlds as concrete and real historical acts rather than as mysterious movements to "weaken" realities (like sexuality and family) nostalgically assumed to have been "stable" before. If we acknowledge women as active and women's concerns as genuinely historical and political, we can see that writers like Woolf and her friend Vita Sackville-West, for instance, have things to say about imperialism and its effects on women; imperialism involves patterns of gender as well as patterns of class and national identity. Writers like May Sinclair and Radclyffe Hall represent women actively struggling to change family relationships and definitions of sexuality. Writers like Rebecca West use experimental techniques to question the division between the public and the private spheres, between masculinity and femininity. Male modernists have no monopoly on either experimentalism or realism; British women novelists of the first half of this century find important work to do in many different kinds of fiction.

The novels of May Sinclair (1863–1946) bridge the transition from the Victorians to the era of modernism. They bring twentieth-century feminism and Freudian thought to bear on the institution of the Victorian family, which Sinclair herself knew all too well. In novel after novel, the outcome is bleak: the family under Sinclair's Freudian microscope seethes with repressed sexuality of all kinds, jealousy, selfishness, and power struggles. But Sinclair, unlike Freud, insists that it is always women who pay most dearly for family life. Although women characters in Sinclair's novels are by no means uniformly innocent of lust, jealousy, or manipulative behavior, their options are fewer, their lines of escape more likely to shut down; when family demands a sacrifice, it is a woman who will make it.

In her earlier novels, from *Audrey Craven* (1897) through *The Three Sisters* (1914), Sinclair worked with a third-person omniscient narrator. Inspired in part by her friend Dorothy Richardson's example in *Pilgrimage*, Sinclair then shifted over to a third-person stream-of-consciousness technique, beginning with *Mary Olivier: A Life* (1919). *The Three Sisters* and *Mary Olivier* are perhaps Sinclair's most interesting novels for critics today: *The Three Sisters* because it is modeled in part on the lives of the Brontë sisters, famous nineteenth-century women novelists; *Mary Olivier*, because (along with Joyce's *A Portrait of the Artist as a Young Man* and Richardson's *Pilgrimage*) it is a compelling autobiographical *Kunstlerroman*.

The Three Sisters are "Mary, Gwendolen and Alice, daughters of James Cartaret, the Vicar of Garth," a parish on the high moors of England— as Charlotte, Emily, and Anne Brontë were daughters of Patrick Brontë, pastor of an isolated Yorkshire parish.[2] Alice, the youngest, is an artist of a kind. Fragile and slight, she plays the piano not expertly, but with a "temperament . . . seeking its outlet in exultant and violent sound" (13). Sinclair characterizes the spiritual and bodily "climax" Alice experiences while playing in virtually orgasmic terms (22). Mary, the eldest, "learned to darn socks for her own amusement on her eleventh birthday" (4). Her goals in life—which she pursues with outward meekness and inward determination—are husband, home, and family. Thoughtful and unconventional, Gwendolen finds space for freedom and passion upon the moors.

Sinclair uses her story's parallels with the Brontë sisters' lives to ask, in effect, how the destinies meted out to different types of women in the early twentieth century differ from those possible to women in the nineteenth century. Her types of twentieth-century women, Jean Radford points out, derive in part from Freudian thought: fragile Alice is driven by "the power of the Id," Mary's determined pursuit of socially sanctioned goals links her to the Freudian ego, and Gwendolen—the central character in the novel—"is dominated by her over-developed consciousness or super-ego."[3]

All three dream of love (10), partly as the only possible escape from their tyrannical father. Each lives out this dream in a different way. Alice eventually makes a happy (and fecund) marriage with a handsome, earthy, dialect-speaking farmer (their relationship has a flavor of D. H. Lawrence about it). Gwendolen gives up the man she loves to her sister Mary; Mary and her husband go on to live in soul-deadening domesticity while Gwendolen sacrifices her own independent life to care for her father. Day by day, night by night, Gwendolen has nothing to do in the end but "wait[ ] for the hour of her deliverance"—the hour when she may go to bed but also, the freighted language implies, the hour of her death. Women's lives and choices in the family, according to Sinclair, seem to have changed little since the Brontës' day.

In *Mary Olivier: A Life*, Sinclair confers broader experiences, both amorous and intellectual, upon her artist-heroine. As a child, Mary hears from her parents that "opinions" are "nasty, dangerous things," especially for girls.[4] Nevertheless, she persists in having them. Her intellectual curiosity and independence struggle with her love for her mother, who approves of Mary only when she sees her "behaving like a little girl" (70). She both loves and hates her mother (Sinclair agreed with Freud's emphasis on ambivalence in emotional life). At 14 and with the onset of menstruation, Mary's ambivalence about her mother (and presumably also about her own female identity) surfaces strongly: "Her thoughts about her mother went up and down. Mamma was not helpless. She was not gentle. She was not really like a wounded bird. She was powerful and rather cruel. You could only appease her with piles of hemmed sheets and darned stockings." Yet "You heard yourself cry: 'Mamma, Mamma you are adorable!' That was you"—this ambivalence, Mary realizes, lies at the core of her being (124).

Young Mary embarks on a course of solitary reading, beginning with her brother's borrowed textbooks, which takes her through theology, philosophy, and finally evolutionary biology in an attempt to understand herself and her world. It is biology, finally (in its then-fashionable deterministic mode) that makes sense of Mary's world to her: "You had thought of yourself as . . . a sacred, inviolable self, struggling against them [her family] for completer freedom and detachment. . . . But it was not so. There were no independent, separate entities, no sacred, inviolable selves. They were one immense organism and you were part of it; you were nothing that they had not been before you. It was no good struggling. You were caught in the net; you couldn't get out" (290).

More ideology than science, evolutionary biology—as Mary interprets it—rationalizes her submission to her family. These patterns of thought bode ill for her independent future. Mary eventually does become a writer: after years of solitary labor also succeeds in publishing a poem of her own (324), then has her work discovered by a well-known scholar, Richard Nicholson, to whom she is acting as secretary. Richard sees to the successful publication of her collected poems and, what is more, falls in love with his middle-aged protégée (344).

Their love is consummated when Richard persuades Mary to leave her mother long enough to visit London (359). We see a life that Mary herself might have enjoyed: the London flat, colorful against the dark bricks of the city, lined with books. But she leaves him to return to her invalid mother, and when her mother dies (372), it is too late; Richard has married. As the solitary years wear on, Mary takes solace in a faith of her own. Not Christian any longer, still she looks for illumination in self-sacrifice and self-surrender, and finds "exquisite clearness and intensity" in her chosen way of life (377).

Most present-day readers will probably find it difficult to accept this as a happy ending. Sinclair herself thought of Mary as a character who creatively sublimated her sexual energies, rather than neurotically repressing them; but her final emphasis is on Mary's sacrifice instead of her active achievements.[5] Like Gwendolen in *The Three Sisters*, Mary Olivier is the most skeptical, intellectually independent woman of her family. But like Gwendolen, she remains trapped in the family, even after her mother's death, by her own active sense of duty, while more conventional, less thoughtful women find ways to escape. As many readers will suspect, Mary Olivier's story was largely autobiographical; Sinclair, too, lived with her mother until her mother's death. Sinclair's novels suggest that while new opportunities beckoned to women in the twentieth century, the women who needed those opportunities most might find themselves unable to step into them, torn by conflicting allegiances.

Like May Sinclair, Radclyffe Hall (1883–1943) shaped her novels partly with reference to ideas borrowed from the newly popular discipline of psychology. Hall's early novel *The Unlit Lamp* (1926), for example, bears a family resemblance to Sinclair's *Mary Olivier* in its heroine's consuming, ambivalent, self-sacrificing relationship with her mother.

Hall ventured into riskier psychological territory with *The Well of Loneliness* (1928), which brought her to the attention of the British censors. The novel's heroine is baptized Stephen Gordon—her parents had longed for and expected a son—and from this awkward beginning other consequences flow. Born "narrow-hipped" and "wide-shouldered," young Stephen grows up tomboyish.[6] In adulthood, she becomes a writer, joins the women's ambulance service in World War I—and loves women. *The Well of Loneliness* became notorious as twentieth-century English literature's first *Kunstlerroman* about lesbian identity.

Hall's ideas about lesbian psychology (which she acted out in life as well as in her art) were derived from those of the famous turn-of-the-century sexologist Havelock Ellis, who contributed a laudatory commentary to the book. Ellis thought of all homosexuals, men and women, as "inverts," souls fundamentally trapped in bodies of the wrong gender. Following Ellis, Hall lays stress on her heroine's "dual nature," the conflict between Stephen's masculine sense of herself and her outward existence as a woman.

Stephen's dual existence is at bottom a tragic condition in Hall's eyes. Stephen desires and wins Mary, a woman more feminine than herself—as Havelock Ellis thought it in the nature of "inverts" to do. Yet in the end Stephen deliberately gives Mary up to a man, Martin, by a sort of inescapable logic: if Mary is feminine, what she desires must be masculine; Stephen is not so masculine as a man; therefore what Mary really must desire is a man. "Suddenly Martin appeared to Stephen as a creature endowed with incalculable bounty, having in his hands all those priceless gifts which she, love's mendicant, could never offer. Only one gift could she offer to love, to Mary, and that was the gift of Martin" (498).

Although Hall could not envision anything but an unhappy ending for her heroine, *The Well of Loneliness* makes a passionate plea for tolerance, ending with Stephen's prayer: "Acknowledge us, oh God, before the whole world. Give us also the right to our existence!" (506). And the novel found defenders during Hall's battle with the British censors. Virginia Woolf and E. M. Forster, among other well-known writers, were prepared to testify on Hall's behalf (despite Woolf's own reservations about the novel's artistic quality).[7] *The Well of Loneliness* has had a cultural impact above and beyond its literary merit, becoming an underground classic of sorts for readers who have variously thrilled to, criticized, and rewritten Stephen Gordon's tragic but lavishly romantic fate.

Where May Sinclair and Radclyffe Hall specialized in novels of consciousness and psychological development, Ivy Compton-Burnett (1884–1969) took a very different tack. The most salient feature of her many novels is their dependence on dialogue. Compton-Burnett herself labeled her fictional technique "something between a novel and a play"; the narrator almost never intervenes with description or commentary.[8] We are never privy to the inward consciousness of her characters. To the contrary: "Miss Compton-Burnett's characters are never allowed to forget—and never allow us to forget—that they are playing a role," and the social role is all that we can know of them.[9]

Compton-Burnett took a degree in classics from Royal Holloway College of London University, and her novels' dialogue seems to owe much to Greek drama, especially its characteristic technique of stichomythia: combative dialogue, alternating line by line, in which adversarial characters twist and turn one another's words. Compton-Burnett's dialogues involve just such swift exchanges—there are very few long speeches—and they are always about struggles for power. To overmaster others' language is to master the others themselves.

The arena of dialogue and struggle is always, for Compton-Burnett, the family, and specifically the upper-middle-class family of the late nineteenth century—"her province," according to Blake Nevius, "because the family then was more closely bound together, its younger members more pliant to authority and therefore more demonstrably at the mercy of tyranny exercised from above" (Nevius, 12).

One of Compton-Burnett's memorable domestic tyrants is Duncan Edgeworth, the patriarch of A House and Its Head (1935). An expert at turning others' civil words against them, beginning with his wife, Duncan rules the house with an acerbic wit that freezes emotion, intellectual curiosity, and acknowledgment of weakness. His children and nephew protect themselves as best they may by assuming language much like his; small rebellions of words are the only kind they can afford.

Compton-Burnett strikes through the novel's surface of acerbic, mannered dialogue with shocking events. Duncan abominably refuses to acknowledge his wife's mortal illness, and remarries a young, beautiful woman all too soon after her death. His second wife presents him with a bastard child, and later runs away with another man. One of Duncan's daughters later arranges for the murder of the child. Yet even here the narrator rigorously abstains from moral commentary. Readers must piece together events and motives from the dialogue, and are left to pass their own judgments on a world in which murder itself cannot for long disarrange the orderly, courteous, everyday affection and hatreds of social intercourse.

The titles of Compton-Burnett's novels—A House and Its Head, Darkness and Day, A Family and a Fortune—invoke the world of Jane Austen's Sense and Sensibility and Pride and Prejudice, but Compton-

Burnett was no simple throwback to an earlier age. Where Austen's novels speak for the possibility of shared moral judgments, Compton-Burnett's novels are terrifyingly silent. And where Austen's happier characters arrive at a workable accommodation between inward consciousness and outward social roles, Compton-Burnett leaves it to her readers to sustain their own faith in consciousness, emotion, and the value of an inner life—if they can.

Jean Rhys (1890–1979) was born and grew up under the name Ella Gwendolen Rees Williams. She spent her childhood in Dominica (in the Caribbean), sailed to England and entered the Perse School for girls in 1907, left school when her father died two years later, and joined the chorus of a traveling musical comedy. She scratched out a hand-to-mouth existence in England and on the Continent for many years afterward, living on odd jobs and on money given her by lovers and former lovers.

In 1922 she met the British novelist Ford Madox Ford, who was then living in Paris. Ford encouraged her to write and chose the new name, Jean Rhys, under which she would henceforth be known. He also took Rhys into his house as his lover, with his wife's connivance, while Rhys's then-husband Jean Lenglet was in prison. In 1925 Rhys began *Quartet* (1928), a novel about her entanglement with Ford. After returning to England in 1927, she published three other novels drawing on her earlier life: *After Leaving Mr. Mackenzie* (1930), *Voyage in the Dark* (1934), and *Good Morning Midnight* (1939).

All of these novels, as Nancy R. Harrison observes, are "cast in the mold of an obsessive autobiography," their common protagonist a woman much like Rhys herself: rootless, passionate, sharply observant, and self-destructive.[10] Yet, as Harrison also insists, "Rhys is writing fiction, no matter how autobiographical much of her material may be" (63). The novels are selective in details, deceptively casual in beginnings and endings. The narrator includes some reactions of others to the autobiographical heroine—reactions that are often damning to both characters.

Rhys was not a novelist of ideas in the sense that Sinclair, for example, was; she would never have been tempted to relate novelistic character to the ideas of evolutionary biology.[11] Dialogue, rather than commentary, matters crucially in Rhys's novels, as it does in the work of Compton-Burnett. But Rhys's dialogue is of a very different kind, technically speaking. Rhys often pits an internal, unspoken dialogue within her characters' minds against the external, actually spoken dialogue between characters

(Harrison, 67–68). In a scene from *After Leaving Mr. Mackenzie*, the protagonist is talking about her despair with a man who is drawn to her and repelled at the same time. "'I see,' said Mr. Horsfield encouragingly"; but then, more cynically, "Mr. Horfield thought: 'Well, nobody can go on for ever.'"[12] Such double-layered dialogue dramatizes, without explicitly moralizing upon, the psychology of hypocrisy and mixed motivation.

At times the narrative voice has the effect of dialogue even when no quotation marks surround her words, as in the last sentences of *After Leaving Mr. Mackenzie*: "The street was cool and full of grey shadows. Lights were beginning to come out in the cafes. It was the hour between dog and wolf, as they say" (191). The narrator suddenly seems to be speaking to us, but also draws in unknown others—"they," whose words she repeats. With its predatory overtones of indignity and hunger, "their" metaphor for the twilight hour sets a seal on the entire world of the novel. And the narrator's casual aside, "as they say," makes her readers party to a faintly sinister ongoing conversation; it assumes that readers are complicit in this world.

After publishing four novels between 1928 and 1939, Rhys was silent for many years. She would draw on memories of her Caribbean childhood in her greatest novel, *Wide Sargasso Sea*, which she began in the 1930s, worked on again after World War II, but did not publish until 1966.

Rebecca West's (1892–1983) writing career began in 1911, when she joined the staff of the *Freewoman*, an important British feminist journal. Born Cicily Fairfield, she took her pen name from a character in Henrik Ibsen's play *Romersholm*, in order to conceal the authorship of her feminist book reviews and political essays from her family.

In 1912 she met the famous novelist H. G. Wells. They began what would be a stormy love affair—not the first for Wells, who had been involved with several other women (novelist Dorothy Richardson among them) over the course of his marriage. In 1914 West bore a son, Anthony West, by Wells. This tangible evidence of their affair changed West's life; she found herself forced to concoct cover stories about the child, Wells, and their relationship for the consumption of friends and neighbors. For all her feminism, West found, the sexual double standard had not quite given up its grip on her own life.

The Return of the Soldier (1918) launched West's career as a novelist. Its plot is simple and short: a British soldier, Chris, is furloughed back to his wealthy home with shell shock. He no longer remembers his pretty but vacuous wife, Kitty; his amnesia has erased the past 15 years. In his own mind he is a young man still enraptured with his first love, Margaret, who is now a faded, work-worn, shabby, but still generous wife to a poorer man. At Chris's insistence, he and Margaret recover something of their youthful, idyllic love. Yet Margaret herself realizes that "The truth's the truth . . . and he must know it."[13] She regretfully collaborates with a psychiatrist in shattering Chris's amnesia, turning him back into a soldier.

As Samuel Hynes observes, *The Return of the Soldier* is "a rare kind of book, a woman's war novel."[14] Written from the point of view of Chris's cousin Jenny (an observant, still youngish spinster who lives in Chris and Kitty's house), the novel—spare as it is—suggests the heavy price men pay for masculinity. Jenny remembers Chris as a golden, imaginative, passionate boy (6) who became not only the cynosure of all the household's female eyes, but also their financial support: "at his father's death, he had been obliged to take over a business that was weighted by the needs of a mob of female relatives" (7). The orderly comfort of the house and her own life there, Jenny understands, was underwritten by Chris's work; she hopes that, in compensation, the women "had made a fine place for Chris," a place "good enough for his amazing goodness" (7).

On his return, however, Chris rejects this implicit bargain between men and women, as he rejects his wife and the improvements made in the house in his absence. In his idyll with Margaret, Chris returns to a time when he was neither soldier, nor dutiful husband, nor provider. But Jenny agrees with Margaret that this idyll must end; if not, "He who was as a flag flying from our tower would become a queer-shaped patch of eccentricity on the countryside, the stately music of his being would become a witless piping in the bushes. He would not be quite a man" (66). To be a man is to be a flag flying from the tower: the image suggests the sacrifice of a human being's three-dimensional freedom to the flat dimensions of a symbol that serves the house. Yet to refuse this role, Jenny thinks, is to refuse adult dignity in favor of second childhood.

"He would not be quite a man." In the novel's last glimpse of Chris, after he recovers his memory, he is—as Jenny tells Kitty—"Every inch a soldier" (68). The phrase itself, and Jenny's hesitancy in uttering it, implies that the recovered soldier leaves little room for the man Jenny had envisioned marching to "the stately music" of his own being. The soldier who must return "to that No Man's Land where bullets fall like rain on the rotting faces of the dead" (67) swallows up any other possible ideal of manhood.

In *Harriet Hume: A London Fantasy* (1929), West pushed divisions between men and women still further, into the realm of allegorical fantasy. Beginning with what seems a romantic but still earth-bound idyll between two lovers, Harriet Hume and Arnold Condorex, the novel becomes a conflict of elemental opposites after Harriet discovers that she can read Arnold's thoughts; she becomes his conscience, his nemesis, ultimately perhaps his good angel.

Harriet is less a real woman than "the embodiment of some principle," as Arnold himself puts it; she replies that she is "all that Arnold Condorex rejected."[15] She incarnates qualities typically thought of as feminine: delicate, beautiful, artistic, devoted to private life, Harriet exists sensually and aesthetically for herself, in her own life and being. Public affairs, to her, are "an amusing appendix to the vastly more important things that happened when she played the piano, bit into an apple, was hot, was cold" (17).

Arnold, by contrast, lives most vividly not in his own life and senses but by virtue of his competitive relationship with other men.[16] Poor and ambitious, he means to rise in the world: "I shall not rest until all men have admitted that I am their peer; ay, and beg me to make admission of equality" (113). West associates Arnold with images of blankness, vacancy, and mirrors; for all its seeming worldly power and solidity, she implies, Arnold's masculinity has no substantial reality of its own.

Reading Arnold's mind, Harriet discovers the betrayals he is willing to commit in order to rise in the world. Their mutual guilty knowledge links them in an indissoluble bond, "a mystical confusion of substance in opposites" (203). West may here be echoing the Platonic myth of creation (from the *Symposium*), in which women and men were said to be the divided halves of one originally unified being, each fated to seek out the other.

Arnold, however, wishes to destroy his opposite rather than live with it (204). Not until the novel's ending (the twists of which readers must discover for themselves) does he learn to avoid "identifying difference with enmity" (271). For her part, Harriet concedes that "Humanity would be unbearably lackadaisical if there were none but my kind alive. 'Tis the sturdy desire you have to shape the random elements of our existence into coherent patterns that is the very pith and marrow of mankind" (267). The opposing principles represented by Arnold and Harriet can be reconciled, West seems to say. The place of their reconciliation is at once utopian and right here in everyday life: a "fantasy," yes, but a "Fantasy of London."

In *The Thinking Reed* (1936), her last novel before the onset of World

War II, West reaffirmed "coherence" as a central value of civilization and returned to the problem of reconciling feminine and masculine values. Compared to *Harriet Hume*, *The Thinking Reed* lies closer to the nineteenth-century realist tradition in the novel. Told in the third person through the consciousness of its heroine, Isabelle Sallafranque, the novel owes much to the example of Henry James.[17] When Isabelle realizes that she wants "life to have a moral beginning and middle and end," wants it "to form part of a pattern," she demands in effect that life attain to the orderly condition of the English realist novel.[18]

Isabelle is a well-off young widow at the novel's beginning and marries an important French industrialist, Mark Sallafranque, whom she comes to love deeply. Threats to order in her world come not from need but from the mindless vacuity of the rich themselves. Happy in each other, Isabelle and Mark disdain this world but remain caught up in it. When Mark, drunk and out of control at a casino, causes Isabelle to lose the child she is carrying (309), she comes close to leaving him.

Isabelle decides to return to the marriage, but remains haunted by ambivalence. "All men are my enemies," she thinks—but "That is why making love is important, it is a reconciliation between all such enemies" (420). She cannot fully understand or forgive him in the end, but cannot imagine life without him: "It struck her that the difference between men and women is the rock on which civilization will split before it can reach any goal that could justify its expenditure of effort. She knew also that her life would not be tolerable if he were not always there to crush gently her smooth hands with his strong short fingers" (431).

In *The Thinking Reed*, West tries to combine an analysis of relations between men and women with a critique of the class system. The idle, complacent rich of the 1920s come in for satire, but the ambitious, envious poor—in the person of Campofiore, a government official—are even more chilling. Mark dismisses his workers' discontent as the work of outside "agitators" (118); Isabelle worries vaguely that Mark cannot see the workers clearly, but the novel never attempts to formulate the workers' perspective on Isabelle and Mark. In the end, we learn that the great crash of 1929 is about to descend, and surmise that this world will be changed utterly. How it will be changed, however, we do not know; and meanwhile, the novel directs our sympathies toward Isabelle and Mark, the most observant, most energetic, and most loving members of the upper class.

West does not manage to bring all the narrative threads and themes of *The Thinking Reed* together in her conclusion. Insofar as they do come together, however, the novel's basic bent is conservative. While the rich can be frivolous, there is no legitimately humane challenge to their dominion; while men can be violent, women can only choose to effect a reconciliation with them. The restoration of pattern, with its orderly beginning, middle, and end, is worth the price—and there do not seem many alternative patterns to choose from.

It is a surprising novel for a onetime radical feminist to write, but perhaps less surprising if we consider its historical context: the Western world still struggling with economic depression, and Hitler looming over Europe. In the following years, West would take her search for moral pattern into nonfictional writing—history, journalism, and political philosophy—before returning to the novel in the 1950s. In 1959, she was named Dame of the British Empire.

Vita (born Victoria) Sackville-West (1892–1962) was a romantic conservative by temperament, and held that oxymoronic combination together in both her life and her art. Her father was an English nobleman, her mother the daughter of a Spanish dancer—hereditary sources, she often said, for her dual character. They lived at Knole, an enormous Elizabethan estate; Sackville-West later wrote of her childhood home, and bitterly regretted that she could not, as a woman, inherit it.

In 1913 she married Harold Nicolson, a young diplomat. While she prized Harold's wit and good humor, she did not care to take on the duties of a diplomat's wife, nor the identity of "Mrs. Harold Nicolson." She had loved women before marrying Harold, and an affair with a former schoolmate, Violet Keppel, almost ended the marriage in the years 1918–21. After Violet, there were other women, although none so all-consuming; Virginia Woolf memorialized her own passionate friendship with Sackville-West in *Orlando* (1928).[19]

Sackville-West won success early in her career as a poet. She generally preferred traditional forms and subjects; *The Land*, a long poem about Knole and the English countryside, won the Hawthornden prize in 1926. Beginning in 1930, however, she published a group of novels that may be her most solid literary achievement: *The Edwardians* (1930), *All Passion Spent* (1931), and *Family History* (1932). As the last title implies, all three of these novels are in some sense family sagas, stories that register historical change through the generations of a single family.

All Passion Spent looks at history through the last days of a magnificent Victorian matriarch, Lady Slane. The novel opens immediately after the death of her husband, a great diplomat and statesman whose career she had followed to India and back. Her cramped, conventional children debate over who shall take responsibility for their mother and what little wealth she has: a small legacy from her husband, and her jewels. Lady Slane confounds them all by simply giving away her jewels and renting a small house in an unfashionable quarter of London, in which she and her maid can live independently.

The rest of the novel mingles Lady Slane's reminiscences of the past with life in her new house and the friends, old and new, who visit her there. Once upon a time, Lady Slane remembers, she had been a girl, Deborah, who dreamed of "escape and disguise; a changed name, a travestied sex, and freedom in some foreign city"—exactly what the younger Vita Sackville-West had escaped to with Violet Keppel. [20] "The image of the girl faded, and in its place stood a slender boy. He was a boy, but essentially he was a sexless creature, a mere symbol and emanation of youth, one who had forsworn for ever the delights and rights of sex to serve what seemed to his rioting imagination a nobler aim. Deborah, in short, at the age of seventeen, had determined to become a painter" (149).

Victoria Glendinning rightly points out that Lady Slane's artistic ambitions here may not have much credibility—we never actually see her try to paint—but that Sackville-West is "making a point here" nevertheless: the artist, for her, is defined by an anticonventional way of being rather than by competitive doing. [21] By that romantic criterion, [22] the house in which Lady Slane spends her last days (like the author's own house, Sissinghurst, with its magnificent gardens) is a genuine artistic achievement. Its "curiously ripened and detached" atmosphere stands opposed to the "animal law" of worldly competition outside (124, 121).

Looking around her in 1931, Vita Sackville-West might well have found reasons to look for detachment from what competition's "animal law" had somehow wrought: war followed by international economic crisis. Lady Slane comes to represent both the world against which Sackville-West had rebelled—the world of Victorian marriage and service to men's public careers—and the world she created for herself in the peaceful detachment of Sissinghurst. Sackville-West's best hope, like Rebecca West's in *The Thinking Reed*, is fundamentally conservative: the balanced, aesthetically pleasing world of a restrained leisure class.

Elizabeth Bowen (1899–1973), like Vita Sackville-West, was a friend of Virginia Woolf; but, like Sackville-West, she was more at home in forms closer to classic realism than with Woolf's experimental modernism. Her novels, as critic Mona Van Duyn notes of *The Death of the Heart* (1938), combine a "tight and studied . . . patterning of characters, setting, narrative organization and prose style" with a consistent "illusion of realism." Retreating from the farther reaches of experimental fiction, Bowen's work imposes a formal, artificial order on life without unseating the reader's habitual faith that novels are simply windows onto everyday reality.[23]

In *To the North* (1932), Bowen's patterning juxtaposes the different characters and fates of two women, sisters-in-law, who share a house in London in the 1920s. Cecilia is a young widow—pretty, sociable, but still "bewildered" and uncertain of direction after her brief marriage and her husband's sudden death of pneumonia.[24] Like other young widows who crop up in the fiction of the 1930s (she resembles Rebecca West's Isabelle, in *The Thinking Reed*, and Evelyn Jarrold, the protagonist of Vita Sackville-West's *Family History*), Cecilia is sexually experienced, has known youthful romance and its loss, but—through no fault of her own—must live on in a world no longer structured by these familiar stories. She and characters like her embody a general question for women (and for fiction): what happens when women's lives go on after the old endings, happy or sad?

If Cecilia represents experience, her opposite in the pattern is innocence. Her sister-in-law, Emmeline, wonders at the novel's outset whether she "would ever love. Nothing could be as dear as the circle of reading-light around her solitary pillow" (26). Emmeline's story in *To the North* is the familiar story of romantic initiation and loss of innocence, at the hands of an ambitious, unscrupulous young man; it counterpoints Cecilia's movement from experience to (perhaps) a kind of sadly diminished innocence in a marriage of friendship and respect, if not romantic bliss.

The contrasting movement of their lives with men tears Cecilia and Emmeline's home apart. "Women are too like each other and far too different," the narrator suggests, to sustain intimacy (133). "She is not my lover; she's not my child," Cecilia says to herself of Emmeline (133); and Emmeline, learning of Cecilia's engagement, reflects that "Houses shared with women are built on sand" (208). Both modern young women are cut adrift not only from conventional romantic marriage, but from the sustaining bonds of nineteenth-century women's "separate sphere" (as feminist historians have recently described them).[25]

Whatever new possibilities have opened for twentieth-century women, Cecilia and Emmeline can only shape their fates, Bowen seems to say, in relation to their male lovers. Emmeline has a job running a travel agency, but loses interest in it as she falls deeper into her affair with Markie. When she kills herself and Markie in a car crash (a quintessentially 1920s disaster, reminiscent of F. Scott Fitzgerald's *The Great Gatsby*), the future is left to Cecilia and her fiancé, Julian. As in Rebecca West's *The Thinking Reed*, we are left with the sense that the old pattern—courtship and marriage—is a diminished thing, but there may not be life outside it.

The Death of the Heart (1938), like *To the North*, tells a story of initiation. Portia, the teenage ward of Anna and Thomas Quayne, falls in love with a young man who toys with her and drops her. Portia's disorders expose the barrenness of the Quaynes' marriage. Anna, we learn, married Thomas only after a long and more significant affair with another man; after marrying Anna, Thomas unhappily finds "himself the prey of a passion for her . . . that nothing in their language could be allowed to express, that nothing could satisfy."[26]

Anna recalls *To the North*'s Cecilia in her social facility and emotional constriction. Portia's innocence recalls Emmeline's, and like Emmeline's, it becomes less automatically sympathetic, more ambiguous—self-involved, willfully obtuse—as the novel goes on.

Yet Portia matters, and the novel does not dispose of her at the end. As her diary (portions of which are recorded in the novel) makes plain, and the other characters finally realize, "She has a point of view" (308); she has the novelist's own ability to get other people "taped" (304). She can use her truth-telling cruelly, as when she shatters Major Brutt's fond belief in Anna's respect for him (288). For better or worse, however, her "point of view"—in a sense, her power of words—gains Portia power over the adult world.[27]

The Death of the Heart offers glimpses of other worlds, in Portia's relationships with her mother and the servant, Matchett. Whether these worlds can be returned to, however—whether there are real alternatives to adult life as a diminished thing—remains a question for Bowen in her novels of the 1930s.

Rosamund Lehmann (1901–90), like her near-contemporary Elizabeth Bowen, admired and learned from Virginia Woolf. Surveying the modern novel in 1946, Lehmann wrote that Woolf's Mrs. Ramsay, in *To the Lighthouse*, was one of the few twentieth-century literary characters whom readers could actually love; the creation of such characters, Lehmann thought, was one of the novelist's foremost duties. She saw "a dismal absence of people to fall in love with" in modern fiction, and complained that "Until the novel gives them back to us, commits itself and them whole-heartedly again, as in the old days, the novel will be small and cold, however sharp and bright."[28]

Woolf's Mrs. Ramsay may well have had an influence on Lehmann's greatest novelistic character: Sybil Jardine, whose doings lie at the center of *The Ballad and the Source* (1944). Like Mrs. Ramsay, Sybil Jardine is an older woman, and a mother figure. As we come to know Mrs. Ramsay in good measure through Lily Briscoe's eyes, so we come to know Mrs. Jardine through the fascinated eyes of the young narrator, Rebecca Landon, and the other women who tell Rebecca Mrs. Jardine's story.[29] And like Mrs. Ramsay, Sybil enjoys scripting other people's lives; she is an artist in what she rather ominously calls "human material."[30]

Yet Sybil Jardine, in the end, is a far more ambiguous figure than Mrs. Ramsay. Rebecca initially adores Mrs. Jardine's capacity to cast a romantic light upon seemingly ordinary events; under the influence of Mrs. Jardine's poetic language, she says, "My form appeared to me in an indistinct but pleasing diaphanous light, moving over the green hillside, spiritually and gracefully gathering blossoms." She is willing, even eager, to "lend myself" to Sybil's imaginative power, to be shaped by her (6)—even though both her parents distrust her.

After this introduction to Sybil's charm, as seen through Rebecca's eyes, the novel incorporates lengthy stories from two other female narrators—Tilly, Rebecca's former nurse, and Maisie, Rebecca's friend and Sybil's granddaughter. From Tilly, Rebecca learns that Sybil had long ago abandoned her own daughter in running away from her first husband, that Sybil had used and betrayed the friendship of Rebecca's grandmother. From Maisie, Rebecca hears of the novel's culminating catastrophe: a tangle of sexual jealousies, madness, and attempted suicide that ensues when Sybil and her daughter at last confront one another. In Tilly and Maisie's stories, Sybil's character emerges in another light—as possessive, disturbingly sexual (given her age), calculating, histrionic, and irresponsible.

The Ballad and the Source asks us to imagine what happens when a strong mother figure is no longer self-sacrificing, asexual, housebound, and domestic in the Victorian mold of Woolf's Mrs. Ramsay.[31] In one moment of self-justification, Sybil presents herself as a kind of late-nineteenth-century feminist pioneer who made it possible for younger women to live "a life in which all your functions and capacities are used and *none* frustrated" (101). Sybil's own attempt to live by this creed of self-fulfillment wreaks a certain amount of havoc in the lives of others; self-delusion and manipulation are among the "functions and capacities" she exploits.

Yet Lehmann does not allow us to judge Sybil easily. For all her faults, she entrances Rebecca, as Mrs. Ramsay entranced Lily Briscoe. And it is Sybil's story, as filtered through the reactions of her granddaughter Maisie, that begins Rebecca's initiation into adulthood—planting "deep within the feathery shifting webs and folds of my consciousness that seed which grows a shape too huge, too complex ever to see in outline, clear and whole: the monster, human experience" (47). In conventional stories of young women's initiation into life, the initiator is more than likely to be a male character (as in Elizabeth Bowen's *The Death of the Heart* and *To the North*). *The Ballad and the Source* recasts this old story for modernity, as a drama whose central characters and narrators are all women.

Sydney Janet Kaplan's comment on Rosamund Lehmann—that she "achiev[ed] a high degree of artistic success through the popularization of previously avant-garde techniques"—could apply with equal justice to many of the writers discussed in this chapter (Kaplan, 114). Other of these writers also prospered by rewriting their modern social concerns—with class and gender conflict, and new ideas of women's sexuality—into more traditional forms. Their very diverse collective achievement suggests that the early twentieth century was both an expansive and an unsettled time for women writers in the British novel, as it was for women in general.

CHAPTER 6

American Fiction: Regions of the National Culture

Like Great Britain, the United States in the early years of the twentieth century saw the emergence of a good many women novelists who were not in the avant garde of experimental modernism, but who nevertheless made important contributions to the twentieth-century novel. In the United States, these novelists allied themselves both with and against certain kinds of "realism," whose contours differed somewhat from the contours of classic nineteenth-century British realism.

Literary realism in the United States was slower in coming of age than it was in England, where the novel had flourished since the eighteenth century. Many of the most famous canonical mid-nineteenth-century American novels are actually romances, it has been argued, rather than realist novels. Works like Hawthorne's *The Blithedale Romance* and *The Scarlet Letter*, Melville's *Moby-Dick* and *Pierre*, are rife with symbolism, allegory, and quasi-supernatural elements; in terms of plot, they tend to favor overtly philosophical quests over realist concerns with marriage and everyday life in human society. Not until Henry James, it is often suggested, is there a full-fledged American inheritor of the classic English realist tradition—and James, of course, gave up on the thin social soil of his native country to spend most of his working life in England, where he thought conditions more favorable to the novelist.[1]

When realism did take hold in American literature, it was closely shadowed by, and often popularly identified with, the later, allied literary movement known as naturalism. Originating in France with Emile Zola, naturalism applied deterministic analyses of society—Social Darwinism, the new disciplines of sociology and eugenics—to the representation of human character and action in the novel, seeing literary characters as creatures of their circumstances and heredity. In the literary history of the United States, Theodore Dreiser, Stephen Crane, and Frank Norris are often labeled as both realist and naturalist novelists.

Thus far, there are no women in this brief history of the realist novel in the United States. And until recent feminist critics took up the issue, women were indeed almost always excluded from standard histories of the Great American Novel. Not that there were in fact no women novelists in the age of Hawthorne and later—to the contrary: Hawthorne himself notoriously complained to his publisher of "the damned mob of scribblng women," lady novelists whose sales and profits vastly exceeded his own. Toward the turn of the century, black American women like Frances E. W. Harper and Pauline Hopkins were active in yoking the forms of nineteenth-century novels to a mission of "social uplift" for all black Americans.[2] But criticism until recently tended to dismiss women novelists of the nineteenth century as sentimentalists, excluding them from the more highly valued—and masculine—critical categories of the philosophical romance and the realist novel.[3]

Feminist critics have come to the defense of the nineteenth-century women's "sentimental" novel, and have also pointed out the considerable extent of women's contributions to one of the major early strands of realism in the United States: the literature of "local color," fiction and sketches that presented life in a particularized place on the immense and variegated American continent. Bret Harte, teller of San Francisco tales, and Mark Twain, with his novels of Missouri, are familiar male writers whose works are often located in the local-color tradition. Less familiar to many readers may be Sara Orne Jewett (1849–1909) and Mary Wilkins Freeman (1852–1930), whose best stories and short novels were written around the turn of the century. Their chosen ground was New England, their central characters most often women of strength and conviction. Eschewing the overbearing Social Darwinism and the urban scenes that were preoccupying many well-known male realists by this time, Jewett and Freeman anatomized life in small-town New England with close sympathy. Jewett's best-known volume of sketches, *The Country of the Pointed Firs* (1896), along with Freeman's collection of stories, *A New England Nun* (1891), treated women's work in maintaining close-knit communities as important in its own right, giving dignity to lives sometimes counted of small importance in the country's grand rush to industrial capitalist development, with its attendant urbanization.[4]

For the women novelists who came after them, Jewett's and Freeman's careers (along with those of many other women writers of their time) were both inspiring and disquieting. Edith Wharton, Ellen Glasgow, Zora Neale Hurston, Willa Cather, and Mary Austin all followed in Jewett's and Freeman's paths—to a certain point—by becoming writers identified with a particular time and place: Wharton with "Old New York" society of the late nineteenth and early twentieth century; Glasgow with the post–Civil War, middle-class white South; Hurston with the all-black township of Eatonville, Florida, and other black neighborhoods of the South; Cather with the prairie and the American Southwest; Austin with California and New Mexico. Yet for the most part they did not locate their stories in communities dominated by women, as had Jewett and Freeman. They sometimes embodied their narrative perspective, or aspects of their own values, in male narrators and characters. They attempted novels of larger scope and ambition than the story collections favored by the earlier local colorists. Most important, perhaps, they asserted their right to deal with matters of sexuality, communal violence, and historical change that had been avoided, some of them felt, by the nostalgic gentility of their precursors.[5]

Of this group of novelists, Edith Jones Wharton (1862–1937) was the eldest and probably the most traditional in terms of both form and subject matter. Her wealthy family belonged to the New York "Four Hundred"—the social elite named for the capacity of Mrs. William Astor's ballroom. Edith Jones's background of privilege, like Virginia Woolf's intellectual Victorian family, was a mixed blessing for a young woman writer, albeit for somewhat different reasons. While a young woman of society enjoyed comparative leisure and access to books, art, and travel, some doors were still closed to her. Although her brothers might attend good schools and go on to university, she would not; she would make her debut and go on to fulfill her "single-minded purpose . . . to make a suitable marriage."[6] In 1878 Edith's mother arranged to have some of her daughter's poetry privately printed, but she would have been surprised and shocked at the idea of rearing a professional author.

Edith apparently fulfilled her expected social purpose in 1885 by marrying Edward ("Teddy") Wharton. By 1889–90, however, she was writing again in earnest and began publishing short stories, some of which would go into her first story collection, *The Greater Inclination* (1899). In 1902

Wharton published her first novel, *The Valley of Decision*, a historical romance set in eighteenth-century Italy. It was after reading—and prais-ing—*The Valley of Decision* that her new friend Henry James gave Whar-ton his famous advice: *"Do New York!"* Cautioning her against his own "awful example of exile and ignorance," James extolled the still-waiting possibilities of "the American subject" for a novelist who knew it firsthand (cited in Lewis, 127).

James's advice may have struck the note of Wharton's own inclination; in any event, Wharton's next novel, *The House of Mirth* (1905), "did" New York, became a runaway best-seller, and established Wharton as a major novelist.[7] The story of a beautiful, perceptive, but aging young woman on the New York marriage market—when we meet her, Whar-ton's heroine is "nine-and-twenty, and still Miss Bart" (38)—*The House of Mirth* maps Lily Bart's inability to find a suitable marriage, to market her charms on terms she can live with. As an orphan without other tan-gible resources, living on the charity of her Aunt Peniston, Lily has no commodity but herself to trade on. Her job, virtually her social duty, is to construct herself as an aesthetic object available for the purchase of the most eligible male bidder, an enterprise that culminates in her starring role in a *tableau vivant* (an entertainment in which costumed players pose as pictures the audience is expected to recognize) at a large society party (133–35).

Lily plays out this role, however, against an inward conflict that sabo-tages her own best efforts to turn herself into an expensive object for someone else's consumption, beginning with her attempt to land the young, innocent, and rich Percy Gryce for a husband. Being such an object, as Wharton makes clear, is extraordinarily demanding work; it involves not just concern and expense for dressing, but the labor of com-posing oneself for the entertainment of one's buyer, enlivening his bore-dom without offending his sensibilities. Yet Lily cannot imagine, indeed is scarcely fitted for, any other kind of work. She can neither imagine for herself the life of her cousin, Gerty Farish, who subsists independently on her own tiny income (7), nor accept being purchased at the hands of the various men—Gryce, Gus Trenor, Simon Rosedale—who in one fashion or another desire her.

The only man who presents an alternative is Lawrence Seldon, through whose eyes we first meet Lily, and who reflects on the meaning of her suicide at the novel's end. Seldon thus—in a limited way—stands in for Wharton's own narrative perspective; he embodies part of Whar-ton's own view of Lily, but his view has its own blindnesses. Reasonably well off by any ordinary standard but not conspicuously rich, Seldon lives modestly, collects books and objects knowledgeably, and believes himself a member of a "republic of the spirit" (68) rather than an oligarchy of wealth. A critical, half-distanced spectator of the society in which he lives, Seldon shares with Lily moments of half-ironic, half-sincere banter about their world, moments that verge on true intimacy (68–74) but never coalesce into romantic commitment. Lily, as both ironically acknowledge, would be too expensive for him.

Yet the failure of their relationship, in the end, is at least as much Seldon's as Lily's. Like other men of his world, Seldon appreciates Lily as a "wonderful spectacle" (66), and keeping her at a distance means that he can enjoy the aesthetic spectacle without risk to himself: "he could give his admiration the freer play because so little personal feeling remained in it" (216). Wharton herself called Seldon a "negative hero," and critic Wai-chee Dimock charges that Seldon's " 'republic of the spirit' turns out to be less a republic than a refined replica of the social marketplace, of which Seldon is a full participating member."[8] Lily's own final rebellion against the social marketplace, her refusal to buy her way back into social favor by relinquishing Seldon's letters to a blackmailer, makes the novel's "most eloquent protest against the ethics of exchange" (Dimock, 789), for Seldon's sake and for her own. He will never learn of Lily's generosity, however, and it is not clear whether that gesture, or the peace Lily dimly feels on the way toward her suicide, or Seldon's own penitence for his missed opportunity, has the power to change their world.[9]

Wharton returned to the figure of the detached male observer in later novels, most notably *The Custom of the Country* and *The Age of Innocence*. In *The Custom of the Country* (1913), the male observer is Ralph Marvell, the loyal son of an old, distinguished, but again not orgulously wealthy New York family. That Ralph cherishes ambitions to be a writer suggests that he, like Seldon, embodies something of Wharton's own perspective on the world of the novel.[10] Unlike Seldon, however, Ralph takes the plunge, marries his aesthetic object, and meets his own ruin in the rapacious vacuity of his chosen love: Undine Spragg, one of Wharton's most astonishing—and most chilling—characters.

The daughter of ineffectual, shadily prosperous midwestern parents whom she has dragged to New York in pursuit of "Society," Undine is named (as her mother explains to Ralph) for "a hair-waver father put on the market the week she was born" (50). Named for an imitation of nature, "Undine was fiercely independent and yet passionately imitative.

She wanted to surprise every one by her dash and originality, but she could not help modelling herself on the last person she met" (12–13). Success for her is a matter of seeking out what to imitate and finding someone to supply the outward trappings to sustain the imitation. Because Undine "is so unfixed herself," because she has no "natural" central self that is not an imitation, she will marry and then discard several husbands, several social identities, in trying to reach the top of the social pyramid, without feeling or caring for the damage she does on the way.[11] Unmoved by what might be supposed to be a woman's "natural" love for her child (she is scarcely interested in her son by Ralph [127]), detached from her own bodily and sexual reality ("her physical reactions were never very acute: she always vaguely wondered why people made 'such a fuss,' were always so violently for or against such demonstrations," 183), Undine typifies "the layers on layers of unsubstantialness on which the seemingly solid scene" of society rests (170).

Undine's strange combination of unreality with destructive power, Wharton suggests, is the result of specifically American—one might add, consumer capitalist—social arrangements. And while it seems that men like Ralph are her victims, they are also to blame. Charles Bowen, a writer friend of Ralph's and a minor character, sums up Wharton's judgment of the situation: "the average American," he says, "looks down on his wife" (128). He will work for her, indeed slave for her, but "the custom of the country" separates the wife's sphere from realistic knowledge of her husband's work. "Why haven't we taught our women to take an interest in our work? Simply because we don't take enough interest in *them*." The American "passion for making money has preceded the knowing how to spend it, and the American man lavishes his fortune on his wife because he doesn't know what else to do with it" (129). Women, as the sociologist Thorstein Veblen put it just a few years before *The Custom of the Country,* had became display objects of "conspicuous consumption" for the leisure class.[12] Where earlier women writers like Jewett and Freeman had often written of women's separate sphere as an Edenic place of precapitalist values, Wharton represents the separate sphere as the gilded cage and ultimate product of consumer capitalism, inimical to women and men alike.

Wharton herself spent most of her working years in residence in France, and her preference for European gender arrangements may have had something to do with her choice. Charles Bowen, again, seems to speak for Wharton in asserting that in Europe woman "is not a parenthesis, as she is here—she's in the very middle of the picture" (129). Even from Europe, however, she continued to do "the American subject." Two short novels from the 1910s, *Ethan Frome* (1911) and *Summer* (1917), extended Wharton's America from wealthy New York to impoverished rural New England, an area Wharton had come to know from the privileged vantage point of her summer estate in the Berkshires of Massachusetts. The title Wharton selected for *Ethan Frome's* French translation, "Hivier" ("Winter") underscores its connection to the later *Summer,* which Wharton herself called "the Hot Ethan" (cited in Lewis, 396). Both stories tell of cramped, embittered lives endured in claustrophobic New England houses. Wharton explicitly contrasted her own realistic vision in these novels with those of earlier women writers, like Jewett and Freeman, who saw "the derelict mountain villages of New England" through "rose-coloured spectacles."[13]

Of the two, *Ethan Frome* is the bleaker. Narrated through the perspective of a visitor to Starkfield (a tactic Wharton picked up from Emily Brontë's *Wuthering Heights,* among other literary models), it presents a somber picture of three people confined to an isolated farmstead: Ethan Frome, a great, half-crippled "ruin of a man"; his wife, Zenobia (or Zeena); and his wife's cousin, Mattie Silver, a querulous invalid.[14] The narrator comes to know Frome slightly, and finally one night, when held over in Frome's house by a snowstorm, meets the other members of the household, and begins "to put together this vision of [Frome's] story" (25). Whether true or false—and the other residents of Starkfield will confirm only a part of his version of events—the narrator's "vision" has a dreadful power.[15] He imagines a love affair springing up between a much younger Ethan and his wife's cousin, come to help the invalid Zeena with the housework; imagines Zeena's jealousy and determination to be rid of Mattie; and imagines the sleighing accident that crippled both Ethan and Mattie on the eve of Mattie's departure as a failed suicide attempt. This part of the narrator's vision, however, will never be confirmed. Nor will Zeena's feelings on hearing of the accident. "It was a miracle, considering how sick she was—but she seemed to be raised right up just when the call came to her. . . . she's had the strength given her to care for those two for over twenty years, and before the accident came she thought she couldn't even care for herself" (179). Zeena draws strength and ascendancy from others' misery; her dark "miracle" suggests that Wharton saw a hideous emotional vampirism in certain forms of women's traditional housebound power.

Told through a more conventional omniscient realistic narrator, *Ethan Frome's* companion novel, *Summer,* presents a more conventional coming-of-age story in some respects. Young Charity Royall, the adopted daughter of a lawyer, dreams restlessly of escaping small-town life; she meets a young man from the city, come to look at New England rural houses. What follows has a certain novelistic inevitability: seduction, pregnancy, and abandonment, as the young man returns to a fiancée of his own class and background. The unusual and gripping elements of *Summer*, however, lie in Charity's relation to her adoptive father, lawyer Royall (as he is known; their names suggestively juxtapose love and law) and in what she learns of her natural mother.

Royall is almost as cramped in small-town New England as Charity; intelligent, bitter, given to drinking, he shares some unspoken under-standings with his ward. One night, however, he tries to turn their awk-ward relationship into something else. Appearing on the 17-year-old girl's bedroom threshold, he asks her to let him in: "I'm a lonesome man."[16] Disgusted more than frightened, Charity bluntly replies, "Well, I guess you made a mistake, then. This ain't your wife's room any longer" (29). Thereafter, Charity keeps her distance in the house, even when Royall directly proposes marriage; in his middle-aged sexuality he seems to her "like a hideous parody of the fatherly old man she had always known" (34).

In the end, however, the "hideous" father is Charity's best refuge. To-ward the end of the book, pregnant and deserted by her lover, she finds her way to the settlement of impoverished outlaws up on "the Mountain," and encounters her mother—or, more accurately, her mother's corpse, dead of drink and hard living (248–49). In their disorder, "herded together in a sort of passive promiscuity in which their common misery was the strongest link" (259), they have given way to everything from which, as Charity now learns, lawyer Royall has saved her (despite his own giving way to sexual disorder). When Royall offers again to marry Charity, knowing of her pregnancy, she accepts. They return from a brief, sexually unconsummated honeymoon, "in the cold autumn moonlight, . . . to the door of the red house" in which they have always lived (291); that door shuts on them and perhaps on their aspirations to escape this house, this town, this place.

It is a profoundly ambiguous ending. Royall's offer of marriage is gen-erous, as is his decision to repect her sexual privacy on their wedding night. It forces Charity to look again at the "hideous" old man, and see him better. Yet the power to do otherwise is in his hands, and if his behavior lets Charity know that "she was safe with him" (284), she still faces the prospect of a future at once barren of sexual pleasure and dependent on the father-husband's forbearance for sexual safety. Their marriage incestuously fixes them in their isolated house, as Ethan and Mattie's accident fixes them in theirs. How high a price does Charity pay for safety, if she is in fact now "safe," and for maturity, if she attains it? Does lawyer Royall pay any commensurate price for his one breach of trust with Charity? If the ending of *Ethan Frome* is bleak without mitigation, the ending of *Summer* presents a more complicated riddle of tone and judgment.[17]

In the greatest novel of her late career, *The Age of Innocence* (1920), Wharton went back to the New York social scene of the 1870s and the drama of the partly detached, observant male character: Newland Archer, through whose point of view the novel is told. Engaged to marry the blandly beautiful and innocent May Welland, Archer meets and falls in love with her cousin, Ellen Olenska. Ellen's family will not countenance a divorce, even though she is separated from her brutal husband (Wharton herself had divorced Teddy Wharton in 1913), and she decides to respect their judgment; Archer drifts helplessly into his marriage. Aware that the two are still drawn to each other, May and the family conspire to separate them, sending Ellen back to Europe with a grandly ritual dinner (Wharton consistently draws on anthropological language—terms like *ritual, ceremony,* and *sacrifice*—in describing the behavior of the New York "tribe"; see Lewis, 432). The dinner, Archer realizes while sitting numbly at the table, "was the old New York way of taking life 'without effusion of blood': the way of people who dreaded scandal more than disease, who placed decency above courage, and who considered that nothing was more ill-bred than 'scenes,' except the behavior of those who gave rise to them."[18]

Yet Archer himself, like Lawrence Seldon and Ralph Marvell, is only partially detached from the society he observes. Along with Ellen, he acquiesces in her exile. Like Seldon, he never commits himself altogether to his love, and is left an onlooker at the novel's conclusion. In *The House of Mirth*, however, Seldon ends up looking on at Lily Bart's deathbed; in *The Age of Innocence*, Archer—some 26 years after her departure—ends by gazing up at the windows of Ellen Olenska's Paris apartment, where she is very much alive and entertaining his son. Archer cannot bring himself to go in. If he is in some ways a "negative hero" like Seldon,[19] the consequences of his failure are less harsh. His own life has been productive, he has lived by his commitments to May, and

Ellen's experience in Paris has probably yielded some riches of its own. Ellen's apartment, indeed, resembles nothing so much as Edith Wharton's own home and life in Paris.

The Age of Innocence "journeys into [Wharton's] own past, a past that she had rejected, in order to recapture a time of lost stability and to achieve a reconciliation with that past" (Fryer, 128). Written in the immediate aftermath of World War I, its errand into the past registers not only Wharton's personal past, but a more widely felt need to come to terms with an America fast vanishing into history. The novels of Ellen Glasgow, Zora Neale Hurston, Willa Cather, and Mary Austin register the same need in different American landscapes.

Ellen Glasgow (1873–1945) descended from an old Virginia Tidewater family on her mother's side, while her father, born to a poor white rural family, became the managing director of the South's largest foundry and munitions supplier after the Civil War. The Old South and the post-Reconstruction South clashed in her own upbringing, as they later would in her fiction. Her early identification with her mother's fragility and depression, along with her alienation from her father's Calvinist rigidity, are constant themes in Glasgow's posthumously published memoir, *The Woman Within* (1954). Her memoir also chronicles Glasgow's favored reading: Darwin, Nietzsche, and Schopenhauer, from whom she imbibed a pessimistic sense of human life as fatally ruled by biology and circumstance.[20]

Divided between nostalgia for the lost South and interest in the commercial vigor and freedom of the new, between determinist notions of history as the survival of the fittest and regret for people plowed under by historical change, Glasgow's novels veer uneasily between ironic and romantic perspectives. She saw her fiction as an attack on the South's misplaced idealism, its stubborn refusal to come to grips with the actual hardship of life; yet the novels betray a conflict between "the novelist she wished to be, indeed believed she was (liberal, nonconformist, realistic)" and "the novelist . . . (essentially conservative, traditional, romantic)" she was in fact.[21]

This conflict is especially acute in Glasgow's novels centered on women characters, *Virginia* (1913) and *Barren Ground* (1925). *Barren Ground* was and remains among the most popular of Glasgow's works; *Virginia* was Glasgow's own favorite among her early fictions.[22] The books present strikingly different heroines. Virginia Pendleton, in the book named for her, is introduced as a pretty and conventional young woman. The narrator ironically comments of this small-town girl that she "embodied the feminine ideal of the ages. To look at her was to think inevitably of love."[23] The first third of the novel chronicles her romance with and eventual marriage to Oliver Treadwell, an aspiring young play-wright and rebellious nephew of the town's only industrial magnate (Cyrus Treadwell, who resembles Glasgow's own father). The narrator, in this section of the novel, divides her ironies impartially between Virginia's blind romanticism and Oliver's ambitious egotism, which easily thinks of women as "an incentive and an appendage to the dominant personality of man" (*Virginia*, 86). There is a hint of Glasgow's own realistic artistic credo, however, in Oliver's determination to bring realism to the Amer-ican drama, "to supplant the pretty shams of the stage by the aspect of sober reality" (96). The would-be artistic rebel himself, however, loses his way in sober reality, "sacrifice[s] art for love" (141), and takes a job in order to marry a woman with whom he shares no real intellectual companionship.

Here the novel shifts narrative gears. Glasgow later wrote of *Virginia* that "Although, in the beginning, I had intended to deal ironically with both the Southern lady and the Victorian tradition, I discovered, as I went on, that my irony grew fainter, while it yielded at last to sympathetic compassion."[24] The second part of the novel features an epistolary chap-ter, told entirely through Virginia's letters to her mother after the mar-riage, that silences the narrator's distanced ironic commentary for a time and makes Virginia into a more accessible and endearing, if still faintly comic, figure. As she has children and becomes increasingly preoccupied with their welfare and the running of the house, Virginia loses whatever common ground she once had with Oliver. At one crisis in the marriage, Virginia chooses to stay home and nurse her son, who complains of a sore throat, rather than go on a pleasure trip with her husband and friends. To Oliver—and probably to most present-day readers—Virginia's maternal solicitude seems obsessive. Glasgow vindicates Virginia's deci-sion, however, by turning young Harry's sore throat into a dangerous bout of diphtheria, which he survives only through Virginia's patient nursing. The narrator's commentary insistently demands sympathy for this gentle, but increasingly invisible, middle-aged woman.

At the novel's close, mother love ambiguously pays off: after Oliver has made a financial success of writing popular sentimental plays rather than scorching realist drama, and has deserted Virginia for his leading actress, Harry saves her from despair by telegraphing word of his instant return to stand by his mother's side. His telegram—"Dearest Mother, I am coming home to you," gives the novel its last words. Is this a happy ending for mother or son? Assuming Harry arrives, what then? Given Virginia's investment of her entire self in her children, it may be fitting that Harry's words, not her own, conclude the novel named after her.

Harry's fidelity suggests that Glasgow is unwilling to let the values by which Virginia has lived go down to conclusive defeat. Two other characters in the novel, however, suggest contrasting possibilities for women. Margaret Oldcastle, the actress for whom Oliver leaves Virginia, is an archetypal New Woman: "The intellect in her spoke through her noble rather than beautiful features, through her ardent eyes, through her resolute mouth, through every perfect gesture with which she accompanied her words. She stood not only for the elemental forces, but for the free woman; and her freedom, like that of man, had been built upon the strewn bodies of the weaker" (364). Glasgow grimly sees the New Woman's victory not as the triumph of women over male dominance, but as the sacrifice of women like Virginia to the laws of "evolution, and . . . the resistless principle of change" as embodied in "free"women (364).

Virginia's childhood friend Susan Treadwell, however, seems to find an independent course between these extremes, and to escape Glasgow's deterministic rhetoric. Independent but loyal, rational but tender (181), Susan wants to go to college, but finds the way blocked by her father (123). Without repining, she continues a slow and comradely courtship with a local man, takes devoted care of her invalid mother, marries and has a family but is not devoured by them. Susan's life suggests the possibility of combining values that the novel elsewhere insists are necessarily incompatible.

If Virginia lives only for the sake of others, Dorinda Oakley, the heroine of *Barren Ground*, painfully learns to rely on her own judgment and labor to shape her life. Like Virginia, Dorinda enters the novel as a young woman in love with love; born to hard work on a struggling Virginia farm, she attaches her longing for "something different beyond the misty edge of the horizon" to a weakly handsome young doctor, Jason Greylock.[25] They become engaged; he jilts her; she learns that she is pregnant, and flees to New York City. Struggling with pregnancy and exhaustion, Dorinda has an accident in the New York streets. A capable surgeon rescues her, treats her, and later offers her work as a receptionist in his office (she has miscarried her child) and babysitter to his family. As Dorinda recovers her health and beauty, and learns sophistication of dress and demeanor, she attracts a younger and eminently eligible doctor in the office: "You ought to marry, my dear," the wife of her employer urges her.

To this point, the plot of *Barren Ground* could seem a standard romantic melodrama of fall, romantic rescue, and star-kissed success in the big world. And if the plot seems stereotypical in certain respects, the alternatives for young city women of Glasgow's time—marriage or the new, feminized forms of clerical work—were real enough. But Glasgow scripts her heroine's choices differently: a good marriage will not be the end of the story. "There must be something in life besides love," Dorinda thinks to herself, and for her there is the family farm she left behind (*BG*, 250), an alternative to dependence upon husbands or male employers. Although word of her father's stroke gives her the final push home (253), Dorinda has researched farming methods in New York and planned her return for her own reasons. Unlike Virginia, Dorinda never lives through or for others: "There's something deep down in me," she reflects, "that I value more than love or happiness or anything outside myself. It may be only pride, but it comes first of all" (325).

What fate does Glasgow assign to this heroine, so different from Virginia? Dorinda indeed makes a success of her farm, and enters a companionable but passionless marriage with a competent local farmer, based on "respect and expediency" (*BG*, 373); she watches grimly over her former lover's decline into drink and destitution. If Glasgow denies Dorinda experiences of buoyant joy, she allows her happiness in successful work: "At middle age, she faced the future without romantic glamour, but she faced it with integrity of vision" (525). While there is something punitive in the fate Glasgow deals out to her heroine, and in the soliloquies on life's meaninglessness the narrator voices through her, still Dorinda belongs in twentieth-century fiction's gallery of memorable middle-aged heroines who exceed the bounds of the traditional marriage plot.

After *Barren Ground*, Glasgow returned to more conventionally middle-class situations. *The Romantic Comedians* (1926), *They Stooped to Folly* (1929), and *The Sheltered Life* (1932) ironically comment upon the tragicomedy of romantic love and the sexual double standard, the scarcely endurable tensions and discontents of traditional family life. Yet her attitude toward modernity and women who, like Milly Burden in *They Stooped to Folly*, assert their right to survive their own sexual "ruin," is—like the narrative stance of many of her novels—fundamentally ambivalent. Attacking sentimentalism, the novels sometimes fall back instead (often via the point of view of an older male character like Asa Timberlake in *This Our Life* [1941]) upon an equally facile stoic determinism, in which every character's desires for autonomy are impartially chastened, and incipient social criticism is turned aside by the rhetoric of fatalism.

Glasgow's fiction prospered in her own lifetime, both critically and financially. Despite a hearing loss that curtailed her social activities, Glasgow was active in the Virginia literary community, and helped organize the Conference of Southern Writers at the University of Virginia in 1931; she won the Pulitzer Prize for fiction in 1942. Her reputation has been sustained by Southern and, lately, feminist scholars,[26] for whom her diverse portraits of Southern women in the grip of historical change are of particular interest.

Zora Neale Hurston (1891–1960) wrote about a South that had very little in common with Ellen Glasgow's faded white gentility. In Glasgow's *Virginia*, the black section of the town of Dinwiddie, "Tin Pot Alley," figures in the margins of the story as a place of "squalid alleys" where "the more primitive forms of life appeared to swarm like distorted images under the transparent civilization of the town" (34). With heavy-handed irony, the narrator reduces the black townspeople themselves to a sociological abstraction, "the Problem of the South sprawled innocently amid tomato cans and rotting cabbage leaves." Born and raised in the all-black town of Eatonville, Florida, Hurston knew black Southern townships like "Tin Pot Alley" from the inside, as places with their own traditions and culture, rather than merely as the nightmarish, "distorted" reflection of white culture.

Yet it was not until she gained some distance from her own world, Hurston found, that she could write about it. She left Eatonville, finished high school in Baltimore, moved to Washington, D.C., in 1918, and enrolled in Howard University—"the capstone of Negro education in the world," as Hurston would later call it.[27] She moved to New York in 1925 and received a scholarship to Barnard College (sister college to Columbia University), where she finished her degree in 1927.

At Barnard, Hurston studied under the famous anthropologist Franz Boas. At the same time, she became involved with the black intellectuals and artists of New York's Harlem Renaissance (see chapter 10), who were intensely debating the merits and importance of traditional African-American folk culture as a source for new black modern art. This vigorous debate, combined with "the spy-glass of Anthropology," gave Hurston a new perspective on her own culture: "From the earliest rocking of my cradle, I had known about the capers Brer Rabbit is apt to cut and what the Squinch Owl says from the house top. But it was fitting me like a tight chemise. I couldn't see it for wearing it. It was only when I was off in college, away from my native surroundings, that I could see myself like somebody else and stand off and look at my garment."[28] Armed with her new, dual perspective on African-American culture (and provided with funding from a wealthy white woman patron), Hurston set off for the South to collect folklore.

Out of this journey came *Mules and Men* (1935), largely written by 1929 but published only after Hurston's first novel, *Jonah's Gourd Vine* (based on her memories of her preacher father, it appeared in 1934) did well enough to convince Lippincott's to take a risk on a less convention-ally structured book. In terms of narrative technique, *Mules and Men* stands somewhere between an ethnographic record of an anthropologist's account of another culture, and a modernist short-story cycle like Sher-wood Anderson's *Winesburg, Ohio*. In ethnographic fashion, it combines recorded folktales with accounts of hoodoo rituals; the tales, however, are recounted within lively communal interchanges that often read like short stories or sketches.

And Hurston herself is not a neutral, detached observer, but a char-acter in the events she describes. *Mules and Men* opens with Hurston's arrival in her hometown: "As I crossed the Maitland-Eatonville township line I could see a group on the store porch. . . . I was delighted. The town had not changed. Same love of talk and song." When she tells the group of men on the porch that she has come to collect their stories, they are skeptical: "What you mean, Zora, them big old lies we tell when we're jus' sittin' around her on the store porch doin' nothin'?" Assured that this is just what she means, one man responds, "Zora, don't you come here and tell de biggest lie first thing" (9–10). Responses like this one challenge the validity of the narrator's newly acquired anthropologi-cal "spy-glass," but at the same time invite her to participate in the group's language games as an insider.

Hurston juggles those two perspectives, the outsider's and the insider's, throughout *Mules and Men*. The book ends with several appendixes—a glossary, a small collection of annotated African-American folk songs, some recorded "formulae of hoodoo doctors"—that seem to reinforce Hurston's status as the careful anthropologist, mediating an "alien" cul-ture for literate, cultured, presumably white outsiders (one note compares a work song to "the Odyssey, or the Iliad" [275]). Hurston's own last words in her persona as narrator, however, are more ambiguous. She ends with the tale of "Sis Cat," who let one fast-talking rat get away from her, but learned from the experience to wash her face and mind her manners after—not before—eating her catch. So, concludes Hurston, "I'm sitting here like Sis Cat, washing my face and usin' my manners" (252). These words are spoken from within, not outside, the culture Hurston has come to study; they coolly challenge her readers to figure out just who has caught whom here, who is studying whom.

Hurston echoed the opening of *Mules and Men* in her next book, by now her most famous novel, *Their Eyes Were Watching God* (1937). The novel begins with a woman's return to her hometown: "So the beginning of this was a woman and she had come back from burying the dead."[29] The men and women sitting on the porches watch her come down the street with no friendly eyes; "lords of sounds and lesser things," after the day's work is done and the boss has disappeared, they exercise their communal power by passing judgment on the woman, Janie, who walks down the street in a "faded shirt and muddy overalls," without pausing (*Eyes*, 10–11).

They pass judgment, but at the same time covet the chance to hear the tale she could tell. Janie does tell her story—not directly to the community of porch-sitters at large, but to her friend Pheoby Watson. In many ways, as critics have pointed out, the novel foregrounds the act of story-telling itself; *Their Eyes Were Watching God* becomes the story of how Janie came to have a story, and came to have the power to tell it when and to whom she chooses.[30]

Janie's story is structured around the pattern of a journey or quest. The quest begins at her grandmother's house, with a sexual awakening inspired not by any particular man, but by nature itself and Janie's own needs: "She was stretched on her back beneath the pear tree . . . when the inaudible voice of it all came to her. She saw a dust-bearing bee sink into the sanctum of a bloom; the thousand sister-calyxes arch to meet the love embrace and the ecstatic shiver of the tree from root to tiniest branch creaming in every blossom and frothing with delight. So this was marriage!" (*Eyes*, 24). This "revelation," however, bears little relationship at first to the actual possibilities of Janie's world. Concerned for Janie's future, her grandmother marries her off to an older farmer, Logan Killicks—not for the sake of love, as she explains to Janie, but for the "protection" he offers (*Eyes*, 30).

The marriage does not prosper, and Janie's grandmother dies soon after, uncertain of what good or evil she has wrought. For Janie herself, Hurston implies, the marriage is a necessary rite of passage into experience: "Janie's first dream was dead, so she became a woman" (*Eyes*, 44). As a woman, then, she leaves Killicks to run away with a "cityfied, stylish dressed man," Joe Starks, who promises her a wider life, a "far horizon" (47, 50).

Joe Starks's promises are not altogether empty. He becomes mayor of all-black Eatonville, Florida, which makes him "uh big voice" as he had hoped. But he expects his wife to bask in his reflected glory; his big voice "makes uh big woman outa you," he tells Janie (74). Marriage in this style, over long years, turns Janie into "the shadow of herself" (119), until one day she rebels. When her husband insults her about her age and appearance in the store they keep, Janie shoots back: "Talkin' 'bout *me* lookin' old! When you pull down yo' britches, you look lak de change uh life" (123).

Janie's retort turns the tables in more ways than one: she not only asserts her right to look at and judge her husband's desirability as he judges hers, but also claims for the first time a "big voice"—a male prerogative—in public talk. With the wind taken out of his sails, Joe Starks declines and dies. Assessing herself in the mirror afterward, Janie sees that the "young girl was gone, but a handsome woman had taken her place" (134–35); her husband's death makes her a prosperous, independent widow.

Gaining a voice leaves Janie with a lingering question: to whom, now, can she talk as an equal? Several suitors try her door, but only Tea Cake—a tall traveling man—really returns Janie's banter, only Tea Cake thinks it natural that Janie should want to play checkers on the porch as the men do. Tea Cake does not represent "protection," nor does he offer Janie upward mobility as the wife of an important man. A neighbor woman warns Janie that "nobody wouldn't marry Tea Cake tuh starve tuh death lessen it's somebody jes lak him—ain't used to nothin'" (156). From another perspective, however, Tea Cake's "nothin'" is exactly what Janie has missed: shared labor, reciprocal pleasure, and companionship.

Their relationship is not perfect; Janie and Tea Cake struggle over trust and over money. It takes time for Janie to establish how much she wants to share with Tea Cake—even down to picking beans on the muck (in the Everglades) with him (*Eyes*, 199). At one point Tea Cake, not fully at ease in their relationship's fluid balance of power, beats Janie (218). What separates them in the end, however, is not their own failing but a hurricane. Fleeing the flood in its wake, Tea Cake is bitten by a mad dog. Janie nurses him, but eventually he attacks her with a gun; she manages to shoot him before he can kill her.

The killing puts Janie on trial before two communities: the white com-

munity, sitting in formal legal judgment, and the black community, passing judgments of its own in the back of the courtroom. Her own voice,
giving her own testimony, saves her legally: "She didn't plead to anybody.
She just sat there and told and when she was through she hushed. She
had been through for some time before the judge and the lawyer and the
rest seemed to know it" (*Eyes*, 278). Although it takes a little longer, Tea
Cake's friends finally extend their forgiveness to her as well.

Their Eyes Were Watching God tells the story of Janie's widening voice:
from talking back in public to her husband, Joe Starks, Janie grows until
she can speak for herself with assurance before everyone in her world,
black and white. In the end, she makes a gift of her story to Pheoby—
and through Pheoby, to the town as a whole. As Marjorie Pryse observes,
"Janie gives Pheoby permission to tell the porch sitters about her life with
Tea Cake, implicitly recognizing that there she, too, will become part of
their folklore."[31] In expanding her heroine's voice, Hurston's narrative
technique—her combination of dialogue with spare realistic narration
and lyric imagery—expanded as well the boundaries of realism for later
African-American women writers.

In *Moses, Man of the Mountain* (1939), Hurston left the realistic setting of Eatonville, Florida, behind to rewrite the biblical book of Exodus
from a black perspective. The story of Exodus had long held special significance for African-Americans: God's promise to bring the Hebrews out
of slavery in Egypt was also a promise made, they felt, to black slaves in
the American South. Retelling the story of Moses in black voices, as
Blyden Jackson points out, Hurston could count on her readers to recognize in it "a story about black America" in which "every Jew in Goshen
is converted into an American Negro and every Egyptian in Old Phar-
oah's Egypt into a white in the America where Hurston's folk Negroes
live."[32] Writing in 1939, Hurston turned the story of Moses and the Hebrew exodus into (among other things) a wry inquiry into the vexing questions of black leadership and black cultural independence that concerned
many African-American intellectuals of the 1920s and 1930s.

Black leadership in *Moses, Man of the Mountain* is male leadership:
Hurston stays close to her biblical precedents in this as in other respects
of the story. She casts Moses' wife, Zipporah, as an ambitious and vain
woman who wants Moses to become king of the Hebrews so that she can
be queen. Aaron's sister, the prophetess Miriam, becomes a jealous,
upwardly mobile rival to Moses' authority who casts snide remarks at
Zipporah, "that dark-complected woman he done brought and put up to
be a Queen over the rest of us women" (*Moses*, 282). Moses publicly sets

her down with a rebuke that echoes twentieth-century dismissals of feminism: "The trouble with you is that nobody ever married you. And when a woman ain't got no man to look after, she takes on the world in place of the man she missed" (*Moses*, 300). Only after punishment and degradation does Miriam attain a "tragic" stature; after asking Moses for permission to die, "She seemed to see something with her eyes. She made deep prints with her feet" (*Moses*, 322–23).

If *Their Eyes Were Watching God* ends with confidence in a black woman's independent power of speech, *Moses, Man of the Mountain* is far more pessimistic about the authority of black women's voices in the community. From whatever combination of personal and historical reasons, Hurston remained silent as a published novelist for several years after *Moses*, and wrote her final novel, *Seraph on the Sewanee* (1948), about a white community.

Like Edith Wharton and Ellen Glasgow, and like many other important African-American intellectuals in the years during and after slavery, Hurston wrote an autobiography relatively late in her career: *Dust Tracks on a Road* (1942). As with many writers' autobiographies, *Dust Tracks* offers a deliberately selective and not always factually accurate account of its subject: Francoise Lionnet notes that "the only events of her 'private' life on which Hurston dwells in *Dust Tracks* are those that have deep symbolic and cultural value" for African-Americans' "collective memory."[33] The title of Hurston's autobiography recalls the pattern of the journey or quest that orders *Mules and Men*, *Their Eyes Were Watching God*, and *Moses, Man of the Mountain*. Like the demure cat at the end of *Mules and Men*, however, the title also challenges Hurston's readers: you will find my tracks here, it says in effect, but do not be too sure of finding me.

Willa Cather (1873–1947) spent her early childhood in Virginia before moving out to Nebraska with her family, and wrote one Southern novel late in her career: *Sapphira and the Slave Girl* (1940), the story of a white mistress's jealousy of her young slave. She spent the greater part of her life, and did almost all of her writing, in New York City. Cather earned her fame, however, primarily with her novels of Nebraska and the American Southwest. Bare, open, dominated by the sky, devoid of conventional attributes of beauty (by nineteenth-century Victorian standards, at least), these landscapes seem to have inspired certain of Cather's own theories of fiction. In an important essay of 1922, "The Novel Demeuble" ("The Unfurnished Novel"), she imagined a novel swept clean of cluttering realist detail and plotting conventions: "How wonderful it would be if we could throw all the furniture out of the window; and along with it, all the meaningless reiterations concerning physical sensations, all the tiresome old patterns, and leave the room as bare as the stage of a Greek theatre, or as that house into which the glory of Pentecost descended; leave the scene bare for the play of emotions, great and little." Like Virginia Woolf, Cather thought "reality" in the novel could and should be something other than journalistic catalogs of brute matter.[34]

Unlike Woolf and Dorothy Richardson, however, Cather did not seek this other sort of reality in the inward reality of consciousness, at least not as they practiced it. The younger writers of her time, Cather thought, were beginning "to present their scene by suggestion rather than by enumeration"; they were learning that the best "processes of art are all processes of simplification" (ND, 40). Cather challenged realism by paring down its detailed, comprehensive plots: her novels often feature intense episodes separated by intervals of time in which realistically important events take place offstage. She also pared down realism's detailed descriptions of social life, in favor of linking her characters symbolically with the landscapes surrounding them. Where realist or naturalist characters would typically be determined by their surroundings, Cather's characters often exist instead in a kind of romantic symbiosis with their environment. Cather's fiction in general blends realistic with romantic impulses more successfully than do Glasgow's novels.[35]

Cather's first novel, *Alexander's Bridge* (1912), tells the story of an engineer and bridge builder, modeled in part after John Augustus Roebling, the designer of the Brooklyn Bridge. A larger-than-life American pioneer, Bartley Alexander is destroyed in the collapse of his bridge.[36] Her second novel and first major critical success, *O Pioneers!* (1913, dedicated to Cather's friend Sarah Orne Jewett), returns to the pioneers Cather knew more intimately: the immigrant farmers who settled the prairie. Centered upon the story of Alexandra Bergson (whose name suggestively recalls Cather's heroic bridge builder), *O Pioneers!* follows the Bergson family from its lean early years, through prosperity, to crisis and loss.

O Pioneers! is not, however, a chronologically detailed realistic family saga; in this novel, Cather first tested the possibilities of a more selective, episodic structure. We see Alexandra as a young woman resolving to hold onto the farm in the teeth of crop failures at the end of part 1, "The Wild Land"; more than a decade intervenes before Cather picks up the narrative again in part 2, "Neighboring Fields."[37] In the meantime, Alexandra has introduced new methods of farming, acquired more land, and made the family rich (*OP*, 83), but Cather omits the realistic details of these operations. Cather also—we might note—skips her heroine over exactly those years in which a heroine is conventionally supposed to be most interesting: years of youth, beauty, courtship and marriage. While Alexandra will eventually marry, both her marriage and the structure of *O Pioneers!* depart from the traditional nineteenth-century marriage plot.

At the novel's end, Alexandra marries a childhood friend, Carl Linstrum, slightly younger than she and by no means outwardly prepossessing. Their unusual, understated love story is set against the romance of another pair, Alexandra's younger brother Emil and their neighbor, Marie Shabata. Emil and Marie also know each other from childhood; beautiful, lively, always drawn to men, Marie marries young and badly. Her husband jealously suspects Marie's vivacity and eventually kills both Marie and Emil—but only after the fated young lovers have come together for the first, and last, time. The story of Marie and Emil is both highly romantic and highly conventional, in literary terms; Cather drew on romantic poetry and other literary sources for the language and symbolism of their passion.[38]

Alexandra's marriage is quite different. Suspecting her interest in Carl, her brothers protest to her that "He wants to be taken care of, he does!" Alexandra retorts, "Well, suppose I want to take care of him?" (167). They think her beyond marrying age; even Emil cannot envision "people who were forty years old imagining they wanted to get married" (179). She chooses someone she knows, rather than a fated romantic image of masculinity, and will preserve her authority over her own land.

The land, in fact, seems to possess Alexandra more erotically than Carl ever will. In her dreams, "she used to have an illusion of being lifted up bodily and carried lightly by someone very strong. It was a man, certainly, who carried her, but he was like no man she knew; he was much larger and stronger and swifter, and he carried her as easily as if she were a sheaf of wheat. She never saw him, but, with eyes closed, she could feel that he was yellow like the sunlight, and there was the smell of ripe cornfields about him" (206). This corn-god out of dream and mythology is the only superior masculine strength Alexandra ever acknowledges or desires.

In her next novel, *The Song of the Lark* (1915), a full-fledged *Kunstlerroman*, Cather attempted to blaze a trail between the prairies and the city. Born in a small Nebraska town, Thea Kronberg eventually becomes a successful opera singer of worldwide reputation. The novel is not usually counted among Cather's great successes; longer and wordier than *O*

Pioneers!, it relies too heavily upon the omniscient narrator's descriptions of Thea at work on her art.

Still, *The Song of the Lark* is a major effort in many ways. Cather vividly reconstructs the checkered cultural landscape of the late-nineteenth-century western United States, its pockets of cultivation and broad plains of dullness, its mixture of old materials with new. The novel creates a mythic story about the possibility of great American artists coming from tiny, dust-swept towns—and about the possibility of the great artist being a woman. Thea becomes a New World artist, paradoxically, in the archetypally Old World form of grand opera. One of her significant rites of passage comes when she attends a concert in Chicago, where she is studying piano and voice. The program begins with Dvořák's symphony *From the New World*. Written—as Cather of course knew—out of the Hungarian Dvořák's experience of a stay in the United States, the music speaks directly to Thea: "This was music she could understand, music from the New World indeed! Strange how, as the first movement went on, it brought back to her that high tableland above Laramie; the grass-grown wagon-trails, the far-away peaks of the snowy range. . . ."[39] The second half of the concert, however, features music from Wagner's mythic, heavily Germanic *Das Rheingold* (252); the new world and the old meet in the concert, and together forge Thea's resolve to "have it, what the trumpets were singing!" She leaves with hands pressed "upon her heaving bosom, that was a little girl's no longer" (255). A musical epiphany, rather than a sexual initiation, marks Thea's emergence from childhood.

In her next novel, *My Ántonia* (1918),[40] Cather found a more suggestive and economical narrative form for her story than the obtrusive omniscient narrator of *The Song of the Lark*. Ántonia is another strong woman from an immigrant family on the Nebraska prairies. We see her, however, through the eyes of a first-person narrator: Jim Burden, who has known Ántonia and loved her in his own way since he was a boy. *My Ántonia* is thus not only Ántonia's story, but also Jim Burden's, and beyond that the story of an entire frontier community over some 30 years. Ántonia helps support her family, falls in love unwisely, becomes pregnant, but survives to marry happily and rear a large family. As a heroine, she combines traits Cather divided between two women, Alexandra and Marie, in the earlier *O Pioneers!*; Ántonia enjoys some of Alexandra's productive strength and sexual blossoming in later life, but shares Marie's vulnerable attraction to a swaggering, no-good man.

If Ántonia is one of Cather's best fictional heroines, Jim Burden is an equally interesting creation as a narrator. His perspective is often between worlds in some way: coming to the prairie from Virginia at the outset (3); on the boundary between prairie and town when his grandparents move (143), or when comparing country girls to town girls (200–201); older than his years, and preferring Ántonia and Lena to girls of his own age (225, 229). He watches, he is often helpful, but he is never completely engaged. He eventually admits—to Ántonia's young sons—that he has always loved their mother; but aside from one kiss, his love finds no sexual expression. His own marriage, we learn at the beginning of the novel, has been unhappy. How do we judge this character, and his point of view?

Jim Burden's story can be read as the tale of a subtle but fundamental failure. Blanche Gelfant, in a well-known essay, suggests that Jim fears and avoids adult sexuality, indeed adulthood itself, by clinging to safely romanticized images of childhood. Gelfant extends this critique to the novel as a whole and to Cather herself, arguing that "My Ántonia engraves a view of the past which is at best partial; at worst, blind."[41] Cather's own brand of romanticism (and perhaps her own consciousness as a lesbian) would question, however, Gelfant's rigid association of adulthood, and adult (hetero)sexuality, with truth and happiness. Moreover, telling the story through a first-person narrator implies that there is no possible view of the past which is not partial (in every sense of the word); we are not to look for the total truth promised by a classically omniscient realist narrator. From another standpoint, the fact that My Ántonia does not center upon a marriage plot—although it does feature married couples in various stages of life, many of them convincingly happy—could be read as both formally innovative and liberating.

Like My Ántonia, A Lost Lady (1923) centers on the relationship between a young man and a woman whom he loves from a distance. Although A Lost Lady is narrated in the third person, its point of view resides for the most part with Niel Herbert; through him we see Marian Forrester, wife of a railroad man, Captain Daniel Forrester. To Niel at age 12, Mrs. Forrester epitomizes grace, hospitality, dignity, fidelity. Later—after Captain Forrester has collapsed, financially and physically—Niel must come to terms with knowledge of Mrs. Forrester's adultery, of her weakness for drinking and need for male admiration. To the end, however, Marian Forrester inspires loyalty even in men whose romantic trust she has disappointed; and she remembers Niel, who "came to be very glad that he had known her, and that she had had a hand in breaking him in to life."[42]

In the great work of her later career, *Death Comes for the Archbishop* (1927),[43] Cather turned to the impersonal, omniscient narrative form of the historical chronicle to tell the story of Jean Latour, first bishop of Santa Fe (based on the historical Father Lamy). She had earlier written about the American Southwest in episodes interpolated into novels set elsewhere: in *The Song of the Lark*, Thea Kronberg renews her vocation on a visit to a canyon pueblo; in *The Professor's House*, Tom Outland's journal tells of his similar explorations in a long-deserted pueblo. Of her own visit to the Southwestern pueblos, Cather wrote that there "you begin to feel that custom, ritual, integrity of tradition have a reality that goes deeper than the bustling business of the world."[44]

In Cather's Southwest, meanings—and even, for Bishop Latour, miracles—inhere in "the most ordinary acts and the most disparate objects: a wooden parrot, a desert rock, a tamarisk tree" (Rosowski, 172). Her narrative does not deny the historical contradictions of the archbishop's time, or of his missionary errand; we hear of corrupt priests, exploitation, conflict among all the parties—Indian, Mexican, Catholic, American— laying claim to this land. But Cather distills conflict into emblematic stories, like the tale of corrupt Friar Baltazar on the rock of Acoma (103– 14), stories that associate themselves with a symbolic place and abstain from moralistic commentary. The Southwestern landscape collaborated with Cather's own aesthetic criteria for the modern novel: it helped her to tell by suggestion and simplification. Despite her complaints about "bustling business," Cather never produced an explicit, sustained critique of modern industrial capitalist life. She directed her romanticism instead toward the representation of past and passing ways of life, of lost habits of meaning, and became the foremost twentieth-century elegist of the American frontier.[45]

Mary Austin (1868–1934) is rather more difficult than Wharton, Glasgow, Hurston, or Cather to classify as a novelist. While she wrote drama and poetry of some interest, her major work may be *The Land of Little Rain* (1903), a volume of nature sketches; while she published several novels, her best (and best-known) "novel" may in fact be her autobiography, *Earth Horizon* (1932), told for the most part in the novelistic third person.[46]

Austin is easily classified, however, as a regionalist. Born in Illinois, in 1888 she became part of the country's great migration westward to

California. Her territory as a writer was the American Southwest, especially Southern California and New Mexico. She lived for a time amid the artists' colony established around the turn of the century in Carmel, California, where she knew the writers Robinson Jeffers and Jack London; in the last decade of her life she built a house in Santa Fe, center of another artists' colony that included, at one time or another, Mabel Dodge Luhan, English novelist D. H. Lawrence, architect Frank Lloyd Wright, photographer Alfred Stieglitz, and painter Georgia O'Keeffe.

Unlike Willa Cather, who was at her most eloquent in describing pueblos long deserted by their original inhabitants, Austin distinguished herself by her sympathy for actual, living American Indians. Rather than looking for a wholly vacant land, onto which the author might project her own meanings, *The Land of Little Rain* describes the beliefs and life of the land's aboriginal inhabitants with sympathy and interest. Indian mythology and symbolism provided Austin with an analogue for her own early mysticism. Austin's biographer and critic, Esther Lanigan Stineman, also speculates that her interest in Indian mysticism and Indian communities "on the fringe of Anglo society" provided Austin in some of her nature sketches with a "mystically gender-neutral" authorial voice, a position from which to criticize male-dominated, industrial capitalist Anglo society indirectly. [47]

In perhaps Austin's best novel of California, *The Ford* (1917), a strong heroine, Anne Brent, manages to save her ranch from the predatory male land barons of nineteenth-century California. Anne Brent's success recalls Alexandra Bergson's skill in holding onto and managing the family farms in Cather's *O Pioneers!*; in her decision not to center her life on marriage and romance, she anticipates Dorinda Oakley, in Glasgow's *Barren Ground*. As *The Ford* suggests, Austin fully intended her writings to revise the stereotypically male myth of the American frontier. Writing in her autobiography of her own pioneering foremothers, among them a Polly McAdams, Austin assigns them generic historical importance: "It is to the things that the Polly McAdamses discovered in their westward trek that Mary's [Mary Austin herself] generation owed the success of their revolt against the traditional estimate of women" (*EH*, 15). Without the pioneering mothers, in other words, no modern New Women. Their stories illustrate for Austin "the predominance of happenings of the hearth, as against what happens on the battlefield and in the marketplace," in the story of the American nation. "What they found out was that the hope of American democracy and the justification of the Declaration of Independence depended precisely on the capacity of the Polly

McAdamses to coordinate society, to establish a civilization, to cause a culture to eventuate out of their own wit and the work of their hands, out of what they could carry with them into the wilderness" (*EH*, 15).

If Mary Austin in fact rebelled against her own stern pioneer mother; if Edith Wharton, Ellen Glasgow, Zora Neale Hurston, Willa Cather, and Austin herself rebelled against some of their pioneering literary foremothers, at least they acknowledged in their different ways the women who came before them. And Austin could be speaking for all five novelists in her regret for what she called her "incomplete adventure," her failure to grasp the elusive essence of the California desert before it slipped away: "I wake in the night convinced that there are still uncorrupted corners from which the Spirit of the Arroyos calls me, wistful with long refusals, and I resolve that next year, or the *next* at farthest . . . and I am never able to manage it" (*EH*, 188–89). As in Jim Burden's salute to "the precious, the incommunicable past" at the close of Cather's *My Ántonia*, as in Newland Archer's vigil outside Ellen Olenska's windows in Wharton's *The Age of Innocence*, as in Hurston's repeated metaphors of journey, the sense of growing distance from another past, another folk, charges these novelists' twentieth-century fictions with irony—and desire.

The reputations of Wharton, Cather, Glasgow, and Austin have gone up and down with the years, as readers have alternately hungered for regionalist fiction about the American past and dismissed such fiction for not being "universal" enough. Hurston died in obscurity, her novels sunk under a double weight of prejudice against black and women writers, until other black women writers began reviving her reputation. The complaint about lack of universality brought against "regional" literature is all too commonly brought against women's literature, and often conceals the assumption that men's stories are universal while women's are only particular to women. If Ernest Hemingway's stories of boyhood in the upper Midwest can be "universal"—meaning, I suppose, worth reading by people who are not boys, nor from the Midwest—so, too, might Willa Cather's stories of boys and girls on the Nebraska prairies. Wharton's New York, Hurston's Eatonville, and Cather's Nebraska are no longer dismissed by many readers as merely regionalist places. If Glasgow's Virginia and Austin's New Mexico do not now have the same ring of familiarity or range of suggestiveness, still they can teach us to beware of easy, hard-and-fast distinctions between major and minor literature, between the centers of life and the margins, between the exceptional and the everyday.

CHAPTER
7

Expatriates and Experimentalists: Gertrude Stein and Djuna Barnes

For American writers of the early twentieth century, born into a society that traditionally deprecated art in favor of money making, Paris beckoned as a capital of the arts and of an artistic style of life in general— more leisured, more nuanced, more open. Museums and cafés were at hand. Post–World War I American dollars went far. For visiting writers at least, worry over censorship and suppression of political dissent—very much in evidence in the United States and England during the war years and after—could recede into the background.

American women writers particularly could see in Paris alternatives to nineteenth-century American culture's exaggeratedly provincial division of men's and women's spheres, as Edith Wharton explored that division in *The Custom of the Country*. If Paris became the home from which Edith Wharton would write many of her elegant traditional novels of New York society, Paris also played host to other expatriated American women writers of the early twentieth century—many of them more conspicuously experimental, in both art and life, than Wharton.[1]

Gertrude Stein (1874–1946) enjoyed a long and famous career at the center of Parisian artistic life, even though she often had trouble finding publishers for her experimental writing. Djuna Barnes (1892–1982), the object of a small but influential circle of admirers in the 1920s and 1930s, wrote memorably of expatriate life in Paris in her *Ladies Almanack* and *Nightwood*. The ups and downs of Stein's and Barnes's critical reputations, and the lack of critical consensus about their importance to modernism, suggest the difficulty—by no means yet resolved—of coming to terms with modernist women's experimental writing. Criticism has usually seen these women as interesting or even lurid characters in the expatriate social scene, but not as major artists in their own right—an estimate that now may be ripe for change.[2]

Arriving in Paris to live in 1903, Gertrude Stein set up housekeeping in an artistic quarter with her brother Leo. Their new address—27, rue de Fleurus—would become legendary in the history of modern art and literature. Born in Allegheny, Pennsylvania, the daughter of a German-Jewish businessman, Stein had attended Radcliffe College (where she studied with the philosopher William James) and Johns Hopkins University (where she dropped out of the medical school). A legacy from their father allowed Gertrude and Leo to begin collecting paintings by then little known modernist artists, among them Matisse, Braque, Gris, and Picasso.

Stein's first published writing, *Three Lives*, appeared in 1909.[3] Written at the same time that Stein was posing for her famous portrait by Picasso, the book presents a triple literary portrait of three women: "The Good Anna," "The Gentle Lena," and "Melanctha" (the middle portrait and by far the longest). Of "Melanctha" particularly Stein would later write that it took "the first definite step away from the nineteenth century and into the twentieth century in literature."[4] Stein's claim is typical of her robust egotism, but she may have had a point. *Three Lives* predated some of the better-known founding works of modernism in the novel—Dorothy Richardson's *Pilgrimage* (1915), Joyce's *A Portrait of the Artist as a Young Man* (1916)—by several years, and its originality belongs to her alone.

The stories in *Three Lives* do owe something to literary naturalism in their choice of subjects. All three protagonists are working-class women of "Bridgeport" (Stein's fictionalized Baltimore), rather than conventionally middle-class heroines; Anna and Lena are German immigrants and servants, and Melanctha is a black woman, child of "a common, decent enough, colored workman" (91), one of "the better sort of negroes, there, in Bridgeport" (86). Each story follows its heroine to her lonely, overworked death, reported without consolation or moralizing.

Unlike the naturalists, however, Stein scarcely presents a sociologically detailed, panoramic picture of working-class immigrant or black American life. In all three of the *Lives*, but especially in "Melanctha," Stein's methods of writing draw readers' attention to the flow and structure of the language itself. Rather than simply looking "through" the words on the page, as if it were a transparent window giving onto the lives of three real women, Stein's readers more typically pause—in pleasure, bafflement, irritation, or thoughtfulness—over the words with which Stein strings together the *Lives*.

This concentration on the medium—on the shape, sound, and disposition of words as entities in themselves, rather than as passive representations of some "real life" thought to be "outside" or "before" language—links *Three Lives* to modernism's general concern with the autonomy of art. Richard Kostelanetz argues that Stein's words are "autonomous objects, rather than symbols of something else."[5] For Stein and other related modernists—including modernists practicing in other arts, like her painter friend Picasso—art was not to be a secondary picture of reality, composed according to agreed-on rules of narration (in literature) or perspective (in painting); rather, art was its own reality. In the technical language of linguistics and literary criticism, such modernist art sets the *signifier* (the word itself, the artistic medium) free of a fixed relation to the *signified* (the thing represented by the signifier), and foregrounds the signifier as a thing in and for itself.

This does not necessarily mean, however, that Stein's writing (in *Three Lives* or afterward) has no relationship whatever to any reality outside itself—that it is, in other words, completely abstract, signifiers without any signifieds around at all. Marjorie Perloff contends that Stein is not out "to pretend that meaning doesn't exist but to take words out of their usual contexts and create new relationships among them."[6] Words do come attached, by convention, to things in the world generally. But for Stein this attachment between words and things, between signifier and signified, is not fixed in stone or dictated by the nature of things. Rather, it is precisely a human convention, a humanly made pattern—one that experimental writing can play with, question, and change.[7]

In *Three Lives*, Stein's experiments with the relationship between words and things take forms so simple as to be, paradoxically, both subtle and crude at the same time. Her favorite device is sheer repetition. Individual words—adjectives like *german*, adverbs like *certainly* and *always*—return time and again. Whole phrases or sentences may be repeated with slight variation (a change in the placement of an adverb, for instance) or none at all. Thus we hear several times, in "The Good Anna," that "The widow Mrs. Lehntman was the romance in Anna's life," beginning on page 30, again on page 34, and so on. *Three Lives* seems constructed of a deliberately narrow vocabulary of simple key words and basic ideas.

Stein also shows a marked preference for certain kinds of verbs. The pages of *Three Lives* abound with forms of the most basic verb in the language, *to be*. Sometimes the verb *to be* carries a sentence on its own, often accompanied by adverbs of stasis or certainty: "And now surely it was all over in Jeff Campbell" (192). As Marianne DeKoven points out, Stein often combines *to be* with "present participles, gerunds, progressive verb forms—'-ing' words for convenience's sake—" of other verbs.[8] Rather than write, for instance, that two people talked, Stein prefers to say that they *were talking*. Her characters, especially in "Melanctha," tend to speak this way: Jeff tells Melanctha, that "people certainly must be thinking each one as good as the other, to be really loving right Melanctha" (192). Stein later labeled this technique the "continuous present"; it conveys a sense of time as ongoing process rather than a series of discrete events.[9]

The formal aspects of Stein's experimental style in *Three Lives*—repetition and a distinct preference for the continuous present—are fairly simple to codify. The really interesting questions, then, become: What does Stein's experimental style come to mean for her readers? What is it like for readers to experience Stein's repetitions and preferred verb forms cumulatively, to live for a time in the peculiar reality of *Three Lives?* How does Stein's experimental style challenge a reader's sense of how words are put together and how they mean in relation to the world at large?

Different critical readers have posed different answers to these questions; there can be no one final answer. To understand the importance of these questions, it helps to look at one particularly insistent and even disturbing group of repetitions: those having to do with words of race and ethnicity.

Time and again in *Three Lives* Stein's narrator explains her characters by referring to their ethnic identity or their race. Anna and Lena are "german." Lena's story begins with the statement that "Lena was patient, gentle, sweet and german" (239) and goes on to tell us that she had a "german voice" (239) and the "unsuffering german patience" of "the working, gentle, german woman" (241). In "Melanctha," the repeated adjectives are *black* and *yellow*; Melanctha's friend is "black Rosie" (85), a "real black negress" (86) like Melanctha's "black coarse father" (90), while Melanctha and her mother are both "pale yellow" (90). Adjectives like *german* and *black* take on nearly the status of epithets in *Three Lives*—that is, they become virtually a part of someone's name or identity.

What effects, then, may this insistent repetition have on the way readers understand words like *black* and *german*? Is Stein, herself the child of German-Jewish parents, prejudiced or racist in defining her characters by ethnic tags? As Stein was growing up, the United States was in the midst of a great wave of immigration, a historical change largely regarded with anxiety by a native-born population eager to defend the supposed superiority of white Anglo-Saxons. How may popular pseudoscientific beliefs about race and ethnicity, or general concern with racial identities, have shaped *Three Lives*?

Some readers find Stein guilty of racism in *Three Lives*. Her repetition of ethnic and racial epithets indicates, they think, Stein's own disposition to see and analyze the world in terms of essentialist categories. In other words, these readers charge, Stein characterizes Lena as "essentially" German, German by virtue of some unchanging natural essence of Germanness in her own makeup; Stein believes that all Germans are German and that a "real black negress" is bound to behave in certain predictable ways dictated by her blackness. We know that Stein, a former student of psychology, was interested in classifying the human mind and human behavior. These readers charge that *Three Lives* classifies in racist terms, reinforcing through its repetitions the notion that a person's identity is determined by adjectives like *german* and *black*.[10]

Not all of Stein's readers, however, agree with this charge. The great black American novelist Richard Wright recalled in 1945 that he found the style of *Three Lives* both "insistent and original," so much so that, "As I read it my ears were opened for the first time to the magic of the spoken word." Although not written in the by then clichéd literary conventions of "Negro" dialect, *Three Lives* nevertheless conveyed to Wright "the magic of the spoken word," suggesting the "deep, pure Negro dialect" of his grandmother. Disturbed by a left-wing review of *Three Lives* that condemned Stein's "tortured verbalisms" as politically retrograde, Wright "gathered a group of semi-literate Negro stockyard workers . . . into a Black Belt basement [in Chicago] and read Melanctha aloud to them. They understood every word. Enthralled, they slapped their thighs, howled, laughed, stomped, and interrupted me constantly to comment upon the characters."[11]

For still other critics, Stein's experimental style in *Three Lives* undermines readers' faith in the explanatory power of words like *german* and *black*. These writers argue that Stein views her narrator's, and her characters', language with skepticism;[12] that the effect of repeating *german* so many times as a descriptive adjective is to empty the word of meaning, to question whether the word actually corresponds to some real thing (the essence of German-ness) in the world. Anna and Lena are both "german"—but what common quality does the word point to, if any? Stein repeats *black* and *german*, these readers argue, until it comes home that these words, along with the unreflective habit of thought that sustain their repeated use, lead to no certain truth. Repetition ultimately makes these epithets tautological: german is german is german (as Stein would later say, famously: a rose is a rose is a rose). Moreover, Stein always lowercases *german* as a descriptive adjective, thus detaching the word from its origins in the proper noun for a nation or a people (Germany, the Germans). *German* comes to refer to itself, tautologically, rather than to a real thing in the world. The repetitive language of *Three Lives*, in this reading, exposes (without explicitly denouncing) the limitations of essentialist thought itself—limitations shared by Stein's characters, who are "painfully aware of the inadequacy of their language."[13]

Racist language? Magical, oral language? Deliberately inadequate, emptied language? The argument over racism and repetition in *Three Lives* illustrates how difficult, even impossible, it is to fix the meanings and effects of Stein's experimental writing. Reading Stein aloud under particular circumstances may yield a different experience from pressing through it silently on the page. Stein in *Three Lives* is scarcely the only modernist whose work prompts questions about her on his relationship to racist thought; T. S. Eliot's and Ezra Pound's anti-Semitism immediately comes to mind. Simply finding that *Three Lives is* racist, however, may be as reductive as finding that Lena is German. Rather, as her favorite verb suggests, Stein's experiments open the very question of what it means, in language, "to be."

After *Three Lives*, Stein's monumental family saga *The Making of Americans* (written from 1903 to 1911, but not published until 1925) continued her interest in ethnicity and the classification of human beings into types. Formally, *The Making of Americans* also continued the repetitive mold established in *Three Lives*, but departed even further from traditional forward narrative time. In *The Making of Americans*, Stein later wrote, "I made almost a thousand pages of a continuous present" ("Composition as Explanation," *SW*, 457)—a daunting prospect to most readers.

Around 1911, her critic DeKoven finds, Stein began to change course, reworking the heavy repetitions of "Melanctha" and *The Making of Americans* into a new style of "lively words."[14] DeKoven links this new style to Stein's decision to live with Alice B. Toklas, her lover and lifelong companion, who entered the household at the rue de Fleurus in 1910, and speculates that their relationship brought Stein to a happier acceptance of her own identity as a woman (DeKoven, 36).

Whatever its impetus, the writing of the 1910s and onward is often exhilarating. It abounds in pleasure: pleasure in domesticity, in objects, in friends, in sexuality, in language. "Susie Asado," a short piece written in 1911, typifies the new style. It is in some sense "about" having tea with the woman of the title: "Sweet sweet sweet sweet sweet tea. Susie Asado." Words for the familiar domestic objects of the tea table—*tea, tray, jelly, pot*—appear in unexpected combinations with other words. Read aloud, some of the combinations make punning sense; "tray sure" forms *treasure*, "sweet tea" an endearment, *sweetie*. Other combinations, like "silver seller" (*Salver? cellar?* the thought of good tea sells silver?) tremble suggestively on the verge of sense (*SW*, 485).

The domestic object-words that crop up in "Susie Asado" figure again in *Tender Buttons* (first published in 1914). Ostensibly divided into the categories of "Objects," "Food," and "Rooms," *Tender Buttons* evokes, only to play with, the reader's expectations of orderly listing, description, and exposition. Stein herself said that in *Tender Buttons* she had "made portraits of rooms and food."[15] Shifting away from the oral style of *Three Lives*, with its indirect suggestions of dialect speech, she tried "to completely face the difficulty of how to include what is seen with hearing and listening," and compared her efforts to those of modernist painters (like her friend Picasso) who reinvigorated the still life (*LIA*, 189).[16]

Here, then, is one of Stein's "portraits" of an "Object"—"A New Cup and Saucer": "Enthusiastically hurting a clouded yellow bud and saucer, enthusiastically so is the bite in the ribbon" (*SW*, 415). As with "Susie Asado," some word combinations come into focus relatively easily: a "yellow bud and saucer" is phonetically close enough to "cup and saucer," and metaphorically suggests a small, delicate cup (a demitasse?). Others are more mysterious, particularly the verb forms and adverbs related to the verbs. Who or what is "enthusiastically hurting"? Such verbs and verb forms without a determinate grammatical subject confer a sense of action and being upon inanimate objects—in something of the way, perhaps, that the multiple perspectives of cubist still-life paintings imply movement.

The nature of an object's being is explicitly the question in one of the more accessible "Objects"—"A Table": "A table means does it not my dear it means a whole steadiness. Is it likely that a change." This portrait merges stability and change in the idea of a table: "there has been a stand, a stand where it did shake" (SW, 419). The table does not just stand there, standing there. It hums, vibrates, lives. We might recall the way Virginia Woolf would later use the image of a kitchen table to exemplify Mr. Ramsay's philosophical work on "subject and object and the nature of reality" in To The Lighthouse (written several years after Tender Buttons). In Woolf's novel, as in Tender Buttons, "subject and object and the nature of reality" are intimately and changefully related.

The speaker in "A Table" addresses "my dear"; this hint of a dialogue suggests that Tender Buttons does not merely catalog things in isolation, but possesses a kind of minimal scenario, even something of a story. Pamela Hadas speculates that Tender Buttons tells the story of how Stein and Toklas set up their joint lives.[17] "A table means necessary places and a revision a revision of a little thing"; so Stein and Toklas had revised their lives and taken a "stand" in making their own "necessary places." Harriet Chessman notes also that "Traditional metaphors for female sexuality abound" in Tender Buttons (roses, boxes, purses, food)—and that the title itself is anatomically suggestive (Chessman, 96–97, 91). Whether or not it is readable as a coded narrative, Tender Buttons surely does abound with a sensuality that spends itself on objects, domesticity, and words themselves.

Other of Stein's works from this period give a more legible sense of her relationship with Toklas. The erotic dialogue of "Lifting Belly" (written 1915–17) is evident enough, and critics have deciphered some of Stein's semiprivate erotic code (cow seems to signify an orgasm; Caesar was a nickname for Stein herself, who was looking rather imperial at the time in her short haircut).[18] Chessman points out, however, that, "Although Stein mentions parts of the body like the lips and the 'belly,' as she renders an intimate situation of asking and responding, she does not allow us to move far enough away from the speakers to see who is speaking, who is kissing, who is being kissed" (101). Reading "Lifting Belly," in other words, becomes an experience of intimacy, rather than a distanced, voyeuristic representation of intimacy.

Stein's greatest fame, along with a real measure of financial success, came in the 1930s. The Autobiography of Alice B. Toklas (1933)—Stein's own memoirs of Paris, written from Toklas's point of view—became a best-seller. Imperturbable, associative, wryly matter-of-fact, the Auto-

biography seems to blend Toklas's accents with Stein's; it allowed many readers access to a notoriously opaque writer.

Stein had met the American composer Virgil Thomson in Paris in the 1920s. Shortly after their meeting, Thomson began setting several of Stein's pieces—among them, "Susie Asado"—to music. In 1927 Stein began writing the libretto of an opera, *Four Saints in Three Acts*, for Thomson. The opera finally made it to the stage a few years later in Hartford, Connecticut. Its opening on 7 February 1934 coincided with a major Picasso exhibition in Hartford, and attracted a fine audience. *Four Saints* went on to play for another month in New York City; its reception, according to James R. Mellow, "was to add immeasurably to what was to become [Stein's] triumphant march across America."[19]

The "triumphant march" was a lecture tour that took Stein to cities all over the United States. She was a hit at Harvard, in Houston, in Chicago; she and Toklas took tea in the White House with Eleanor Roosevelt. Asked by a reporter, Joseph W. Alsop, Jr., "Why don't you write as you talk?" she replied "Oh, but I do. After all, it's all learning how to read it" (Fellows, 380). For many in her audiences, listening to Stein read her own writing was a revelation: the simple vocabulary, the repetitive sentences, were clearly the work of a woman thinking aloud, and thinking about thinking, in unfamiliar ways.

Stein's last major work was another opera libretto for Virgil Thomson: *The Mother of Us All* (written 1945–46), about the life and work of American feminist Susan B. Anthony.[20] It was an interesting choice of subject for Stein, who never sympathized with political feminism (or with any other sort of organized politics). In the text, Anthony muses on the mixed results of her work on behalf of women's suffrage; speaking from behind a statue of herself, she measures the difference between desire and achievement.

As Harriet Chessman points out, Anthony "resembles her creator," if "only partially" (199). As her fame grew, many visitors to Paris had compared Stein herself to a statue—monumental in girth, solid, with a profile like a Roman emperor. She had lived (sometimes gracefully, sometimes testily) with her own legend for years. A few months after imagining the dead Susan B. Anthony's relationship to her own monument, Stein herself died of cancer in Paris.

The daughter of wildly eccentric parents who educated her at home, Djuna Barnes began her writing career as a journalist in 1913, earning respectable money from several New York newspapers and magazines.

Her most notorious journalistic accomplishment in these years was the story on force-feeding she wrote for the *New York World* (6 September 1914). Imprisoned suffrage activists in England, on hunger strike, were being force-fed—a combination of medical treatment and punishment; the procedure was by all reports excruciating. Barnes underwent force-feeding herself, with a photographer standing by, and wrote about the experience for the *World's* curious readers. Well known for her bravado in what we would now call "participatory journalism," Barnes had other talents as well. She illustrated many of her newspaper articles with her own drawings: extravagant, faintly sinister, sinuous, and stylized, her pictures of half-human, half-animal figures owed a good deal to the example of Aubrey Beardsley.

Her first independent publication, the pamphlet-sized *Book of Repulsive Women* (1915), featured both poems and drawings.[21] The lesbian erotic imagery of several poems in the *Book*, like that of Gertrude Stein's erotic poetry, somehow escaped American censors; the *Book* became an underground hit in Greenwich Village, and established Barnes's local reputation as an artist.

In 1920 Barnes joined the great American postwar exodus to Paris, where she soon met American artist Thelma Wood, the great—and destructive—love of her life. They visited Berlin, knowing that their American dollars would go far in a city ravaged by postwar inflation, and sampled the fabled decadence of Berlin nightlife. After returning to Paris, Barnes published her first major collection, simply entitled *A Book* (1923), which combined drawings and poems with plays and short stories.[22]

Barnes finally ran afoul of the American censors with her novel *Ryder* (1928), a Rabelaisian family chronicle, once again illustrated with Barnes's own drawings, and centered on the adventures of its aggressively masculine patriarch, Wendell Ryder (modeled on Wald Barnes, Djuna's father).[23] The novel became an unexpected popular success, but not before Barnes reluctantly replaced certain scatological passages and drawings with asterisks—allowing readers to imagine for themselves what might have been.[24]

Her next work, the *Ladies Almanack* (1928), never came to the attention of American censors; it was privately printed and sold around the artistic quarters of Paris. A bawdy, affectionate portrait of Natalie Barney's lesbian salon, the *Ladies Almanack*—like *The Book of Repulsive Women*—became a great local favorite, as readers matched characters in the *Almanack* with their originals (among them novelist Radclyffe Hall, journalist Janet Flanner, and poet Mina Loy).

The *Ladies Almanack* is still readable (an American edition finally appeared in 1972), not only for its gossip value, but for its mock-heroic, risqué celebration of lesbian sexuality.[25] "Evangeline Musset" (Natalie Barney), the central character, is "a witty and learned fifty" years old, but still "much in Demand . . . for her Genius at bringing up by Hand" (9). "Bringing up by hand" is a stock British phrase for physically disciplining children (it figures importantly in Dickens's *Great Expectations*); Barnes's characterization at once casts Evangeline as an erotic tutor to younger women, tinges her pedagogy with sadism, and hints at the specifics of her sexual techniques.

The *Almanack* draws on then-current ideas about lesbian identity: Evangeline is said to have "been developed in the Womb of her most gentle Mother to be a Boy" (7), a theory advanced by some psychologists to account for the "invert," the person whose desire turned toward members of the same sex. But Barnes spoofs the heavy aura of pathology surrounding such theories. Emerging "an Inch or so less" than the boy she was meant to be, Evangeline "paid no Heed to the Error, but . . . took her Whip in hand, calling her Pups about her, and so set out upon the Road of Destiny" (7). Like the Elizabethan hero/heroine of Virginia Woolf's *Orlando* (published in the same year as the *Almanack*), Evangeline goes on to cut a wide, mock-heroic swath through her crowd of admirers—and through conventional binary gender divisions.

Barnes's always stormy relationship with Thelma Wood came to an end in 1931. Out of it came the work for which she is best remembered, the short novel *Nightwood* (1936). Appearing with a laudatory preface by T. S. Eliot (who had persuaded his publishers to take the manuscript), *Nightwood* garnered respectable reviews, and, although never a best-seller, has remained in print.[26]

The novel tells the stories of a motley group of expatriates, wandering in the flotsam-and-jetsam underworld of postwar Europe. Felix Volk-bein, heir to a shady baronetcy, is burdened with "an obsession for what he termed 'Old Europe': aristocracy, nobility, royalty. . . . He felt that the great past might mend a little if he bowed low enough, if he succumbed and gave homage" (9). He marries Robin Vote (modeled after Thelma Wood), who leaves him for Nora Flood (Barnes's own alter ego in the novel). Robin then betrays that relationship with another woman, Jenny (as Thelma had). A renegade doctor, Matthew O'Connor, functions as a sort of confessor and chorus to the others; given to long rhetorical flights of soliloquy, the doctor was T. S. Eliot's favorite character.

Nightwood is epigrammatically brilliant, like Barnes's own conversation, and darkly obsessive in its vision of passion. "If one gave birth to a heart on a plate, it would say 'Love' and twitch like the lopped leg of a frog," O'Connor tells one character (26–27). His prophetic observation that "though those two [Nora and Robin] are buried at opposite ends of the earth, one dog will find them both" (106) is borne out by the novel's surrealistic ending. Alerted by her dog's barking, Nora tracks Robin to a church, where Robin has set lighted candles, along with "flowers and toys"—a private sacrifice to their love?—in front of a statue of the Madonna (169). Interrupted, Robin collapses to the floor and crawls after the dog, barking and weeping.

Barnes's original title for *Nightwood* was *Bow Down*. The novel's ending implies that Felix Volkbein's forlorn desire to find some genuine royalty before which to bow, some genuine past in postwar Europe, has reduced itself to Robin's bestial posture before the altar of this deserted church. Nor is lesbian sexuality the romp that it was in the *Ladies Almanack*; obsessional desire unto death, rather than the endlessly repeated comedy of sexual fulfillment, dominates the novel. *Nightwood*, as Donna Gerstenberger concludes, "stakes out the same territory" as T. S. Eliot's *The Waste Land*—the territory of "a civilization (particularly Western Europe) in decay, an aristocracy in disarray, a people estranged from a sense of identity."[27]

After *Nightwood*, Barnes lapsed into a prolonged silence. Her poetic drama *The Antiphon* appeared in 1958, to generally unfavorable reviews. She died at 92 in Greenwich Village, impoverished and obscure but not wholly forgotten. Her modernism belongs to the strain of Joyce (whom she deeply admired) and Faulkner (whose "prose style manifestly owes her more than a little" [Fields, 20]). Conspicuously rhetorical, mobile, punning, allusive, given to wide-ranging stylistic parodies of English literature, Barnes's experimental style could not be further from the monumental simplicity of Stein's words. Their differences stake out the wide range of twentieth-century women's experimental writing.

Short Stories and Detective Fiction: Women and the Question of Mass Culture

The short story and detective fiction are distinctively modern literary genres that have flourished, in the twentieth century, from roots sunk in the nineteenth century. To understand how and why these genres came to be so popular in the twentieth century—and why they have been slower than poetry and the serious "art" novel to receive much sustained critical attention—we must look not just at individual writers' achievements in isolation, but at the historical contexts in which detective fiction and short stories were written, published, and read.

The Short Story

The modern short story owes much of its shape and popularity to a modern cultural institution: the magazine or periodical, reading material organized and distributed on a regular basis and featuring a variety of contributions from different authors. As commonplace as magazines may now seem to us, they have a distinct history and depend for their existence upon a distinct set of social conditions.

Magazines and periodicals, in order to be profitable, must be relatively cheap to produce and distribute. Printing technology must therefore have reached a certain stage of development; even more important, there must be reliable national mail service for the circulation of magazines beyond urban centers. Eighteenth- and nineteenth-century improvements in the British mails did much to foster periodicals in that country. In the nineteenth-century United States, transcontinental railroads and telegraph lines began to make a common print culture possible across the forbidding distances of a continental nation.

Railroads and the post might bring relatively inexpensive periodicals to every household door, but only if someone in the household was literate and had time to read them—and only if contributors could be found to fill them. The nineteenth-century spread of mass education in England and the United States expanded both the potential public for magazine consumption and the potential authorship of magazine contributions. Conspicuous among the literate and (relatively) leisured publics open to magazine publishers were middle-class women. Periodicals addressed to women, often written and edited by women, flourished; they featured poems, articles, sketches, sometimes household hints and fashion information.

The phenomenal expansion of advertising and consumer-goods production in the latter part of the nineteenth century set the fundamental pattern that most mass-market periodicals still follow today: text interleaved with pages of elaborate advertising, advertising that partly offsets the cost of paying contributors, producing the magazine, and distributing it. Readers became accustomed to juxtapositions of "art" and commerce, and interruptions of "art" by commerce, that they likely would not tolerate in printed books—although publishers, as I write, are pressing on these boundaries with the insertion of advertising into bound books.

The huge, advertising-driven expansion of the magazine market, however, also helped generate some alternatives to the mass-market magazine. In business terms, the market "segmented," producing more specialized wares for specialized audiences. The phenomenon was particularly marked in the United States, where a "dearth of established forms and institutions" combined with a national economic explosion to speed the growth of mass culture.[1] Readers began to face a "three-part structure" of "mass circulation magazines such as the *Saturday Evening Post*" or *Ladies Home Journal*; "the little magazines, including *Partisan Review* . . . deliberately minuscule in their circulation, yet with an informed and passionate purpose; and the literate, middle-range magazines

. . . comparatively small in circulation but large in influence," like *Harpers* in the United States or the *London Mercury* in England.[2]

Writers of short fiction had inevitably to negotiate with the evolving structure of the periodical magazines in conceiving and publishing their work. From at least Herman Melville forward, many writers of short stories who thought of themselves as producers of serious literature have struggled with the way mass-market periodicals turned their fiction into a commodity alongside other commodities. Some made a qualified peace with mass-circulation magazines or sought the middle ground with reputable reviews. Others, out of conviction or necessity, placed their work in small-circulation avant-garde or academic journals. Some managed to publish short-story collections as books without entering the magazine market first, but by and large "it was very hard in the first half of the century, as it is now, to publish, in book form, a collection of short fiction for which an audience had not been already created by a reputation made in the periodicals" (Stevick, 10).

There is, as I have already hinted in connection with women's magazines, a gendered subtext to this literary history of short stories and the magazine. Andreas Huyssen argues that late-nineteenth- and twentieth-century modern writers have often personified their cultural adversary as feminine,[3] and perhaps nowhere more so than in thinking about the magazine. "Mass culture as woman," as the stereotypical magazine reader consuming stories along with fashion hints, has been the enemy to many a struggling modern writer even while he or she hoped to have a story accepted at the rates paid by the mass magazines. A common cultural thread links Nathaniel Hawthorne's notorious complaint about the "damned mob of scribbling women" to the famous comment of Harold Ross, founding editor of the *New Yorker*, that he was not out to please "the little old lady from Dubuque"—even though the *New Yorker*, then as now, certainly made appeal to wealthy women consumers in its advertising pages.

This gendered subtext of the modern short story left its mark in different ways on male writers, many of whom seemed anxious to divorce themselves and their work somehow from mass culture's stereotypical femininity. But where did it leave women writers?

This chapter will explore that question through the careers of five women known chiefly for their work in the short story: Katherine Mansfield, Katherine Anne Porter, Dorothy Parker, Kay Boyle, and Mary Lavin. These writers do not by any means exhaust women's twentieth-century productivity in the short story. Among the writers I have already discussed as novelists, Elizabeth Bowen, Rebecca West, Ellen Glasgow, Willa Cather, Edith Wharton, and many others also published short stories. I have omitted Caroline Gordon and other less familiar writers who were known for their short fiction, and writers like Flannery O'Connor, Elizabeth Taylor, and Eudora Welty, who were at the beginning of their careers in the 1940s. Between them, however, Mansfield, Porter, Parker, Boyle, and Lavin not only produced a compelling body of short stories, but also represent well the variety of ways in which early-twentieth-century women writers of short fiction shaped their careers in relation to the possibilities of the literary marketplace.

Katherine Mansfield (1888–1923), born Katherine Mansfield Beauchamp, was the difficult, rebellious daughter of a prosperous New Zealand family. Sent off to school in London in 1903 under the chaperonage of her aunt, she edited the college literary magazine and began writing stories about her childhood. After three years in England, her parents demanded that she return to New Zealand. Upon her return to England in 1909 she married one man but abandoned him without consummating the marriage, became pregnant by another, and went off to Germany to await what turned out to be a miscarriage; in 1910 she began calling herself Katherine Mansfield, the name under which she would publish her stories.

One of Mansfield's earliest stories, "The Tiredness of Rosabel" (1908), was a fictional commentary on the milieu of urban mass culture—the very soil in which the short story flourished—and its gendered subtext. At the story's beginning Rosabel, who works "in a millinery establishment," is going home hungry, having divided what money she has between the purchase of a bunch of violets and a scanty tea.[4] Like the many young single women who flooded British and American cities around the turn of the century, she struggles to live alone on inadequate wages. She lurches home on the omnibus, gazing at the familiar advertisements and at her seatmate, "a girl very much her own age who was reading *Anna Lombard* in a cheap, paper-covered edition" (*SKM*, 4–5).

Advertising and mass-market romance together ("it was something about a hot, voluptuous night, a band playing, and a girl with lovely, white shoulders") foster and delimit Rosabel's desires. Arriving at "her own room at last!" she falls asleep by dreaming herself into the place of a wealthy woman on whom she had waited at the hat store, earlier in the day. Rosabel herself may be aware of her dream's incongruity—at one point she laughs aloud at its stereotyped diction and outcome, which combine her observation of the other woman with the words of the romance novel (*SKM*, 7, 8). Her cramped life, however, has no other anodyne.

Rosabel virtually embodies "woman as mass culture." Yet "The Tiredness of Rosabel" suggests that there is more to women's consumption of mass culture than either optimistic advertisers or hostile (and potentially misogynist) critics of it might guess. Rosabel is a victim of her circumstances but not a mindlessly passive victim; the story's third-person narrator ends (perhaps too sentimentally for some readers) in sympathy for her subject.

Mansfield followed "The Tiredness of Rosabel" with a group of stories set in Germany and drawn from her experiences during her pregnancy. Originally published in the *New Age*, they were collected into a volume, *In a German Pension* (1911), which her publisher advertised as a "six-shilling novel"—probably hoping to capitalize on the prestige novels enjoyed over disparate collections of stories. Mansfield herself later rejected these satiric pictures of bourgeois German life as "positively juvenile," but the volume did well both critically and in terms of sales.[5]

It was also in 1911 that Mansfield met John Middleton Murray, then an Oxford undergraduate. Murray soon became her lover (in 1918, her husband), and he and Mansfield together edited *Rhythm*, one of modernism's many "little magazines." The first story she published in *Rhythm*, "The Woman at the Store," ventured into new fictional territory for Mansfield. Set in the isolated wilds of Mansfield's native New Zealand, the story begins with three riders, two men and a woman (the story's narrator), approaching a desolate frontier outpost. One of the men, Jim, knows the territory and assures the others that they will find whiskey, provisions, a place to camp—and a woman "with blue eyes and yellow hair" (*SKM*, 125).

When they arrive, the woman is a weather-beaten wreck of her former self: "her front teeth were knocked out, she had red pulpy hands, and she wore on her feet a pair of dirty Bluchers" (126). The narrator shudders to imagine her loneliness; Jim, at a loss to explain the metamorphosis, guesses that the woman's husband has abandoned her (129). Her appearance notwithstanding, Jo butters her up and sleeps with her, leaving the other two to stay in the store with the woman's six-year-old daughter. Resentful of their presence, the daughter draws a cartoon for them that suddenly brings the situation into focus: "the picture of the woman shooting at a man with a rook rifle and then digging a hole to bury him in" (134). Mansfield allows her readers to fill in the rest: domestic violence, loneliness, finally murder.

Mansfield returned to her New Zealand youth, although not quite to the raw naturalism of "The Woman at the Store," in several major stories of the following years, among them the long "Prelude" (first published in 1918 as a booklet by Leonard and Virginia Woolf's Hogarth Press), its sequel, "At the Bay," and "The Garden Party." Taken together, Rhoda Nathan suggests, Mansfield's New Zealand stories form a bildungsroman cycle comparable to other great twentieth-century portraits of the young artist (Nathan, 13).

"Prelude" begins as the Burnell family is moving from a house in town to a grander house at some remove in the country. Lottie and Kezia are left behind to be picked up later as their mother, grandmother, and sister Isabel ride off on a loaded buggy for the new house. The incident typifies their position in the family: their languid, indifferent, beautiful mother favors the tattletale Isabel, and their father, Stanley, a complacently virile man of business, loves his wife first and the son he does not have second (*SKM*, 244). Their single aunt Beryl—a more privileged version of Mansfield's earlier Rosabel—is indifferent to all the other members of the family with whom she lives, dreaming of a romance that will take her away. The story ends with Kezia playing with, and dropping, the lid of a jar of Beryl's face cream. Her awkwardness seems to portend other kinds of unhappiness with conventional femininity.

"At the Bay" picks up with the Burnell family on vacation at the shore. The son Stanley longed for has arrived, but his wife still fears further pregnancy and acknowledges to herself that she has little love for her children (*SKM*, 278–79). Beryl, discontent as ever with her life and looking for romance, falls into a sexual triangle with a married couple, the Kembers; leered at admiringly by Mrs. Kember (276), she ends by refusing the advances of Mr. Kember.

If Mansfield's New Zealand stories can indeed be described as a bildungsroman, they are unusual in that they "show all the stages of growth and development at the same time in the same household" (Nathan, 32). The several female characters of the stories "are different aspects of Mansfield herself," Nathan suggests, perhaps vehicles through which Mansfield explored different possible resolutions for women's development and women's adult sexuality.

Mansfield published some of the New Zealand stories in the *Athenaeum*, a relatively prosperous and stable journal that John Middleton

Murray began to edit after *Rhythm*, the *Blue Review*, and the *Signature*—all avant-garde little magazines on which Murray and Mansfield worked—folded. Two more collected volumes of stories, *Bliss, and Other Stories* (1920) and *The Garden Party, and Other Stories* (1921) appeared before her death from tuberculosis in 1923. In her short career, Mansfield—like many of the best short-fiction writers of her generation—had managed to cross the literary boundaries between precariously supported little magazines, respectable literary reviews, and successful published collections.

Katherine Anne Porter (1890–1980) distanced herself and her short fiction from the mass culture of the magazines more consistently, perhaps, than any other American woman writer of her generation. Although she did publish in periodicals—beginning with "Maria Concepcion," her first acknowledged short story, in *Century* (1922)—she is best known for prestigious, cohesive collections: *Flowering Judas* (1930, revised and expanded 1935); *Pale Horse, Pale Rider*, a volume of three long stories or novellas (1939); and *The Leaning Tower and Other Stories* (1944). Her work was praised from the start by an influential group of critics, among them Yvor Winters, Allen Tate, and Robert Penn Warren.[6]

Many of these critics were associated with what has come to be called the New Criticism, a movement in American literary studies that began in the late 1930s and called for criticism to focus closely upon the symbols, paradoxes, and metaphors that were, according to New Critical doctrine, the defining features of poetic language and indeed literature generally. Many of the New Critics were practicing poets, and tended to write the kind of poetry their criticism was best prepared to appreciate: dense with metaphor, intellectual, tightly crafted. Poet-critics like Tate and Winters recognized the forms of symbolism they most admired in Porter's short fiction, and hailed her work; poet, critic, and novelist Robert Penn Warren explicitly dissociated Porter's craft from the kind of short story "the magazine has corrupted."[7]

Porter's flair for symbolism shows in "Flowering Judas" (first published in 1930) and "The Grave" (1935), both stories of initiation. "Flowering Judas," set in Mexico, centers on Laura, an idealistic 22-year-old American woman who has come to Mexico to teach children and work for the Mexican revolution. Virginal and grave, she bewilders the Mexican men, and they her.[8] Laura cannot understand the codes by which they mix sexuality with politics; "She is not at home in the world"; her "talismanic word," repeated inside her like a charm against otherness, is "No. No.

No" (CS, 97). The name and appearance of the flowering Judas tree suggest her sense that her idealism is betrayed by the sensual life around her (96), but the betrayal is ultimately a self-betrayal as well. The colors of the Judas tree insinuate themselves into her thoughts (96), and the story ends with Laura eating the flowers of the Judas tree in a dream—flowers that turn into the "body and . . . blood" of a revolutionary she has visited in prison. Laura cannot hold herself completely apart from what she rejects; her own unconscious mind betrays her into "monstrous" minglings of "love with revolution, night with day, life with death" (101).

In "The Grave," a 12-year-old boy and his 9-year-old sister visit the old family cemetery, from which their ancestors' bodies have been taken up for reburial in the public plot (CS, 362). Combing through the freshly turned earth, each finds a token: Miranda, a small silver dove; Paul, a "ring carved with intricate flowers and leaves" (363). Each wants what the other has, and they make the exchange; Paul, it turns out, has recognized and desired the dove as the screw head from a coffin.

Their bargain resembles a wedding, and foreshadows what follows. Paul shoots a rabbit, who turns out to be pregnant. Seeing the "bundle of tiny rabbits" in the mother's womb, Miranda (whose name recalls the heroine of Shakespeare's *The Tempest*) learns something she has not known before. This is her initiation into female sexuality, and it links birth to death, womb to tomb (DeMouy, 139–44). Exchanging her coffin-dove for a ring carved with designs of nature and life, Miranda has still—unavoidably—made a compact with death.

Porter's longer stories are less compacted with weighted symbolism, but never abandon it altogether. "Pale Horse, Pale Rider" (first published in 1938) is a long and in many ways realistic story about a wartime love affair between Miranda (an older version of the girl in "The Grave," perhaps) and Adam. Both contract influenza in the terrible epidemic of 1918, and Adam dies of it while Miranda makes a slow and reluctant recovery. Woven into the story's realism, however, are symbolic passages of Miranda's dreams, even delirium, as she struggles with her illness; "Pale Horse, Pale Rider" manages to link the symbolic story of a young woman's initiation with a realized historical context.

Porter's interweaving of symbolism and realism in this story deserves comparison to Rebecca West's *The Return of the Soldier*, another long story (or short novel) about relations between men and women on the home front in World War I. We feel the historical climate of wartime America in "Pale Horse, Pale Rider": working on a small salary, living in a boardinghouse, Miranda is pressured to buy war bonds she can't afford under threat of being thought unpatriotic (CS, 271). When dissenters and conscientious objectors are losing their jobs or being thrown in jail on vague charges, this threat seems real indeed to Miranda. She does women's war relief work, yet cannot dispel her own unvoiceable skepticism about its value, about women's false relations to wounded soldiers (276) and to war rhetoric more generally.

In this repressive climate, Miranda meets and falls in love with Adam (another suggestive name)—a strong, handsome, and gentle soldier. Adam cannot allow himself to think what Miranda thinks of old men spouting war rhetoric (294–95); he holds himself, she imagines, "Pure . . . all the way through, flawless, complete, as the sacrificial lamb must be" (295). After she contracts influenza, he nurses her selflessly. She dreams of him in a forest, shot through with arrows, rising alive and whole, only to fall again and rise again, until she comes between him and the arrow demanding why he must "always be the one to die" (305). The dream-arrows then go through them both, but kill only him.

Preparing to leave the hospital after she has learned of Adam's death, Miranda asks a friend to buy her "One lipstick, medium, one ounce flask Bois d'Hiver [winter wood] perfume, one pair of gray suede gauntlets without straps, two pairs gray sheer stockings without clocks," and an elegant walking stick. The 1920s, Porter seems to suggest, were born here. "No one need pity this corpse," Miranda says to herself in the mirror, "if we look properly to the art of the thing" (316). Art (as self-creation, even dandyism) will henceforth substitute for the life that is missing; her dream of the deadly wood and its arrows will be transmuted into an expensive French fragrance.

Male writers of World War I saw one world destroyed and another one born in the European trenches. In "Pale Horse, Pale Rider" Porter's blend of realism and symbolism astonishingly succeeds in compressing that history—with its political, aesthetic, and sexual dimensions—into a love affair lasting a few weeks in a small Colorado town.

The most productive years in the life and work of Dorothy Parker (1893–1967) were centered in New York City. Born Dorothy Rothschild, she grew up in prosperity—her father was a successful garment manufacturer—but was left suddenly unprovided for by his death in 1913. Casting about for work, she published some poems in Frank Crowinshield's *Vogue*, was given a minor editorial position on the magazine, then accepted Crowinshield's invitation to become the drama critic for *Vanity Fair*, soon to be one of the most glittering success stories of American magazine publishing. She also married a stockbroker with three names, Edwin Pond Parker II, the first of many such WASPs with whom she would fall madly in love. The marriage fell apart soon thereafter, but she preferred Parker to her own Jewish surname and kept it as her professional and social identity for the rest of her life.

Parker leapt to fame as a merciless critic and founding member of the Round Table, a group of wits who met for lunch at the Algonquin hotel. Usually one of very few women in a group of men, Parker shot off scores of memorable remarks at others' expense and her own; she made her own incorrigible romantic and sexual neediness fair game. Her reputation for mordant wisecracks preceded the publication of her first, wildly popular volume of light verse, *Enough Rope* (1926). During the midtwenties, however, Parker's energies turned increasingly toward short fiction. Her friend Harold Ross founded the *New Yorker* in 1925, and from 1926 on Parker was a frequent contributor to the magazine, helping to shape what came to seem the magazine's distinctively urban economy and wit.

One of Parker's favorite fictional forms was the monologue. "The Waltz" and "A Telephone Call," perhaps her two most famous such stories, work by dramatizing the internal conflicts of a witty but needy woman who wonders at her own willingness to play the games she plays with men. The speaker of "The Waltz" graciously accepts the invitation of a hopeless dancer. Her polite social patter contrasts with her sarcastic inner monologue about her partner's inadequacies; she herself cannot understand why she did not find an excuse for not dancing; yet at the story's end, she cannot stop her own voice, like a broken record, from flattering her partner into another turn.[9] In "A Telephone Call," a woman alternates between trying to prevent herself from phoning a male lover who has not called her, and trying to persuade herself that she has nothing to lose by doing so (*PDP*, 119–24). The story's fascination lies in the mental ingenuity the speaker invests in the process of disguising her situation from herself.

In a sense, both "The Waltz" and "A Telephone Call" are extended wisecracks at Parker's own expense, dramatizations of the hard-living, urban, cynical, but helplessly romantic persona on which Parker traded in art and life. Yet their popularity suggests that Parker gave an acceptable voice to more general anxieties about the meaning and consequences of the sexual revolution, such as it was, of the 1920s. Desperately liberated and desperately dependent at the same time, her female speakers would be difficult to hear out were it not for their wit, which protects both them and Parker's readers from the consequences of their feelings.

Parker wrote out her most sustained, least self-protecting encounter with this aspect of her life in the long short story "Big Blonde" (first published in the *Bookman*, 1929), which won the O. Henry competition for best short story of the year. Hazel Morse, the story's heroine, prides herself on being a "good sport" with men: "Men liked her, and she took it for granted that the liking of many men was a desirable thing" (*PDP*, 187). Her marriage and subsequent relationships come apart, however, when men discover the day-to-day lapses in the good sport's emotional armor. Hazel drifts into alcoholism for anesthesia and eventually attempts suicide. When her attempt—like Parker's own attempts—fails, Hazel wakes up again to a life more trapped than ever by the need to pretend good spirits.

Like many other American writers and intellectuals, Parker was politically radicalized in her own way by the trial and 1927 execution of Sacco and Vanzetti. She joined the picketers at the Massachusetts State House in Boston to protest the pending executions and was arrested. Although she never completely left behind the world of the *New Yorker*, Parker began injecting sharper social contrasts into her satire.[10]

In "Horsie," for example (written during 1932, in the depths of the Depression), a wealthy young couple, after the birth of their first child, engages a nurse temporarily to look after mother and baby. Generous after the way of their world, the husband correctly invites the nurse to eat dinner with him. As the weeks stretch by, this dinner becomes an ordeal; making conversation with "Horsie," as he and his wife jokingly call the long-faced Miss Wilmarth, is excruciating. He does his best to conceal the fact from her, and buys her a small corsage of gardenias—an afterthought to the immense bouquet he presents to his beautiful young wife—when she finally goes. The small courtesies of departure bring him face to face with what he would rather not know: that the nurse is returning to a life in which she has but two dresses, no room of her own, and no possibility of escape (*PDP*, 274). For her, this job has been an idyll, and his half-hearted kindness the most significant gallantry she has ever known. Peeping at her flowers in the car on the way home, Miss Wilmarth is momentarily transfigured. "It would have been all fair then for a chance spectator" (275) who could have seen a woman in that moment, not a caricature. But, of course, spectator there is none—unless Parker's readers embrace that position, with all its mingled potential for compassion and condescension.

Parker's more politically pointed stories, as the conclusion of "Horsie" suggests, do not always escape bathos. And given the context of their publication—often in mainstream, if not mass-market, magazines like the *New Yorker*—perhaps it makes sense that these stories work best when pricking their readers' sense of comfort in their own worlds, rather than when exploring other worlds. Parker did write one convincing sketch of another political world: "Soldiers of the Republic," one of several stories drawn from her 1937 trip to see the Spanish Civil War firsthand. Her friend Harold Ross accepted the Hemingwayesque "Soldiers of the Republic" for the *New Yorker,* after rejecting a string of Parker's other politicized stories (Meade, 305).

"Soldiers of the Republic" in the *New Yorker* of the late Depression, surrounded with luxury advertising: the inescapable historical ironies of such a juxtaposition frame Parker's life and career. Her most typical work—in "A Telephone Call" or "Horsie"—speaks with the ambiguous wit of a divided conscience, aware of and trapped in her world's sharp contradictions, but unprovided with a solution to them.

Kay Boyle (b. 1902) learned both literary and political radicalism at her mother's knee. Katherine Evans Boyle defied her husband and father-in-law's disapproval not only by "running for election to the Cincinnati Board of Education on the Farmer-Labor ticket," sheltering protesters, and working for radical labor organizers in Cincinnati, but by reading Gertrude Stein aloud at dinner parties and taking her daughter Kay to the 1913 Armory show in New York, which introduced modernist painters like Picasso to American audiences. Not surprisingly, Kay Boyle grew up assuming that modernist aesthetics and radical politics went hand-in-hand.[11]

During the 1920s, Boyle's own work centered on aesthetic radicalism. She published poetry, some short fiction, and aesthetic manifestos in some of the period's most influential avant-garde little magazines—*Poetry, Broom, Contact, transition*—alongside modernists like William Carlos Williams, Marianne Moore, and James Joyce.

In the 1930s, however, Boyle's work changed directions. Confronting the economic needs of her growing family on the one hand, and world depression and the rise of fascism in Italy, Germany, and Spain on the other, she began writing more realistic, accessible stories. Her work began appearing in mainstream magazines—from the *New Yorker* and *Harpers* to those bastions of mass circulation, the *Saturday Evening Post* and *Ladies' Home Journal* (Spanier, 2, 94–95). This change of direction gave Boyle herself and some of her admirers misgivings; Edmund Wilson later damned her 1944 novel *Avalanche* by associating it with *Saturday Evening Post* illustrations.[12] But her new style succeeded well enough with other readers to win Boyle two O. Henry awards, for "The White Horses of Vienna" (1935) and "Defeat" (1941).

Her 1930 collection, *Wedding Day,* included several powerful stories originally published in the little magazines, many of them written in an urgently Joycean stream of consciousness. Compiling an edition of her stories many years later, however, Boyle omitted her most experimental work. Her *Fifty Stories* begins with the more realistic "Episode in the Life of an Ancestor," which also introduced *Wedding Day*—an indication that Boyle's priorities were heading away from radical formal experimentation as early as 1930.[13]

Modeled after one of Boyle's own grandmothers, "Episode" presents a rebellious daughter locked in silent conflict with an authoritarian father. They live on the Kansas frontier, where the daughter rides horses over the prairie. (Boyle's admiration for D. H. Lawrence betrays itself in these human-animal bonds.) Her father admires her "feminine ways" in church (FS, 17) but mistrusts her passion for riding, which has "rubbed any tenderness out of her flesh" and left instead a sense of power, arrogance, and pleasure in her mastery over the animals (19).

The father considers marrying his daughter off to the schoolmaster, the only eligible man around. Searching through her room, however, he comes upon a copy of Milton's *Paradise Lost*, signed in the schoolmaster's hand and open to the scene of Adam leading Eve to "the Nuptial Bowre" (*FS*, 21). Enraged with what he takes to be the schoolmaster's effort to seduce his daughter with filth (Spanier observes [51] that the father does not recognize the lines as Milton's), the father vows not to allow the marriage, and imagines that his absent daughter is even now meeting the schoolmaster out on the prairie.

The father's rage seems to stem from unacknowledged jealousy over his daughter's sexuality. What he imagines is, in fact, untrue; the daughter is not in the possession of any man. Instead, she is racing her horse, in a way "that is unmistakeably sexual—with the female in the role of mastery" (Spanier, 51). At this point in the story, Boyle's narrator begins to call the daughter by another name, "the grandmother"—thus assigning her in advance the "power and stature" of an older woman (Spanier, 51). When "the grandmother" returns home, she sees her book at the table where her father is sitting, and reclaims it with silent contempt. He wilts in fear of her; as he earlier displaced his own sexual desires onto the schoolmaster, he now imagines that she has somehow injured the school-master (*FS*, 24). In fact, she has diminished *him*; the grandmother-to-be towers over the father.

With its examination of sexual feeling in the confines of the family, "Episode in the Life of an Ancestor" probably owes something to the Freudian social climate of the 1920s. But Boyle turns Freud on his ear, in at least one way, by stressing the father's jealous desire for the daughter rather than the daughter's for the father. Nor does Boyle seem to imply—as an orthodox Freudian would—that the grandmother's riding is a sub-stitute for possession of a real man, or a symptom of penis envy. The grandmother's lonely experience on the prairie is her best reality, not a substitute for anything else.

"Episode" explores the hidden involvement of sexuality in the will to dominate. Sexuality and power are intertwined again, with the additional complication of race, in another story, "Black Boy" (sold to the *New Yorker* in 1932). The narrator, a well-off young white girl, visits the shore with her grandfather, who "takes his pick of the broad easy chairs and the black boys" to wheel him along the boardwalk (*FS*, 50). There is a hint of homoerotic feeling, expressed through class privilege, in the grandfath-er's selection of his "boy," and an explicit display of power in the names he calls the boy, without ever finding his real name (51).

The narrator, however, strikes up a friendship of sorts with the black boy. Her grandfather warns her against him, suggesting that the boy might knock her down and rob her (53); what other possibilities lurk be-hind that image, he does not spell out. She disobeys him, riding her horse once more down to the boy on the beach. Given a chance to try the horse, he rides beautifully, without laying on hand or whip. The narrator offers to show how the horse jumps, but her own dogs startle the horse, and she is thrown. Lying on the sand in semiconsciousness, she hears voices of love and feels comforting hands—hands that must belong to the boy; he picks her up to carry her home. But when the grandfather "met the black boy carrying me up to the house, he struck him square across the mouth" (55).

There the story ends, and Boyle allows readers to make their own con-nections. The grandfather's prejudice is on one level obvious and deplor-able, at least to the broadly liberal readers of the *New Yorker*. Yet his reaction seems overdetermined—shaped, that is, by more than one mo-tive. Racial prejudice is complicated by what might be called male dom-inance more generally (the grandfather's power to tell the narrator where she may and may not go) and by the implicit erotic entanglements suggested in the narrator's nascent attraction to the black boy, the grand-father's visceral reaction against that possibility, the grandfather's own taken-for-granted privilege to "pick" black boys to serve him. "Black Boy" is more subtle than any simple synopsis of its plot might suggest.

Whatever Boyle lost or gained by moving away from her 1920s period of formal experimentation and the little magazines in which that exper-imental work was published, clearly her mainstream magazine fiction is not trivial. Her subtlety did not desert her when she turned, in the mid-thirties, to the political situation in Europe.

"The White Horses of Vienna," her O. Henry Prize story of 1935, hauntingly evokes a world in which Nazism seemed attractive to people not devoid of humanity. As the story opens, a doctor in a small Austrian town in the mountains has badly wrenched his knee while climbing a mountain at night. The narrator does not disclose the purpose of his night climb, but the glimpse of men and women "carrying a knapsack of can-dles . . . climbing through the twig-broken and mossy silence in the dark" (FS, 151) is both mysterious and beautiful.

Only later do we learn that the doctor and his wife climb the mountain to light swastikas with candles, visible for miles. Part of a Nazi group, he will eventually be arrested and imprisoned by the Austrian authorities. A sturdy, in many ways decent man, the doctor has a passion for cleanliness and for the purity of his native mountains. He meets his opposite in the young doctor who arrives from the city to help him: Heine, a Viennese Jew. To the older doctor and his wife, Heine stands for all the interrelated disorders of modernity: the city, cultural miscegenation, and the leveling powers of money (FS 156–58). Heine, for his part, feels desperately iso-lated on the mountain and longs for the culture of the city, "indoors, with the warmth of his own people, and the intellect speaking" (164).

In terms of the story's ending, the older doctor is history's victim, hauled off to prison for insurrection. Boyle already knew in 1935, of course, what would become even more obvious in time: that soon the younger doctor and his people would become the Nazis' victims on a scale without precedent. "The White Horses of Vienna" could be said to sympathize with Nazis; one of the O. Henry competition judges, in fact, objected to the prize on those grounds.[14] It might be more accurate to say that the story does not demonize Nazi sympathizers; it instead grounds the evils of Nazism in particular and complicated social condi-tions. Boyle evokes a magically beautiful, traditional society on the mountain, whose members have retreated in fear from the hunger and depression below. She locates their antagonism toward modernity in love for a particular, concrete way of life. Yet this very love rejects and will destroy Heine, the "wanderer," the unsettled outsider; on their beloved mountain, the swastika burns.

In "The White Horses of Vienna," Boyle—once the quintessential 1920s modernist—grasps the heart of fascism's antimodernist appeal, its warped and vicious form of populism. The story empitomizes Boyle's complicated, changing, lifelong dialogue between rebellion and tradition, elite and mass culture, aesthetic modernism and social activism, a dialogue that would continue well beyond 1945 and the scope of this book.

Mary Lavin (b. 1912) has enjoyed a distinguished reputation as a writer of short stories on both sides of the Atlantic. Born in Massachusetts, Lavin at the age of nine moved with her parents to their native Ireland. She began publishing short fiction in the late 1930s; her early stories appeared both in mainstream American periodicals like the *Atlantic Monthly* and in the Irish *Dublin Magazine*, before being collected as *Tales from Bective Bridge* (1942).

Lavin's range in this first volume extends from realistic stories in the mold of Joyce's *Dubliners* to more fantastic stories invoking traditions of Irish folklore. "At Sallygap," on the realistic side, begins with a conversation on a bus: Manny Ryan from Dublin, with "the urgent respectability of his striped city suiting and his very slightly mildewed bowler hat" confides to his seat companion that once upon a time he almost made it to "Gay Paree."[15] The Irish band in which Manny once played fiddle had booked passage to Paris, hoping to play to new audiences. But Manny's girl, Annie—now his wife—had come to the dock in tears, and Manny had fought his way off the boat to her; his fiddle, thrown off after him, was smashed.

Manny and Annie now endure a loveless marriage in Dublin. At Sallygap, walking about the small town, Manny experiences a Joycean epiphany in which he imagines changing his life right there in the Irish countryside rather than in distant and magical Paris. His return home to his bleak rooms, cheerless supper, and frustrated wife scotches this hope; he realizes that the sacrifice of his dreams has issued only in his wife's smoldering hatred.

Ranging away from realism toward Irish folklore, "The Green Grave and the Black Grave" opens with a memorable sentence: "It was a body all right" (*Tales*, 33). The Irish fishermen who find this body floating on the waves act throughout the story as a kind of chorus of lament, interpreting the drowning of Eamon Og Murnan through the perspective of traditional Irish language and beliefs. He was a newly married man, we learn, married to an "inland woman" (37) with an inland woman's dread of the sea and a dread that her husband might drown and never be recovered—his body consigned to "the green grave," the open sea—instead of going down to "the black grave," on land, where they could lie together (38).

When the fishermen bring Eamon's body ashore and try to find the young wife, she is mysteriously absent. Eventually we learn from the older women that the wife insisted that night on going to sea with her husband, to share whatever fate was his. Ironically, then, it seems that the wife's insistence on a shared fate may have separated them; his body is recovered, hers is gone. Returning to the shore, however, where they had left Eamon's body, the fishermen find that the tide has taken it: husband and wife will share the green grave. In the chanting, powerfully formulaic language exchanged between the fishermen and the women, "The Green Grave and the Black Grave" takes on the dimensions of myth.

Lavin followed *Tales from Bective Bridge* with several other well-received volumes of short fiction through the 1940s, 1950s, and 1960s, and was honored as president of the Irish Academy of Letters from 1971 to 1973.

Detective Fiction

Crime has been a staple of mass culture since well before this century. Eighteenth-century London printers hawked broadsides featuring the last words and grisly deaths of executed criminals. Daniel Defoe's novel *Moll Flanders* (1722), the narrative of a prostitute and thief who becomes a respectable woman in the end, is only the canonized tip of an iceberg. Criminals' "true confessions" were an immensely popular eighteenth- and nineteenth-century literary genre among newly literate urban publics; and those who could not read might have the latest read to them.

In 1841 Edgar Allen Poe introduced a new element to the literature of crime: his detective, C. Auguste Dupin, who solved crimes with reason rather than brute force or luck. Toward the end of the century, Arthur Conan Doyle created Dupin's heir, Sherlock Holmes, another reasoning detective. By the 1920s, the market for crime fiction in England and the United States was so large that it segmented, like the magazine market (with which it was intimately related, of course): readers could choose between police stories, classic detective stories focused on deduction, and the new "hard-boiled" American school of tough, professional detectives who solved murders dangerously on the street, instead of safely in the library.

As with other developments in mass culture, the story of crime fiction has a gendered subtext. Where, in these developments, have the women been? In many respects, crime fiction has been a hospitable area of mass culture for women. As Kathleen Klein observes, most readership studies have concluded that "detective fiction is read by both women and men," unlike many other popular genres—the romance, the western—whose readership is strongly segregated by gender.[16] Moreover, two women would appear on almost anyone's list of the early twentieth century's best-known mystery writers: Dorothy Sayers and Agatha Christie, who may yet turn out to be the best-selling author of this century. Many other women writers on both sides of the Atlantic—Mary Roberts Rinehart in the United States, for example, and Josephine Tey (one of the pen names of Elizabeth Mackintosh, who also wrote under the male pseudonym of Gordon Daviot) in Great Britain—were important contributors to what is often called the early-twentieth-century "Golden Age" of the mystery.

The success of women writers in the genre of crime fiction is in some ways surprising, even paradoxical. "After all, this fiction is primarily a man's story . . . with major female roles limited to villain or victim (Klein, 9). Women traditionally are not supposed to be interested in or capable of violence, nor do they often have the direct professional experience of murder, mayhem, and investigation that some male writers have drawn upon. As a consequence, perhaps, the most popular early-twentieth-century women writers in crime fiction tended to specialize in classic stories of deduction—which can take place in the library of a country house or even at a dinner table—rather than in the more male-dominated, action-oriented genres of hard-boiled detective fiction or spy thrillers.[17]

One of the things drawing these women writers to crime fiction, we might surmise, was the opportunity to write stories focused on work, money, power, and the public realm instead of traditional romance plots. Oftentimes, however, the working, professional, paid detectives they created were men. Women detectives have appeared in stories by women and men since at least 1864 (Klein, 18), but they tend to be amateurs rather than professionals, and "women detectives—even the amateurs—do not appear frequently on readers' polls of all-time favorites" (Klein, 8).

If many women do read detective novels, if women successfully write them, still there seems to be a lingering resistance to the idea of women emerging out of the categories of victim and villain to take justice into their own hands. Agatha Christie and Dorothy Sayers, whose writing featured both male and female sleuths, found ways of overcoming this resistance in the course of their successful careers.

Agatha Christie (1891–1976) began her writing career in the 1920s by producing a series of murder-and-espionage novels that drew vaguely on current political events—Red scares, general strikes, conflict between England and Ireland—for the impetus to (or at least the atmosphere of) crime. Her first novel, *The Mysterious Affair at Styles* (1920), also introduced her most important male detective, Hercule Poirot of the Belgian police. Christie and Poirot became the talk of England when readers by the thousands tried to figure out whodunit in *The Murder of Roger Ackroyd* (1926). This book, notes Robert Barnard, also "established the typical milieu for a Christie detective story—the small English village."[18] moving Christie away from a world she did not know, the realm of international intrigue, to a no less intriguing world she did know, that of a gossipy, tight-knit, middle-class small town.

This is the world for which Christie invented her famous female detective, Miss Marple, first introduced in *The Murder at the Vicarage* (1930). Like most of the relatively popular women detectives in the genre, Miss Marple is an amateur, not a detective in the strict sense at all. A village gossip and a spinster, she has learned what she needs to know in order to solve crimes simply by watching what passes under her nose in St. Mary Mead. Miss Marple by and large solves crimes by simple knowledge of human nature, not through professional expertise, and she need not poke around, climb trees, or peer over windows to do it; indeed she can find the villain while doing her after-dinner knitting (and does so several times, in *The Tuesday Club Murders*, 1932).

In some senses Miss Marple could be called a feminist heroine. She quietly challenges the notion that women's sphere, the stereotypically private sphere of the home and garden, contains nothing that could possibly foster deductive intelligence. At the same time, however, she never openly fights with the boundaries of that sphere; and her ability to solve crimes simply by knitting and nodding her head can make her seem more a fictive dea ex machina, the fantasy of an all-seeing mother, than a rounded character.

The Moving Finger (1943), a Miss Marple novel, exemplifies both the strengths and the limitations of Christie's writing.[19] Like Dorothy Sayers's *Gaudy Night*, which it postdates, *The Moving Finger* is plotted around a poison-pen case, anonymous notes that initially seem noxious but trivial, only to bring genuine violence in their wake. As in *Gaudy Night*, the problem of trying to find the writer of the notes is partly shaped by Freudian assumptions—that sexually frustrated women (but not men) are likely to do these things—that are at least partly disproved by the novel's end, appropriately enough with Miss Marple's help. Also like *Gaudy Night*, *The Moving Finger* ends with a marriage between two of the characters. But this marriage is far more conventional than in Sayers's novel, and the village's sexual norms are never fundamentally called into question. Christie's Miss Marple operates from a special but comfortable place within things as they are, rather than imagining things as they might be.[20]

Dorothy Sayers (1893–1957), like Christie, found popular success with both male and female fictional detectives: Lord Peter Wimsey, the blond son of a duke, shares the investigative honors with Harriet Vane, the obscure, often awkward daughter of a provincial clergyman (and with some other, minor sleuths). And like Christie's Miss Marple, Harriet Vane is, strictly speaking, an amateur as a detective.

There, however, the resemblance ends. If Harriet Vane is an amateur detective, she is very much a professional as a writer of mysteries, a woman who earns her living by her own wits. She is sexually experienced, although unmarried for most of her fictional career, and uncertain of her own position as a woman in the world. Moreover, her counterpart, Lord Peter Wimsey, is every bit as much the amateur, with the added experiential handicap of never having needed to earn his own living. Finally, Sayers brings her two detectives together in an elaborate love story, strung across several novels, that asks and answers the question of whether the male detective can truly respect the woman's work while loving the woman.

Sayers inaugurated the love story of Harriet Vane and Lord Peter Wimsey in *Strong Poison* (1930). As the book begins, Harriet Vane is on trial for the murder of her estranged lover, Philip Boyes. Sayers puts the burden of exposition into the mouth of the judge, who is summing up the evidence for the jury; this narrative move not only acquaints readers with the basic information of the story, but allows Sayers to dramatize men's basic power to judge women through gender stereotypes. The ancient judge makes clear his lack of sympathy for modernist notions of "free love," modernist literature in general, and women who have sex with men without benefit of marriage—all part of the same noxious package, he believes, and almost reason enough to convince the jury of guilt beyond a reasonable doubt. [21]

Fortunately, two people in the audience disagree with the judge's authoritative male narration: Miss Climpson, a spinster sitting on the jury, and Lord Peter Wimsey, a spectator in the gallery. Miss Climpson's refusal to convict hangs the jury; Lord Peter's conviction of Harriet's innocence sends him out to find the true killer. He has also fallen instantly in love with Harriet, and means to marry her.

Lord Peter eventually does find the killer, with the help of both Harriet (from her prison cell) and Miss Climpson, who runs a detective service disguised as a secretarial bureau (with Lord Peter's aid and subsidy). The fate of his love for Harriet, however, remains in the balance. Lord Peter wants to love her as an equal, but both are painfully aware that it would be unsatisfactory and unequal for Harriet to feel obliged to love him out of sheer gratitude. Given her painful recent experience, Harriet also mistrusts men who merely appear to honor women's equality; furthermore there is the formidable problem of the objective differences in their social stations. Modern artistic bohemias, Harriet has learned, are not oases of gender equality (Sayers's view of "advanced" young people is almost as dim as the old judge's, if for rather different reasons), but neither is traditional marriage. Are there enough independent people in the world, whatever their social location—strange allies like Miss Climpson, Harriet, Peter, and some of their friends—to make the difference that would make Harriet and Peter's love possible?

In *Have His Carcase* (1932), Sayers allows Wimsey and Vane to work on another case together, solving the murder of a young gigolo at a seaside resort. As the novel begins, Harriet finds herself unwillingly notorious for her recent murder trial. Sensitive about her reputation, she wryly accepts the boost in sales it gives her writing, and resolves to maintain her independence. The murder throws Harriet and Lord Peter together again but does not settle the question of how, and in what social world, they might be together on terms of equality.

Sayers explored that problem most fully in her most ambitious novel, *Gaudy Night* (1936). A workable mystery (although it does not quite obey the murder mystery's requirement of beginning with a corpse), *Gaudy Night* is also, and more importantly an intricately sustained meditation on twentieth-century women's struggle to combine love and work. [22]

Attending a reunion at her old Oxford college, Shrewsbury (a fictional name; Sayers's Oxford college was Somerville), Harriet receives an unpleasant anonymous note. She ascribes it to her own unhappy notoriety, having received many such since her trial—until the college dons inform her that the college has been besieged with such notes, some of them truly damaging, and asks her to investigate a pattern of behavior that threatens to tear the college apart or undermine its reputation in the eyes of the male-dominated university.

Harriet and the dons begin the investigation with the assumption (underwritten by Freudian psychology) that the perpetrator is likely to be a member of the college itself, part of its celibate community of women. They suspect about themselves, in other words, exactly what the culture at large does: that women in the absence of men are neurotic, twisted, repressed; that the women's community of the college is in some way unnatural. Harriet cannot see the investigation clearly until she discards this assumption, and she cannot readily discard it because she fears its implications for herself.

It is Lord Peter who at last points out to Harriet that her "fears are distorting [her] judgment" (GN, 295). He exposes the sexism of popular psychologizing, the way it is applied to women but never to men: "If every frustrate person is heading straight for the asylum I know at least one danger to Society who ought to be shut up" (295)—meaning himself. He accepts her right to take both her writing and her investigation seriously, even to the point of courting physical danger. He shows his respect for the college's community of scholarly women and his sense of their mission's importance. As they solve the Shrewsbury case together, Lord Peter demystifies Harriet's fears both of love and of celibacy. Able to see her own choices clearly at last, Harriet can accept his offer of marriage, an offer tendered in the language of the scholarly community they have defended: "'Placetne, magistra?' 'Placet'" ("Does it please you, my [female] teacher?" "It does" [GN, 457]).

Sayers followed up Gaudy Night with Busman's Honeymoon (1937), in which—predictably enough—Lord Peter and Harriet find themselves faced with a murder to solve on their honeymoon. They also find themselves working to fit an egalitarian relationship into the framework of "repressive words" like husband and wife.[23]

Although this conclusion seems flat to some readers after Gaudy Night, Susan J. Leonardi eloquently defends Sayers's achievement in the Wimsey-Vane series of novels. Their marriage, she points out, "is a creative act, not a real or a social one, and the object of that creativity is marriage itself. Harriet, reborn of a world of women, marries Peter, whim of a woman, to make concrete a vision, not of things as they are, but things as they might be."[24] Detective novels are seldom thought of as a utopian genre, dependent as they are upon crime and destruction; at most, they assert only that a fragile social order can be defended with reason and care. Sayers's distinctive achievement lies in turning detective fiction's defense of an endangered stability into a vision of social transformation.

Mass or popular culture, according to some critics, is distinguished from real "literature" (among other things) by its drive to pigeonhole writing into marketable segments: romances, detective fiction, westerns, science fiction, and so on, each with even more specialized subheadings, each with magazines and publishers catering to readers' specialized—and thereby predictable—needs. In contrast to this kind of cultural production, these critics suggest, "literature" is universal and does not minister to readers' slavishly specialized, predictable generic expectations.

I have argued in this chapter that there is some basis in historical fact for this view of mass culture; the early twentieth century exacerbated an already existing segmentation of the literary marketplace. But this phenomenon resists easy after-the-fact judgments about "real literature" versus all other writing. As we have seen, women writers could cross some of the internal boundaries of the literary marketplace. Sometimes mass magazines published serious and radical stories by serious writers. Sometimes writers stretched the boundaries of popular genres, as Dorothy Sayers did in the mystery.

As Andreas Huyssen argues, we must question rather than simply assume the division between mass culture and elite culture if we are to understand modernism, and we must question the gendered subtext that assigns women to the side of mass culture in this division. Twentieth-century women writers of short stories and detective novels actively positioned themselves in relation to this division through the diverse and fascinating strategies of their own writing. It is worth trying to recover an appreciation not only for the formal qualities of their stories as art, but for their perspectives on literary history's "great divide" between modernism and mass culture.

CHAPTER 9

Women Playwrights and
Modern Drama

The first half of the twentieth century was a time of great change for American and British drama. At the beginning of the century, the theater enjoyed more respectability and financial profitability than ever before. Nineteenth-century audiences had become steadily larger and more prosperous, even though there was a relative dearth of important original playwriting in English during the early to mid-nineteenth century. By the turn of the century, those audiences were seeing challenging works by new playwrights: names like G. Bernard Shaw and John Millington Synge appeared on playbills in England, Ireland, and the United States. By 1945, however, theater was staggering under the challenge from a new source of entertainment, the movies. The years in between saw changes indeed.

The kings of the theatrical world in the late nineteenth century were men like Sir Henry Irving, actor-managers who controlled their own companies. Like Irving, some of them were eventually knighted. Their prominence helped erode some of the ancient prejudices attached to theater, especially in countries with a Puritan heritage—England and the United States among them. Acting, directing, and playwriting became more professional as they became more respectable; it became possible for aspiring young dramatists to attend professional schools, and various professional associations for people involved with the theater began to appear.

The early years of the twentieth century, however, also saw the beginnings of a now-familiar split between commercial theater and artist-controlled theater. Commercial productions—associated with the West End district of London or New York's Broadway—became increasingly expensive to mount, and therefore fell more and more under the control of specialized commercial managers and the financial backers to whom they answered.

Some actors and writers responded by organizing theater companies of their own. Many, like the Provincetown Players in the United States, were dedicated to the production of original works by their members. Others, like the Abbey Theatre in Ireland, also introduced the radical new playwrights from Europe—at first Ibsen and Strindberg, later Cocteau and Brecht—whose work had little appeal to commercial investors. The black American activist and intellectual W. E. B. Du Bois founded the Krigwa players in Harlem to produce the work of new, mostly African-American, playwrights. Repertory companies sprang up outside the major commercial theatrical centers, performing both modern works and older standards in the light of new ideas about staging. Companies attached to universities and colleges also sponsored new playwrights.

Many of the artists' companies, like the Group Theater and the New Playwright's Theater in the United States, had leftist political agendas. For political radicals in both England and the United States, theater as a genre was especially attractive. By its very nature, drama is public rather than private: even amateurs can perform it and help shape it, rather than passively consuming the words of an unknown, distant author; it thrives on the representation of conflict, and so takes up themes of political struggle with ease. When out-of-work performers and directors flocked to the Federal Theatre organized by Franklin D. Roosevelt's Depression-era Works Progress Administration (WPA), the U. S. Congress became so suspicious of its leftist fervor that congressional committees inquired into its activities and eventually cut off its funding.[1]

The changes that shaped early-twentieth-century theater had mixed but generally positive consequences for women's participation, especially women's participation as playwrights. More than other forms of authorship, perhaps, playwriting benefits from some form of practical apprenticeship—experience in the theater, learning how written words are embodied on the stage. Changing conditions for drama in the twentieth century opened up new ways for potential women playwrights to acquire that necessary apprenticeship, but did not eliminate all the old obstacles to authorship.

The increasing prestige and respectability of the drama made it possible for more women to consider entering the profession. The old aroma of immorality hanging around the theater (at one time, to be an actress was considered tantamount to being a prostitute) was slowly dissipating. But it was not altogether gone, as the persistence of old jokes about chorus girls, and the time-honored institution of the casting couch, still testified. Women hoping to enter the theater were probably still at greater social and personal risk than men.

The transition from actor or playwright to artistic director or producer, an important one for men like Irving, Harley Granville Barker, and John Gielgud, seems to have been more difficult for many women to make; stereotypes about actresses and reluctance to give women authority over mixed groups may help account for it. Few women, too, although they might be in demand as actresses, could hope to carry much decision-making weight in the rarefied financial world of Broadway and West End commercial productions. Some women did act as patrons of alternative theaters, most notably Annie Hornimann, who funded both the Abbey Theatre in Dublin and the Gaiety Theatre in Manchester.

Many of the alternative theaters, like the Provincetown Players, the Krigwa troupe, and the Abbey Theatre, were distinctly hospitable to women as playwrights. Others, for whatever reasons, seem not to have been. A theater group's left-wing politics alone did not guarantee women's participation—which is not surprising, given Marxism's relative lack of interest in feminist issues during the 1930s and 1940s. Yet women writers like Lillian Hellman sustained their work in leftist contexts during the same period, and a woman, Hallie Flanagan of Vassar College, energetically directed the left-leaning Federal Theatre Project.[2] In some cities, the Federal Theatre sponsored all-black theater groups; one of them, the Chicago Negro Unit of the FTP, was headed by the black playwright Shirley Graham. The most vigorous circles of early-twentieth-century African-American drama, however, centered upon the Harlem Renaissance and its Krigwa players, and the writers associated with Howard University in Washington, D.C. (see chapter 10).

The women playwrights whose work I will survey in this chapter— Lady Gregory of Ireland; Elizabeth Baker of England; Rachel Crothers, Susan Glaspell, Shirley Graham, and Lillian Hellman of the United States—represent a range of dramatic styles and degrees of political commitment, and illustrate the diversity of methods women found to make their way as writers into the venerable but fast-changing world of early-twentieth-century theater. The women playwrights of Harlem and the

Howard University circle will be central to the story of the following chapter on the twentieth-century African-American women's literary renaissance.

In 1902 Lady Augusta Gregory (1852–1932), along with the poet William Butler Yeats, helped found the Irish National Theatre in Dublin. Better known as the Abbey Theatre—so christened in 1904 after Annie Horni-mann, the noted theater patroness, presented the group with a building of its own—the company became the center of the early-twentieth-century Irish literary renaissance and remained so for many years. From its founding until 1927, Lady Gregory not only helped provide the Abbey with artistic direction, financial support, and fund-raising, but also wrote for the company many plays based on Irish myth, history, oral tradition, and rural life.

Lady Gregory began her playwriting career by collaborating with Yeats on a poetic drama, *Cathleen ni Houlihan* (1902), before moving on to her first independently written play, *Twenty-Five* (1902). She was most successful with one-act dialect comedies of Irish village life, among them *Hyacinth Halvey* (1906) and *The Jackdaw* (1907). *Hyacinth Halvey* fol-lows the travails of an ordinary young man, the new sub-sanitary inspec-tor for the town of Cloon, who arrives preceded by an extravagant set of testimonials to his good character. The people who meet him embroider still further on his supposed virtues, driving him to try to ruin his repu-tation in order to live normally. Every attempt he makes to blacken him-self, however, backfires; by the play's end he is held up as a would-be martyr and example to the whole town.

Hyancith Halvey pokes fun at the Irish love of verbal one-upmanship, the inability to leave a testimonial or a story alone without trying to top it. More seriously, the play's verbal and physical farce shows how the villagers, perhaps without consciously intending to do so, throw sand in the wheels of Great Britain's imperial bureaucracy. By stealing a sheep to blacken his character, Hyacinth comically saves Mr. Quirke from the inquisition of Sergeant Carden, ordered to search Quirke's establishment for unwholesome meat. Mr. Quirke stints on the provisions he sells to England's troops: "Is it to encourage them to fight the poor Indians and Africans," he asks, that he should provide good meat to the army at bot-tom prices?[3] Mr. Quirke, in his own sly way, defeats empire at home—with Hyancinth's unwitting help.

Lady Gregory wrote other kinds of plays with more explicit Irish na-tionalist themes. In *The Gaol Gate* (1906), a peasant woman learns of her son's execution for refusing to inform on other Irishmen, and composes a mourning song, or keen, to tell the world that "Denis Cahel died for his neighbor!" (*Seven Short Plays*, 194). *The Deliverer* (1911) explores the career of Charles Stewart Parnell, the famous statesman who worked for Irish nationalism until his career foundered in the aftermath of a divorce suit. Her published journals and memoirs later provided an invaluable firsthand account of the Abbey Theatre's work.

Elizabeth Baker (1879–1962) helped bring the new realism of Continental drama and its critique of middle-class life to the English stage with *Chains* (first performed in 1909) and *The Price of Thomas Scott* (1913).

Chains, Baker's most famous play, treats a few days in the life of a lower-middle-class suburb of London. Mr. Tennant, who boards with Charley and Lily Wilson, precipitates the action of the play by announcing his intention of emigrating to Australia. His decision forces Charley to face the monotony of his working life and helps Maggie, Lily's sister, realize that she is thinking of her impending marriage only as an escape from her dreary work as a sales girl.[4] Maggie breaks off her engagement, but Charley—on the verge of taking flight for Australia with Tennant— is pulled back by his wife's announcement that she is pregnant, and is once again trapped in the life he knows only too well.

Baker analyzes the misery of both women and men of the lower-middle class in *Chains*. Young women's only alternative to low-paid service work is marriage, but marriage is scarcely a romantic idyll; struggling to make ends meet, Lily must take in boarders and work to feed and house them. Charley chafes at his own inability to live out the old proverb that a man's home is his castle. When all the local men clerking at his office are forced to take a pay cut, they swallow the decisions of a faceless Board (27). As white-collar slaves (Charley enters and exits the play pulling irritably at his office uniform of collar, silk hat, and cuffs), they lack even the potential solidarity of working-class men, and are prepared to do one another out of a job rather than challenge the system (37). Middle-class relations between women and men (67) contribute to this cycle of fearfulness, stagnation, and thwarted dreams of escape.

The Price of Thomas Scott was first produced in Manchester, England, by the Gaiety Theatre, another of Anne Hornimann's projects. One of the important new repertory companies in early-twentieth-century England, the Gaiety from its founding in 1907 enjoyed "a reputation for disciplined, sincere realism."[5] *The Price of Thomas Scott* was perfectly suited to the Gaiety's style.

Set in Thomas Scott's seedy London draper's shop, the play turns on Scott's rejection of an offer to buy out his decaying business. Scott needs money for his and his wife's retirement, and could send his son on scholarship to a good school with a few extra pounds. His daughter Annie, who has a fine eye for trimming hats, longs to see the family settled so that she can escape to Paris. Scott finally rejects the offer of £500, however, because the would-be buyers intend to turn the premises into a dance hall. Scott abhors drinking and dancing, and will not sacrifice his staunchly Puritan, chapel-going conscience for financial security.

Baker does not make Scott either an idealistic hero or a figure of fun. The church he serves is riddled with hypocrisy; his decision sharply narrows both his son's and Annie's futures. His religious strictures forbid his children to participate in either dancing or the theater—central forms of amusement for the growing urban youth cultures of modern cities. Yet he is no simple domestic tyrant, but a father concerned with giving his daughter a fair share of the money her work brings in.[6] Baker's dramatic realism observes both Scott's narrow integrity and his daughter's conflicted admiration for him with compassion.

Rachel Crothers (1870–1958) made her way into the theater through a path that typified some of the evolving local and professional institutions of American drama around the turn of the century. Born into a middle-class family in Bloomington, Illinois, in her twenties she founded and wrote plays for the Bloomington Dramatic Society, one of many such groups around the United States. She then left for the East Coast to study professionally, spending four years as a pupil and instructor at the Wheatcroft School of Acting in New York City, where she began to direct as well as write her own plays. She made her professional debut as a playwright in 1902 with *The Rector*, a one-act comedy, and continued to send plays—many of which she directed herself—to the New York stage at regular intervals for the next three decades.

Crothers avoided the cramped, lower-middle-class settings of a realist like Elizabeth Baker. She excelled instead at "country house" plays, a favorite genre of middle-class theatergoers in both England and the United States, in which a group of beautiful and leisured people gather at a country estate to play and, of course, expose all their emotional entanglements with one another. Crothers used the genre to explore the familiar social issues of pre– and post–World War I America: the sexual double standard, marriage and divorce, the behavior of the Bright Young

Things of the 1920s. Her dialogue often manages to suggest real cruelty in the limited social world of the country house; her resolutions, how-ever, tend to find conservative solutions for the problems opened in the plays.[7]

Let Us Be Gay (first performed in 1929) begins with a prologue in which Kitty Brown, a young and innocent wife, has just learned of her husband's infidelity. Bob insists that it is meaningless, she that it irrev-ocably alters the meaning of their love; she will not take him back, and she sues for divorce. Three years later, the action picks up in a country house to which the hostess has invited both Bob and Kitty—without knowing of their previous marriage.

Kitty now enters the scene as a hardened flirt, thoroughly disillusioned after the divorce, drawing all the men around her with practiced skill. Her hostess, in fact, has asked her there for just these skills; she wants Kitty to detach Bob from another young woman, Deirdre, who is infa-tuated with him. Kitty and Bob encounter one another awkwardly, but Kitty refuses to allow Bob to make a clean breast of the affair to the entire house party. She treats Bob to a dose of his own medicine, allowing him to think that she is embarking on an affair with one of the other guests. Finally, however, Bob confesses that he still loves her, cracks Kitty's fa-cade of cynicism, and they agree to remarry.

Let Us Be Gay in many respects anticipates the divorce-and-remarriage comedies that would be filmed in Hollywood during the 1930s and 1940s—movies like *The Philadelphia Story* and *The Awful Truth*. Like those movies, it asks whether women and men might be able to know their own feelings more clearly through loss and sexual experimentation, in the wreckage of the double standard that allowed such experiences only to men.

Kitty's rather improbable transformation from wronged wife to hollow flirt, however, suggests that there is no viable middle ground between wronged innocence and disillusioned cynicism—disillusionment itself being only another form of self-delusion. For both Bob and Kitty, know-ing through experience turns out to mean knowing that Kitty was right the first time: "Bob, marriage means just one thing—complete and ab-solute fidelity or it's the biggest farce on *earth*."[8] Experience can teach only that experimentation is empty; Kitty ends by disavowing that quin-tessential social virtue of the 1920s, gaiety.

Susan and God (first performed in 1937) also looks at a troubled mar-riage, although this one is saved before coming to a divorce. Susan

Trexel, a flighty society woman, has driven her husband, Barrie, to drink and her teenage daughter Blossom to lonely despair by her utter neglect of them. At the opening of the play, she arrives at a country house party from the Riviera, bursting with enthusiasm for a vaguely religious "movement" run by a Lady Wiggams. Having discovered God and the virtues of honest confession for herself, Susan proceeds to urge her new faith upon the other guests.

She gets her comeuppance when her husband, drunk, devoted, and angry, finds out where she is and bursts in on the scene. Barrie actually takes her enthusiasm seriously, and proposes that they try to redeem each other and their marriage by opening up their disused country house and giving Blossom a real home for the summer. Susan reluctantly agrees, and finds she almost likes her newly domestic way of life; Blossom blossoms for the first time, becoming sociable and pretty; Barrie stops drinking. But Susan cannot quite give up her dream of becoming a public figure in her religious "movement": "I can't go back to being an ordinary woman again.—Lady Wiggam says I have a *very rare power.*"[9] She makes one more attempt to break away, and almost loses Barrie before realizing that love, and God, reside in their marriage rather than somewhere in the outer world (164).

Susan and God hands down an obviously conservative moral: a woman's real duty lies at home, and dreams of public life and authority are only a self-serving distraction from that mission. More so than in her earlier plays, critic Lois Gottlieb finds, Crothers here "records a sense of disillusionment with the women's movement, and a tendency to blame it for deficiences in woman's emotional life."[10] The play's resolution suits the tenor of the 1930s, when many voices urged women to stay at home and avoid competing with men for scarce jobs and resources in the depressed world economy. Yet Susan is a powerful figure, at her most impressive and witty when she is being cruelest to her husband and child—just as Kitty, in *Let Us Be Gay,* steals the show not as the dutiful wife but as the heartless flirt. It is hard to reconcile such vital, if thoroughly unpleasant, figures with the traditional happy endings Crothers doles out to her characters; yet Broadway audiences as well as critics heartily appreciated Crothers's contradictory dramatization of current social issues.

Susan Glaspell (1876–1948) began her writing career as a journalist, author of short stories, and novelist. Like Rachel Crothers, she was a native Midwesterner; born to an old pioneer family in Davenport, Iowa, she drew on her knowledge of rural life in her early fiction and some of her later plays. In 1910 she joined the "Monist Society" of Davenport, a group of radical intellectuals; among its members were Floyd Dell, who would become one of the best-known American socialists of the 1910s and 1920s, and George Cram Cook, whom Glaspell would later marry.

In 1911, Glaspell moved to New York's Greenwich Village. After their marriage in 1913, she and Cook established the pattern they would follow for the next several years: winter in the bohemian colony of Greenwich Village, summer in the small artistic resort town of Provincetown, Massachusetts. It was in Provincetown, during the summer of 1915, that Cook brought a group of artists and writers together to perform original plays. He and Glaspell contributed a satiric one-act comedy they had written, *Suppressed Desires*, about the modest havoc wrought by the introduction of psychoanalytic ideas into a modern household. Other writer friends turned out also to have plays sitting in their desk drawers; and so was born the Provincetown Players, one of the most important little theater groups in early-twentieth-century America.

The Players wrote, acted in, and produced their own plays. Eugene O'Neill and John Reed were among the most famous writers associated with the group. Edna St. Vincent Millay acted with the Players, who premiered her own poetic drama, *Aria da Capo*, in the 1919–20 season. Susan Glaspell, however, remained among the most active contributors to the group; between 1915 and 1921 they performed eight plays by Glaspell and two short comedies (*Tickless Time* and *Suppressed Desires*) coauthored by Glaspell and Cook.

Glaspell's first independent play, *Trifles* (first performed in 1916), was also in many respects her most successful.[11] A tight one-act play set in a desolate farmhouse, *Trifles* pits the law as administered by three heavy-handed men against the insight of two women. The men have come to the farmhouse to investigate the death of its master, John Wright, found strangled in his bed; the women are there to fetch some clothing for Mrs. Wright, in jail under suspicion of the murder. The male investigators are at a loss for the motive that will persuade a jury to convict the woman. After commenting dismissively on Mrs. Wright's housekeeping and her concern with domestic "trifles" in the midst of a murder case, they go upstairs to the bedroom in search of the sort of objective evidence—facts about the rope, the window, the bed—they think will make sense of the case.

Meanwhile, however, the women left downstairs are finding their own way into the murder. To them, "trifles" speak volumes: the stitching gone awry on a quilt; an empty bird cage; the body of a canary hidden away, its neck wrung. They put together a story of domestic cruelty, isolation, and desperate rebellion. Horrified at both the untold story and its grisly ending, they reach an unspoken decision not to confide their reconstruction of the crime to the men; there, the play ends.

Trifles makes chillingly economical use of Glaspell's Midwestern experience, and points to feminist arguments about power and misery in marriage without preaching. It also inaugurates an important pattern, one that Glaspell would repeat in other plays, of setting a "theme into action and dialogue through a heroine who never appears on stage."[12]

In *Bernice* (first performed in 1919 [*Plays*, 157–230]), the heroine—a young woman of elusive grace, charm, and generosity—is dead of a mysterious ailment before the action starts. Bernice's death gathers the family together around her body: her father; her philandering husband, Craig, a writer; her good friend Margaret; her husband's sister, Laura.

The play's first crisis comes when Abbie, Bernice's loyal maid, reveals to Craig that Bernice committed suicide. Craig, who has long resented Bernice's elusive freedom ("I never *had* Bernice," he complains [173]), remorsefully concludes that Bernice died for love of him and despair at his faithlessness. Margaret, to whom he confides his secret, is thrown into turmoil at the idea of Bernice—Margaret's personal icon of life and happiness—taking her own life. Eventually she wrenches from Abbie a further confession: that Bernice actually did die of natural causes, but made Abbie promise to tell Craig otherwise.

This new revelation is even harder for Margaret to accept. Could Bernice have been so mean-spirited as to turn her own death into a lifelong punishment for her husband? At the play's end, however, Margaret realizes that Bernice has been even more insightful, and more generous, than Margaret knew: Bernice intended that Craig's remorse at the idea of her suicide would make a more serious man and artist out of him. Sacrificing her own integrity and vision of life, Bernice has cannily used Craig's egotism—anticipating that he would believe his wife died for love of him—against itself. And like the women in *Trifles*, Margaret decides to keep Bernice's secret rather than betray her to the man who unknowingly receives Bernice's last act of generosity.

Bernice's convoluted psychological drama constructs a complicated allegory of relations between modern women and men. Bernice and Craig are a modern couple: he justifying his extramarital affairs in the name of a liberated new morality, she eluding her husband's masculine will to possess her. In the end, however, a purer woman sacrifices herself to redeem a man. If the means of his redemption belong to twentieth-century psychology, still the basic pattern of redemption recalls the nine-teenth century's faith in the powers of womanly sacrifice.

The Verge (first performed in 1921) is Glaspell's most ambitiously ex-perimental play.[13] Its elaborate settings of fantastic plants and towers, along with its occasional ventures into poetic dialogue, draw on Freudian ideas of symbolism and the practices of European expressionist drama (Waterman, 82). Its heroine, Claire, is a dark version of Glaspell's absent Bernice. Like Bernice, she is mysteriously full of life and grace, an icon of life itself; like Bernice, she eludes possession by any of the men who desire her. Claire is present throughout the play's action, literally speak-ing; yet she grows more absent psychologically to the other characters, as she loses her hold on sanity. In the end she, like Bernice, becomes a kind of sacrificial figure, someone who dares to shatter familiar patterns of life. But where Bernice in her death redeems the man who desires her, Claire's madness finally kills Tom, the man who comes closest to understanding. her vision.

The Verge takes one strain in Glaspell's own temperament, her roman-tic idealism, to a deadly conclusion. Claire is a figure of the romantic artist as woman: a breeder of plants, she has striven for years to perfect an exotic blossom she names "Breath of Life." As her godlike ambition is on the verge of being fulfilled, however—the plant is finally in bloom—she realizes that even a completely new form is still a form, a prison, once realized: beautiful, but a trap (80). Moreover, "Breath of Life" lacks scent, a trait Claire hoped to bring into it through another plant, "Rem-iniscence." Glaspell's symbolism links the scent of "Reminiscence" to the humanizing properties of memory, connection, and sympathy; without those properties, she implies, Claire's quest after an absolute work of art, like her quest for absolute life, is admirable—but doomed to fail.

Glaspell returned to social realism and Midwestern settings in her other major work of 1921, *Inheritors*. The play's first act, set in 1879, sets out the founding of a small college in a frontier town. The plot then leaps forward to 1920 and the college's fortieth-anniversary celebrations. Ambitious to expand the college into a major university, the president pleads with the legislature for funds—and agrees to suppress campus dis-sent and muzzle the lone faculty radical. The play then comes to center on the president's niece Madeline, who finds herself unable to accept her uncle's actions. Arrested for defending the right of Indian students to protest against British imperial rule in their home country, Madeline, through her emerging political consciousness, is brought to the brink of prison by the play's end.

Inheritors, like much vital political drama of the 1920s and 1930s, vigorously critiques America's post–World War I climate of political repression. Glaspell uses the two-part temporal structure of the play to co-opt the label of "true American" for the radicals of the 1920s: the pioneers who founded the college were revolutionaries and political exiles in their own time, whose legitimate heirs in the play are Americans imprisoned for asserting their American right to free speech and redress of grievances.

Cook helped disband the Provincetown Players in 1922. They had become, he thought, the victims of their own commercial success, with Broadway producers eager to cannibalize their writers' productions. Glaspell accompanied Cook to Greece in 1922, and wrote only one major play thereafter: *Alison's House*, based on the life of Emily Dickinson and the family drama surrounding the publication of her work, won the Pulitzer Prize in 1931. Glaspell worked for part of the 1930s as a director of the Midwest Play Bureau, an arm of the New Deal Federal Theatre Project. In her last years, she returned to the novel, publishing four more books before her death in 1948. Glaspell's novels are now little read, but a few of her short stories remain memorable, and her plays continue to be revived for production.

Shirley Graham (1896–1977) came to theater through music, which she studied first in Paris, at the Sorbonne, and later at Howard University and Oberlin College in the United States. Even as a child, she later wrote, Paris was "a city in which I had boundless interest. This may have been because I had read *Les Misérables* and *A Tale of Two Cities*, as well as because Father had told us that in Paris there was no discrimination against black people."[14] Graham's sojourn in Paris, during its 1920s heyday as a capital of international modernism, helped set her direction as a musical playwright. Like many other modernists, both black and white, Graham was drawn to African culture. Combining her formal musical training with what she learned about African music from African students in Paris, she composed a major musical drama about African-American musical culture, *Tom-Tom*, which "was produced during the spring of 1932 at the Cleveland Stadium in Cleveland, Ohio, before a crowd of 25,000."[15]

From 1936 through 1938, Graham successfully headed the Chicago Negro Unit of the Federal Theatre Project; among the company's productions was Graham's own *The Swing Mikado*, a jazz musical play based on Gilbert and Sullivan. She spent the next two years at Yale University on a creative writing fellowship, where she wrote *Dust to Earth*, *I Gotta Home*, *It's Morning*, and *Track Thirteen*, a radio play.

It's Morning (1940) draws on Graham's musical talents. A short one-act play in two scenes, *It's Morning* tells the story of a slave mother who kills her daughter rather than let her be sold downriver; Union soldiers liberate the plantation only in time to witness the mother carrying the bleeding body of her child. The play's characters sing both old spirituals and music of Graham's own composition. They also speak, much of the time, in dialect arranged in loose blank verse—a surprisingly effective combination of black oral tradition with formal literary convention.

I Gotta Home (1939), by contrast, works in a tradition of realistic domestic comedy, enlivened by Graham's own autobiographical recollections of her youth as a preacher's child. The Reverend Elijah Cobb heads a large and struggling black family in a Midwestern town. His wife and children resent their lot of moving from parsonage to parsonage with the minister's fading fortunes. "I thought he was going to be something," Cobb's wife complains, "a Bishop, maybe, or something—but he just goes on preaching . . . dragging his family from pillar to post—."[16] A gentle and unworldly man, more comfortable with books than with fundraising, Cobb has little power with the overbearing, hypocritical elders of his church. His children dream of other lives: Mirah thinks of marrying ("Some day I'm gonna have a home of my own and I'll do just what I want to in it" [231]); E. J. tries to make money as a numbers runner; Toussant wants to emulate his namesake as a black political leader; Ben Hur imagines himself a businessman; and Lilacs wants to be a dancer on stage—a particularly suspect ambition in a preacher's household.

The arrival of Mattie, Cobb's sister, turns the household upside down. A former dancer and maid to a Hollywood star, Mattie comes to the door pestered by photographers and preceded by the story that her former employer left her a fortune. The rumor of money soon has the church's head elder pursuing Mattie, despite her scandalous past; Mrs. Cobb takes the opportunity to snub Mrs. Swan, a middle-class doctor's wife whose mission in life is to "keep our culture pure" (244). For all the other Cobbs, Mattie's fortune represents hope and the chance to know the outside world.

In fact, Mattie possesses no fortune: her actress employer had none to leave. Yet she does bring fortune and the outside world to the Cobbs. Her friends Jasper Jones and Peewee, "gentlemen of Harlem" dressed in Seventh Avenue city suits (225, 265), turn up in the Midwestern town, determined to share in the booty; Mattie buys a sweepstakes ticket from them, and takes the third prize on the dark horse, Raven—$50,000, enough to set up the Cobbs for life. For Elijah Cobb (kept innocent of the money's source), the windfall is manna from heaven, like the food the ravens brought to his biblical namesake in the desert (279). For Mattie, the rest of the family, and the play's audience, the windfall pays comic tribute instead to the mutual loyalty, optimism, and resourcefulness of an extended black family that can come together, by the play's end, to sing an old song—"I gotta home in that rock"—with new meaning.

After her years at Yale, Graham abandoned playwriting for journalism and biography. The unequal treatment meted out to black soldiers during World War II aroused her indignation; her own son's death, following abuse and lack of medical attention in an army camp, confirmed her growing political consciousness. In 1942 she went to work for the National Association for the Advancement of Colored People (NAACP) in New York City. In 1951 she married the famous activist and intellectual W. E. B. Du Bois, and saw him through his trial and acquittal (one of many such trials held during the postwar McCarthy anticommunist fever) on charges of being an "unregistered foreign agent."[17] In her last years, she traveled in and wrote about Africa, coming to know firsthand the cultures that had first drawn her in the Paris of the 1920s.

Lillian Hellman (1906–1984) is far and away the most famous American woman playwright of the first half of the century. Her career combined the popular appeal of Broadway with the leftist politics that inspired so much innovative twentieth-century American drama. Hellman scored major successes with *The Children's Hour* (first performed in 1934) and *The Little Foxes* (1939). *Watch on the Rhine* (1941) also did very well; her only real failure was *Days to Come* (1936), an unwieldy story of a strike in an Ohio town.

Hellman came to her career as a playwright through a different path than either Crothers, Glaspell, or Graham. She served an important part of her apprenticeship in the twentieth century's new artistic medium, the movies. During a 1930–31 sojourn in Hollywood, she took a job reading and summarizing potential movie stories for MGM. Writing two or three summaries a day, Hellman without realizing it "was learning script writing in a disciplined fashion."[18]

It was also at this time that Hellman met Dashiell Hammett, author of *The Maltese Falcon* (1930) and other works in the new genre of hardboiled detective fiction. Hellman and Hammett became lifelong on-again, off-again lovers; Hammett also became Hellman's best writerly mentor, pressing her to complete her work and helping her tighten her dialogue.

The Children's Hour, Hellman's first and stunningly successful play, treated a topic so controversial that it was difficult to cast actresses in the first Broadway production (Rollyson, 70). Briefly, a manipulative adolescent girl accuses the two women who run the school she attends of an "unnatural" relationship. Her grandmother, Mrs. Tilford, believes her and spreads the story; the two women lose all their pupils and are left alone with each other, their only supporter a young doctor to whom one of the women, Karen, is engaged.

Although both Karen and her friend Martha know the accusation is, technically, untrue, Martha realizes her own feelings under pressure: "*I have loved you the way they said,*" she confesses to Karen, who cannot reciprocate or even acknowledge Martha's words.[19] Martha commits suicide; Karen's doctor retreats from their engagement; Mrs. Tilford arrives to tell Karen that her granddaughter's accusations have been exposed as lies, and to accept her responsibility in the disaster.

The Children's Hour has sometimes been faulted for shifting its focus from the girl's lie to the dynamics of the relationship between Karen and Martha, with an ending tacked on to return the issue to the original false accusation. Certainly the girl, Mary Tilford, is a gripping character: wily, shrewd, alarmingly powerful. Compared to her, Karen and Martha come closer to stock characters, the "normal" woman and the "repressed lesbian"—that new creature of popular psychology. (D. H. Lawrence's short novel of 1923, *The Fox*, featured a roughly similar couple.)

But all of the play's conflicts bear on issues not just of honor generally, but of honor and truth between women specifically. Mary Tilford's manipulations rely on the jealousy and competition of an enclosed community of girls. She finds it easy to turn her grandmother's conventional womanly morality against two outsiders, working women, self-supporting in the world. Martha's confession to Karen opens questions of how much honesty bonds between women can bear under these circumstances, and of where honesty with herself can lead in a brutally heterosexist world.

The Children's Hour does not answer any of these questions in systematic or political terms. The plays following *The Children's Hour* increasingly do rely upon political terms of analysis, political ways of delineating good and evil, but Hellman's political vision concerns itself primarily with class rather than gender or sexuality. In company with Dashiell Hammett, a committed Marxist, and other leftist writers and intellectuals of the 1920s and 1930s, Hellman studied Marxism and the Soviet Union, wrote and spoke in defense of the Soviet experiment, and looked at the United States through Marxism's framework of class struggle leading to international revolution.

In *The Little Foxes*, Hellman returned to the American South of her own childhood—she had divided her schooling between family in New York and New Orleans—with a critical eye. As the play opens, the Hubbard family is about to conclude a deal with a Chicago manufacturer to bring a cotton-processing plant to their small Southern town. To come up with their own financial stake in the deal, the Hubbard brothers need a contribution from their sister Regina's husband, Horace. Regina promises his cooperation, but Horace, near death from a heart ailment, is sick of their exploitative schemes for fattening their fortunes on cheap labor (*Four Plays*, 219).

The Hubbard siblings concoct a scheme for getting the money that involves, among other things, planning to marry off Horace and Regina's gentle daughter Alexandra to her no-good first cousin. Each of them tries to cheat the others; Regina finally triumphs, after driving her husband to death in the process. Although her brother Oscar has lost in the deal, he accepts his defeat as temporary, reasserting his own faith in the world as a dog-eat-dog competition he intends to win (245). Alexandra, however, articulates a different vision in the end, vowing to fight the system in which "there were some people who ate the earth and other people who stood around and watched them do it" (247).

Alexandra's last-act conversion to political consciousness may seem forced. It does, however, affirm that there is a political alternative for women under competitive capitalism, that women who fight the class system need not become passive victims of their own gentleness, like her aunt Birdie, nor objects of monetary exchange among men, as her uncles planned for her, nor players wicked enough to compete with men, like her mother, Regina. But Regina's role, rather than Alexandra's, is the dramatic heart of the play. First performed on Broadway by the brilliant and temperamental Tallulah Bankhead, it has been a durable role for actresses ever since, including Bette Davis, who starred in the 1941 film version of the play.

Women's roles receded somewhat in Hellman's next play, *Watch on the Rhine*, which opened in New York on 1 April 1941. The center of the play is the conflict between Kurt Muller, a German refugee and member of the anti-Nazi resistance, and Teck de Brancovis, a treacherous Romanian aristocrat in exile. Kurt's wife, Sara, supports his antifascist work with all her considerable heart and mind, despite the risk. Fanny, the matriarch of the wealthy Washington family with whom the Mullers are staying, eventually responds to Kurt's predicament with courage and generosity. But women are supporting actors in the struggle, not the main participants.

Written at a time when isolationist feeling in the United States still ran high, *Watch on the Rhine* attempted to engage American support for the war against Germany. In hindsight, Hellman's efforts were well-timed indeed; by the end of 1941, the United States would be at war with both Japan and Germany. In early 1941, however, matters were less clear. Not only did many Americans oppose intervening in the European war, but Communists and fellow travelers (and Hellman was certainly the latter and probably the former) were hampered in their opposition to Nazism by the Hitler-Stalin pact, still in effect. Not until Germany invaded Russia, in June 1941, could American Communists officially "rehabilitate" their opinion of the play (Rollyson, 177). Thus vindicated by history with audiences both right and left, *Watch on the Rhine* was selected for a command performance during President Roosevelt's 1942 birthday celebration and filmed in Hollywood that very year, as well.

Hellman would return to the Hubbard family and the New South in her first postwar play, *Another Part of the Forest* (first performed in 1946), which was also the first of her own plays she directed. (Later she would agree with critics that direction was not her strong suit.) But her energies were increasingly turned in other directions, as she was called to testify before the House Un-American Activities Committee, forced to prepare a defense, and blacklisted in Hollywood. She would look back to these and earlier times in her published memoirs: *An Unfinished Woman* (1969), *Pentimento* (1972), and *Scoundrel Time* (1976).

Hellman's dramatic technique is often summed up—and sometimes dismissed—as political melodrama. If melodrama is understood broadly, as a kind of drama depending on the plots of clear-cut villains and intended to evoke strong emotions, this summary judgment has its uses. In writing political melodrama, however, Hellman tries to locate evil in social structures that her audiences can learn about and fight, rather than in mysteriously wicked individuals.[20] That her plays continue to be revived in reading and performance, and that movies based on her plays remain popular in revival, suggests that political melodrama's appeal to audiences, its ability to connect strong feeling with social thought, is far from exhausted.

Drama, more clearly than any other form of literature, is always and necessarily a social practice, something that people collectively make in a variety of ways. It loses much when its history is written only in terms of isolated individual authors—a Henrik Ibsen here, a Eugene O'Neill there—without consideration of the collaborative institutions, both formal and informal, that make theater possible. Women of the early twentieth century in particular often vanish in such capsule histories of great individual playwrights. Searching out the women playwrights of these years, and locating them in their historical contexts, does more than redress an important omission about women in literature; it also helps to restore an important element of historical drama to the drama itself.

CHAPTER 10

Women in the
Harlem Renaissance

Modernism is a movement often associated with the great cities of Western Europe, England, and the United States; it is a word that conjures up images of Paris, especially, but also of London, New York's Greenwich Village, and postwar Berlin. Unlike nineteenth-century English and American romanticism, which typically valued rural settings and landscapes of natural sublimity, modernism often celebrated technique and human artifice and condemned rural life as stultifyingly conventional; its practitioners frequently drew on the conjunction of many arts—visual, musical, and literary—and many cultural traditions. While the twentieth century was hardly the first era in history in which artists flocked to urban centers, modernism nevertheless saw a real efflorescence in urban bohemia—a word that had come into use in English in the mid-nineteenth century to describe the quarters of the artistic and the unconventional. Artists, writers, and intellectuals gathered themselves into enclaves in the great capital cities of modernism, eager to live by their own standards and draw inspiration from one another's work.

One of those urban capitals of modernism—often neglected in canonical literary histories, but now beginning to receive its due of critical attention—was Harlem, the major residential neighborhood for African-Americans in New York City. By the beginning of the twentieth century, New York, along with Chicago, Detroit, and other Northern cities, had become a magnet for black Americans fleeing the legal segregation, antiblack violence, and economic oppression of the post-Reconstruction Southern states. Initially crowded into the Tenderloin district of Manhattan, New York's black citizens began moving north to Harlem in large numbers around 1904–5, aided in part by a depression that created vacancies in the hitherto largely white neighborhood. Their numbers included merchants and professionals, intellectuals, musicians, and writers. They soon created "the largest, most exciting urban community in Afro-America—or anywhere else, for that matter."[1]

Commentators from both inside and outside the Harlem community began to speak of it, in the 1920s, as a phenomenon: the Harlem Renaissance. The expectation of an African-American cultural renaissance was not unique to Harlem, or to the 1920s; as early as 1901 William Braithwaite had announced in the *Colored American Magazine* (published in Boston under the direction of novelist Pauline Hopkins) that "we are at the commencement of a 'Negroid' Renaissance . . . that will have in time as much importance in literary history as the much spoken of and much praised Celtic and Canadian renaissance."[2] The renaissance could be said to have begun in Boston and extended down the eastern seaboard of the United States, through Harlem to the historically important black community of Philadelphia to Washington, D.C., home of Howard University. Still, Harlem was widely recognized as its center and the home of the two major black magazines of the 1920s, *Crisis* (published by the NAACP under the direction of W. E. B. Du Bois) and *Opportunity* (published by the Urban League and edited by Charles S. Johnson). It was after an awards banquet sponsored by *Opportunity* in 1925 that the *New York Herald Tribune* announced to all the city that "a Negro renaissance" was underway (Lewis, 116).

By this time, the Harlem Renaissance had attracted the interest of many white writers and intellectuals—"Negrotarians," as Zora Neale Hurston bitingly called them—of mixed motives and sincerity. Aspects of both African and African-American culture enjoyed a kind of vogue in the years after World War I; after the turn-of-the-century heyday of imperialism, Western museums began to fill with exhibitions of art looted from the African continent, artifacts that intrigued artists like Picasso, writers like André Gide, and dealers like Paul Guillaume. Jazz became popular both overseas and in its native United States and finally gave its name to the whole decade of the 1920s. And white "writers of postwar America, in their revulsion both against the machine and against the Victorian prudery that still dominated small-town life, often came to look on the Negro as a kind of noble savage whose primitive spontaneity had been left untouched by the horrors of the civilization they were condemning."[3]

Not surprisingly, black writers of the Renaissance themselves had mixed reactions to modernism's idealization of "the primitive." Many of them embraced African art and African-American folk culture, seeing them as potential wellsprings of both new art forms and new forms of African-American political identity; others were less sanguine about the identification of black people with the exotic (and frequently sexualized) primitive, and promoted instead literary forms that emphasized black writers' access to all the old and new resources of Western culture. This divide often coincided with a related (but not identical) debate between the values of modernist, self-justifying "art" versus uplifting "propaganda": propaganda might address itself to educating both black and white readers in liberal middle-class values, but "art," its advocates said, could and should seek out vitality regardless of its potential for edification.[4]

These simmering disagreements played themselves out in incidents like the controversy over the little magazine *Fire!!*, a one-issue sensation in November 1926. *Fire!!* featured drawings, short fiction, and poetry by artists identified with the "folk" and Afrocentric wing of the Renaissance—among them Zora Neale Hurston, Gwendolyn Bennett, Countee Cullen, and Langston Hughes. Its editor, Wallace Thurman, proclaimed a few months later that *Fire!!* "was not interested in sociological problems or propaganda. It was purely artistic in intent and conception. Its contributors went to the proletariat rather than to the bourgeoisie for characters and material."[5] It was intended to shock the black bourgeoisie, and it did; some black journals (mostly outside of Harlem itself) obliged with antimodernist condemnations.[6]

The irony of Thurman's aesthetic modernist position, however, is obvious: his "purely artistic" defense of *Fire!!* itself resorts to the categories of sociology (*bourgeoisie* and *proletariat*) that it purports to ignore. In actual practice, as many black intellectuals of the renaissance realized, divisions between art and propaganda, between folk or Afrocentric and Eurocentric culture, could seldom be hard and fixed for African-American literature. What made the modernism of the Harlem Renaissance so productive was arguably the vital tension between these poles, rather than the ultimate victory of one or the other—its inveterate "cultural dualism," in critic Jean Wagner's phrase (Wagner, 168), the double perspective of which Zora Neale Hurston wrote in the opening of *Mules and Men* (see chapter 6).

If Zora Neale Hurston is now one of the most famous voices for this aspect of the Harlem Renaissance, still other women writers explored the questions of cultural dualism in their own ways, some of which critics are only now being to appreciate after decades of neglect. As writers, as editors, and as patrons and sponsors of new writing, women of all kinds and degrees of fame played essential roles in the renaissance. To take only three of many possible examples, from the famous to the obscure: novelist Jessie Redmon Fauset was literary editor of *Crisis* from 1919 to 1926; Georgia Douglas Johnson encouraged young women playwrights at her salon in Washington, D.C.; Ernestine Rose, librarian at the Harlem branch of the New York Public Library, organized literary readings with the assistance of writers like Fauset and Gwendolyn Bennett.

In the ensuing decades, however, women's contributions to the Harlem Renaissance tended to be forgotten or devalued. Black women suffered, of course, from the general neglect of African-American writers and literary communities in canonical (and even some feminist) histories of modernism, but sexism contributed to their neglect in complicated ways as well. As Gloria T. Hull points out, women writers of the renaissance were frequently at a disadvantage in the networks of patronage and influence run by black men not immune to sexism; Alain Locke, a professor at Howard University, was one of the worst offenders in this respect.[7] Later male critics, black as well as white, often lumped most black women writers of the renaissance together as members of the "genteel tradition," claiming that this tradition ignored or disguised its black authorship altogether. Thus Arthur P. Davis and Michael W. Peplow, editors of a pioneering 1975 anthology, *The New Negro Renaissance*, judged that "Most of the better-known 'lady poets' of the period . . . tended to produce raceless verse"; and "If one knew black life only through Jessie Fauset's fiction, one might easily conclude that the middle-class Negro was simply a 'tinted' middle-class white."[8]

More recently, feminist critics of the Harlem Renaissance have argued strenuously against such dismissals of women's writing. They find in women's writing of the renaissance an exploration of the complicated meanings of both race and gender: judging women's poetry "raceless" implies that the judger knows with some certainty what it means to write *with* race, but—as feminist critics have pointed out—women and men have sometimes lived out the meanings of race differently. Modernism's idealization of the "noble savage," for example, the primitive and sexualized Negro, might well have been received and reenacted differently by black women writers than by black men. If cultural dualism energized the renaissance, women writers conscious of both racism and sexism may well have been particularly sensitive to its dilemmas. In resurrecting and rereading the women writers of the Harlem Renaissance, black feminist critics have opened an immense field whose outlines can only be sketched in the remainder of this chapter.

During the brightest years of the renaissance, from 1925 through the end of the decade, Jessie Redmon Fauset (1882–1961) may well have been its most famous woman writer of fiction, in addition to her prominence as an editor and woman of letters. Her fame as a novelist has since been eclipsed by that of Zora Neale Hurston, who cut an important figure in New York in 1925–27 but returned to the South for the setting and the writing of her most important work in the 1930s. Hurston's explorations of African-American folk traditions have intrigued later writers searching for a distinctive African-American aesthetic, while Fauset has been cast for many years as the arch-representative of the "genteel tradition," supposedly given to emulating white middle-class standards of social and literary correctness.

Fauset and Hurston are admittedly very different novelists, but an element of sexism (in addition to modernist denigration of the middle class), as critic Deborah McDowell notes, inflects such judgments. When Claude MacKay "described Fauset as 'prim and dainty as a primrose,' and added that 'her novels [were] quite as fastidious and precious,'" he participated in a long-standing male critical tradition of identifying women authors bodily with their books, and slighting both in stereotypically feminine terms.[9] What writers like MacKay and critics like Arthur P. Davis overlook in Fauset's work, McDowell argues, is "her examination of the myriad shadings of sexism and how they impinge upon female development," an examination that widens into a "critique of the relations between money, sex, and power" in the urban America of the 1920s.[10]

In her first novel, *There Is Confusion* (1924), Fauset painted on a wide canvas the relationships among several young men and women dividing their time between the black communities of New York and Philadelphia.[11] Joanna Marshall, the most important of the central characters, is also the most ambitious; driven from her middle-class childhood to do something great, she becomes a concert singer and eventually a dancer. She loves Peter Bye, the handsome and feckless son of a proud black Philadelphia family, and tries to motivate him through medical school. Out of her own snobbery, Joanna discourages Maggie Ellerley, a poor friend of the family, from marrying her brother Phillip, a political and cultural activist in the mold of W. E. B. Du Bois. Their paths (along with those of several other minor characters) meet, diverge, and cross again until at last, in the aftermath of World War I, Joanna gives up her career for the sake of her husband's dignity, while Maggie and Phillip come together briefly before Phillip's death from the lingering effects of poison gas.

There Is Confusion works hard to integrate its divergent plots and sub-plots; World War I comes along almost as a convenient deus ex machina, sorting out the characters and sending them on their way enlightened. (In the crowning coincidence of the novel, Peter Bye crosses over to Europe on a troop ship with a white man who turns out to be his half brother, Meriwether Bye, whose death in combat finally allows Peter to exorcise his inchoate resentment of, and emotional dependence on, the white world.) But its re-creation of middle-class urban black life, and the impact of World War I on that life, is nevertheless vivid and convincing. Fauset's urban communities debate whether it is worth fighting for a seg-regationist country; they buzz with concern over word from the South of new lynchings and new repression during the postwar hysteria; they share information about how to cope with the daily indignities of unofficial segregation in the North—all of which the novel's broad canvas is well equipped to register.

Fauset's treatment of her female characters, on the other hand, is prob-ably harder for most present-day readers to accept. She does not consign them uniformly to a destiny of middle-class house and home: Joanna redirects her ambition into shaping Peter's life, but Maggie takes the op-posite course, learns to abandon her lifelong habit of dependence on men, and becomes a shrewd, successful, independent businesswoman after Phillip's death. If Fauset does not press all her women into one mold, however, her plot nevertheless suggests that whatever women want most for themselves is somehow wrong and must be corrected. Neither Joanna nor Maggie gets what she initially dreamed of, nor is she allowed to combine her first dream with later desires. Combining love with am-bition outside the home seems a forbidden resolution for the heroines of *There Is Confusion,* as it was difficult for many early-twentieth-century women in real life.

There Is Confusion generated great interest when it first appeared (un-der the auspices of the important modernist publishers Boni & Liveright). A dinner held on 21 March 1924 in honor of Fauset and her first novel, organized by Charles S. Johnson and attended by many other famous editors and publishers, black and white, would go down in literary history as one of the inaugural events of the Harlem Renaissance.[12] Some four years later, Fauset brought out *Plum Bun* (1928), her best-known novel today. Unlike *There Is Confusion*, *Plum Bun* is centered firmly around the fortunes of a single heroine, Angela Murray, who leaves behind her black middle-class origins in Philadelphia to seek her artistic fortunes "passing" as a white woman in Greenwich Village. *Plum Bun*, along with Nella Larsen's *Quicksand* and *Passing* (1929), was one of several novels written during the Harlem Renaissance on the theme of light-skinned African-Americans passing as members of the white world. But *Plum Bun*, as Deborah McDowell points out, belongs to another and older literary tradition as well—the bildungsroman, like Dorothy Richardson's *Pilgrimage*.[13]

Like Fauset's earlier heroine, Joanna Marshall, Angela Murray wants to be an artist and has a genuine gift—in Angela's case, for portrait painting. Yet Fauset idealizes Angela less than she did Joanna; Angela herself realizes that "for the vanities and gewgaws of a leisurely and irresponsible existence she would sacrifice her own talent, the integrity of her ability to interpret life, to write down a history with her brush."[14] Angela's flight from black Philadelphia to white Greenwich Village is prompted by an assortment of mixed motives: hope of evading discrimination in her artistic studies, but also craving for sheer physical luxuries and social ease. More than this, even, Angela longs to shed what she experiences as the burden of perpetual self-consciousness about race: to walk down the street without wondering whether she can enter a restaurant or a store, to cease monitoring white stares for signs of hostility, to step out of the place of the "other" and simply be.

The irony of passing, however, is that in the long run it inevitably heightens rather than diminishes Angela's consciousness of race. At times this heightened self-consciousness brings Angela pleasure and a sense of power, especially erotic power: "Stolen waters are the sweetest. And Angela never forgot that they were stolen. . . . The realization, the secret fun bubbling back in some hidden recess of her heart, brought colour to her cheeks, a certain temerity to her manner" (123). This sense of erotic power, however, does not last; and what Angela ultimately takes from her love affair with a rich white man is an awareness of "the casual link between money and power and the white male prerogative of monopolizing both"—an awareness, that is, of sexism as well as racism.[15]

Angela ultimately acts on her enlarged awareness of race and gender in several ways. She speaks in defense of a fellow art student denied a prize because of her race, and in the process discloses her own identity as "colored." Her self-disclosure paves the way for a full reconciliation with her sister Virginia, now a teacher living in the burgeoning, vital Harlem community, and incidentally helps Angela sort out true friends from false among her white artistic and bohemian connections. Despite losing her own fellowship to France, Angela manages to scrape together money to study independently in Paris. Compromised as Angela's artistic vocation has sometimes seemed in the novel, Fauset allows her, unlike Joanna Marshall, to stay with it.

Yet Fauset does supply, at the same time, an improbable romantic resolution to Angela's story. Angela loves a fellow artist, Anthony Cross, who initially was also passing as white (and whose artistic vocation, unlike Angela's, seems fully idealized by Fauset). By an improbable set of co-incidences, Anthony is engaged to her sister; by another set of plot ma-neuvers, Fauset extricates Anthony, establishes Virginia with her true love, and clears the way for the right couples to get together. Like the World War I ending of *There Is Confusion*, the ending of *Plum Bun* works hard to tie up its romantic plot threads. Unlike *There Is Confusion*, how-ever, *Plum Bun* does not do so wholly at the expense of its heroine's independent identity.

Fauset published two more novels after *Plum Bun*, *The Chinaberry Tree* in 1931 and *Comedy: American Style* in 1933. Neither attracted the attention of her first two. Some of the energies of the Harlem Renaissance had waned or dispersed by the 1930s; the Depression hit black commu-nities, always living on a narrow economic margin, particularly hard. After giving up her position as literary editor of *Crisis* in 1926, Fauset had sought but could not find work in publishing or as a social secretary. Ultimately she turned to teaching junior high school French to make a living. Her relative literary silence after the early 1930s tragically echoes that of many young women writers after the heyday of the renaissance, when opportunities for publication and production became fewer and sheer economic survival more taxing for many black women.

Although few of their names are widely recognized today, black women playwrights were numerous and active in the theater of the Harlem Renaissance. As we have already seen, drama as a genre posed special difficulties for early-twentieth-century women writers: commercial the-ater had for many years been an alien world for "respectable" women, and—more important—getting plays produced in popular venues took substantial financial backing that women were unlikely to have. Obstacles like these were doubled for black women, who faced discrimination on grounds of race as well as gender, and who were even less likely than white women to have access to financial resources for production.

Nevertheless, black writers and intellectuals of the 1920s felt that it was essential to develop an African-American theater, and they developed cultural institutions in which black women's playwriting flourished. In 1925, both W. E. B. Du Bois at *Crisis* and Charles S. Johnson at *Opportunity* announced contests for the best one-act plays of the year. The contests ran in both magazines through 1927, and in every year "women outnumbered men in submitting plays, and most of the winners were women."[16] Following the success of the first year's *Crisis* contest, Du Bois organized the Crisis Guild of Writers and Artists in Harlem— soon known by the acronym Krigwa—to produce the work of the new playwrights. Krigwa's Harlem outpost did not survive for long, but other cities took up the call, and "Krigwa Players groups were organized in such cities as Washington, D.C., Denver, and Baltimore" (Perkins, 6).

This wide dispersal of the black theater movement was important for black women writers because, as in other literary genres of the renaissance, black women playwrights were perhaps best represented outside the centers of Harlem itself, especially in Washington, D.C. Women were particularly active as playwrights and producers in both the Washington and the Baltimore Krigwa groups. Moreover, playwrights as well as other black writers in Washington drew sustenance from Howard University, whose program in theater was one of the most advanced at any university in the nation, black or white. "It was through the Howard Players that many black women received their initial training in playwriting. This opportunity allowed black women to see their works produced throughout the northeastern portion of the country" (Perkins, 7). Black women's plays, in fact, numerically dominated among those produced by Howard students, as they did in the submissions to the *Crisis* and *Opportunity* contests. Some of the black women so educated went on to distinction in other literary genres; Zora Neale Hurston was among the young writers whose literary careers were launched in Howard's theater program.

The poet and playwright Georgia Douglas Johnson (1880–1966) lived and worked in the heart of Washington, D.C.'s black cultural renaissance, running a famous literary gathering at her home, the "S Street Salon," where she received and encouraged many black women writers.

Most of the many plays she wrote during her lifetime remained unpublished, but two received *Opportunity* awards for best new play and were printed in that magazine: *Blue Blood* in 1926, and *Plumes* in 1927.

Plumes, a "folk" one-act set in the poor rural South, became Johnson's best-remembered play. Its action centers around Charity Brown and her 14-year-old daughter Emmerline, who is dying offstage of an unnamed illness. Charity and her visiting friend Tildy debate the merits of allowing the local doctor to operate on Emmerline. To pay the doctor his fee for the operation, $50, is to use up the entire family savings; if Emmerline dies, nothing will be left for the "shore nuff funeral, everything grand,— with plumes" that Charity has her heart set on for her family.[17]

Unfamiliar with the doctor's scientific knowledge and uncertain of the odds of his success, Charity and Tildy resort to folk knowledge—reading the coffee grounds in Charity's cup—to show them the way. When the omen is bad, Charity hesitates before allowing the doctor to fetch his instruments; while he is gone, Emmerline dies. Perhaps the doctor was right, and delay was fatal. Or perhaps Charity's intuition, confirmed by the omen, was right all along: "He can't save her—don't even promise ter. I know he can't—I feel it . . . I feel it" (30). Johnson's realistic play passes no explicit judgment either way. Her audience may identify with the doctor's impatient, rational authority, but they may also feel the power of the two older women's ritually dignified approach to life and death.

With the end of the *Opportunity* and *Crisis* playwriting contests after 1927, Johnson found fewer publishing outlets for her work. During the 1930s, she tried without success to interest the Federal Theatre Project in producing some of her more overtly political plays, among them *A Sunday Morning in the South* and *Blue-Eyed Black Boy*, on the topic of lynching, and her historical drama *Frederick Douglass* (Perkins, 22).

Although her own plays remained within the traditions of realism and black folk drama, Johnson helped launch the career of a more experimental young playwright, Marita Bonner (1899–1971), a member of the Washington Krigwa group who attended Johnson's S Street Salon. Bonner's *The Purple Flower*, an allegorical one-act about race relations, took the *Crisis* award for best play in 1927.

The play represents a rivalry between a group of "Sundry White Devils," encamped on the top of the hill where the purple flower grows, and "The Us's" down in the valley. The Us want to ascend the hill, and quarrel among themselves over how to do it; their debate satirically reproduces

1920s arguments among black Americans over strategies of upward mobility. The dream of an "Old Lady," however—"I dreamed that I saw a White Devil cut in six pieces"—precipitates a change of goals.[18] An old conjure man, hearing her dream, declares "Thank God! It's time then!" and demands that everyone bring something to his iron pot: dust, books, gold, and finally, blood. "If I can do this," he says, "God will shape a new man Himself" (197). From the Us will come a wholly new people, not just envious competition for the White Devils. But where is the necessary blood for the conjuring to come from? The play closes with the intimation that either the White Devils, who "built up half their land on our bones," must provide it, or the Us themselves; but whoever spills it, "Blood will be given!" (199).

Bonner's elaborate allegorical casting, and the stage machinery it required, may have prevented *The Purple Flower* from ever being staged. Under cover of allegory, however, Bonner allowed herself to ask a disturbing question: must the birth of the "New Negro" in America be attended with violent rebellion? The dramatic structure of *The Purple Flower* leaves the question open, just as the more realistic structure of Johnson's *Plumes* in a different way leaves open the audience's ultimate judgment of its rural Southern characters.

Few black women playwrights of the 1920s and 1930s followed Bonner's lead in experimental drama. Working in realistic theatrical idioms for the most part, they struggled not so much with modernist formal innovations as with the vexed relationships between art and propaganda, theater and strategies of racial uplift. Eulalie Spence (1894–1981), like Johnson and Bonner, won awards in the *Crisis* and *Opportunity* competitions, and was an early member of Du Bois's original Krigwa troupe in Harlem. Eschewing both Bonner's experimentation and Johnson's concern for current social issues like lynching and miscegenation, Spence typically wrote well-crafted domestic plays with lively dialogue.

Fool's Errand, first published in 1927, turns on a church council's interrogation of a young woman thought to be pregnant. Egged on by Cassie, the community's self-appointed guardian of morals, the parson, his council, and Maza's father try to force the young woman to name the child's father. Her steadfast refusal earns Maza a loyal outburst from one of her male friends, Frank. At the play's denouement, Maza's mother reveals that it is she, not Maza, who is pregnant; Maza and Frank, along with her parents, cement their relationships in defiance of Cassie and the church council.

Fool's Errand paints the black church as a place in which women can exercise considerable powers of speech, but not always to good ends and only with the collaboration of the authoritative male minister. In the end, however, the council seems to exorcise Cassie and her tale-telling ways with its own traditional verbal challenge and response. The play ends with a chant, sung offstage, about a sister who gossips about another woman: "as soon as mah back wuz turned / She scandalize mah name." Is that a sister? the singer asks; "No! No!" the council chants in response.[19]

As Kathy A. Perkins observes, Spence's plays tend to feature "the strong female character and the weak male" (Perkins, 106). In *Fool's Errand*, Cassie abuses her power and preys on the anxieties of Maza's father, but Maza's mother is strong enough to say the day. In *Undertow* (1929), matters end less happily. The matriarch of a middle-class urban family, Hattie indulges her son Charley and regards her husband, Dan, by contrast, as a serviceable workhorse. Her world is turned upside down when Dan fails to come home to dinner one night and Charley informs her that Dan is having an affair with another woman.

The other woman, Clem, comes to the house to beg Hattie to grant Dan a divorce. The conflict between the two women seems painfully unequal at the outset: Clem not only has Dan's love, but also looks, prosperity, and confidence. "Yuh doan' need Dan an yo' son doan' need him. . . . Ah's gwine take him frum yuh," she tells Hattie.[20] But Hattie has a dark power all her own, inhering in words rather than appearance or social prestige. Learning that Clem wants the divorce in order to allow her daughter of years ago by Dan to think of her as an honest woman, she refuses to let Dan go. She mocks Clem's upwardly mobile aspirations to respectability and calls down a curse upon both Clem and Dan. Enraged, Dan responds with action rather than words. He strikes Hattie down, accidentally killing her; thus the curse takes its victims.

In both *Fool's Errand* and *Undertow*, Spence's strong women struggle with one another over definitions of familial and community respectability. Not always admirable, they reflect the extent to which African-American women in the early twentieth century did feel responsible for binding families together and keeping them upwardly mobile. The ties that bind, however, can also divide: Cassie's will to police her community sets women against one another, and Clem's desire to present a conventionally moral front to her successful daughter divides Hattie's family. If Spence's plays do not directly participate in the 1920s politics of racial uplift, if they are not dramas of protest, they do dramatize relationships within black communities—relationships that helped shape and were in turn shaped by those wider public agendas.

Most of the poetry published by women writers during the Harlem Renaissance appeared first in the major black magazines of the 1920s, *Crisis* and *Opportunity*, or in important anthologies of poetry edited by male writers of the Renaissance: *Caroling Dusk* (1927), edited by Countee Cullen, and *The Book of American Negro Poetry* (1931), edited by James Weldon Johnson. Some of it, like Angelina Weld Grimké's love poems to another woman, remained unpublished until very recently. Thanks to Maureen Honey's anthology *Shadowed Dreams: Women's Poetry of the Harlem Renaissance* (1989), however, it is now possible to read women's poetry of the renaissance as a collective body of work in which recognized names, like Grimké and Alice Dunbar-Nelson, complement lesser-known writers like Clarissa Scott Delany and Marjorie Marshall. [21]

Along with Honey, critic Gloria T. Hull has done the most to resurrect this work from its obscurity and to defend it against the charge that it is "genteel," formally conservative, and excessively oriented toward white European literary traditions. Hull points out the ideological preeminence of poetry as a form during the modernist period generally and the Harlem Renaissance particularly, "based on its universality, accessibility for would-be writers, suitability for magazine publication, and classical heritage as the highest expression of cultured, lyric sensibility" (Hull, 13). Lyric poems about nature and love, Honey argues, served black women writers in many ways. Nature poetry drew on the rebellious energies of nineteenth-century romanticism, a valuable model because "the Romantics saw art and truth as connected, a viewpoint that echoed their own sense that the ills of modern life stemmed from a coarsening of the human spirit due to acquisitive, aggressive domination by a white ruling class." Love poetry, too, bore more than vapidly conventional meanings for black women; "a fundamental tenet of white supremacy was that Afro-Americans were not capable of fine, romantic feelings," a tenet implicitly refuted when black women wrote moving love poems (*Dreams*, 7, 20).

Georgia Douglas Johnson and Alice Dunbar-Nelson (1875–1935) were the elder mentors of the renaissance generation of black women poets. Wary of combining racial issues with poetry, Dunbar-Nelson wrote some of her best-known poems protesting other ills than racism; "I Sit and Sew" is the dramatic monologue of a woman stifled by the "pretty futile seam" she works on, conscious of "The panoply of war, the martial tread of men" outside her "homely thatch" (*Dreams*, 74). The poem's "impassioned commentary on the narrowness of culturally defined sexual roles" (Hull, 80) is clear, as is the connection it draws between those sex roles and militarism. In "The Proletariat Speaks" (*Dreams*, 75), Dunbar-Nelson challenges the period's stereotypical leftist image of the proletarian as a burly, half-naked industrial worker. Her proletarian is a woman, an office worker whose daily confinement is painfully at odds with her yearning for "beautiful things"—the consolations of art and the sensual pleasures of a middle-class dream-life. Like her poetry, Dunbar-Nelson's political activism encompassed many forms of oppression: as public speaker and writer of fiction and journalism as well as poetry, she worked for women's suffrage, in peace organizations, and in antilynching campaigns. [22]

Georgia Douglas Johnson's poems tended to be more formal, less drawn from folk traditions, than her plays. More so than Dunbar-Nelson, however, Johnson made a conscious decision to blend poetry with issues of race, and issues of race with those of gender. Looking back at her own work, Johnson wrote that after her first volume of poems, *The Heart of a Woman* (1918), was criticized for having "no feeling for the race," she then "wrote Bronze [1922]—it is entirely racial and one section deals entirely with motherhood—that motherhood that has as its basic note—black children born to the world's displeasure" (cited in Hull, 160). The woman who speaks in "Motherhood" tells her unborn child not to "knock at my heart, little one"; she cannot release the child into a world of "monster men" (*Dreams*, 64).

More retiring than Georgia Douglas Johnson, Angelina Weld Grimké (1880–1958) also lived in Washington, D.C. Her complex ancestry included the famous white abolitionist and feminist sisters Sarah M. Grimké and Angelina Grimké Weld; her father, a lawyer, married a white woman. Angelina Grimké's own strongest emotional bonds were with women, and many of her love poems to women remained unpublished in her lifetime despite her solid reputation as a poet and playwright (her play *Rachel* was staged by the NAACP of Washington in 1916). [23]

Grimké's lyrics venture further into modernist free imagistic forms than Dunbar-Nelson's or Johnson's. "A Mona Lisa," which Grimké did publish, can be read both as a poem about the painting and a love poem. "I should like to creep / Through the long brown grasses / That are your lashes," the speaker begins, but she fears the outcome may be drowning, leaving "only white bones / Wavering back and forth" in the beloved's eyes (*Dreams*, 147). Traditionally, the famous women of Western art are assumed to pose for (beckon to, or hide their secrets from) desiring male eyes. This poem imagines a different possibility, that the Mona Lisa's mysterious gaze invites another woman, but the poem's ending implies that this possibility is uncertain, perhaps threatening.

Grimké wrote little of what could be called "protest poetry"; poems like "The Black Finger" and "Tenebris" rely on natural imagery rather than discursive argument or human pathos for their effect. In "Tenebris," a tree's shadow "Against the white man's house" seems to "pluck" at its bricks by night (*Dreams*, 185). As Maureen Honey points out, this natural image bears a heavy freight of human history: "The portrait of a house built with blood-colored bricks evokes memories of the big house on a plantation maintained by the blood and sweat of slave labor" (*Dreams*, 12). The house's power seems virtually nonhuman, a part of nature, but it is nightly undermined by the tree's resistant dark shadow— an image that might also be taken for Grimké's own poetic strategies of concealment and indirection.

While Dunbar-Nelson, Johnson, and Grimké all remained at a certain distance from Harlem itself, a few woman poets of the renaissance did either live in Harlem or work more closely with projects identified with it. Gwendolyn Bennett (1901–81) lived in Washington, D.C., as a professor of art at Howard University (until she was fired in 1927 for marrying a student), but served at the same time as an assistant editor for the Harlem-based *Opportunity*; she was also a member of the small group that brought out *Fire!!* She dedicated her poem "To Usward," first published in *Crisis* in 1924, to Jessie Fauset in honor of *There Is Confusion*. "To Usward" begins with a racial imperative cast in a modernist image:

> Let us be still
> As ginger jars are still
> Upon a Chinese shelf.
> And let us be contained
> By entities of Self. . . .
> (*Dreams*, 104)

The poem's conclusion exuberantly imagines black identity as a sealed, spicy treasure about to be opened "With pungent thrusts of song"; Bennett's response to Fauset shows us a younger, more experimental black woman writer in friendly dialogue with her older, more conservative precursor.

Finally, Mae V. Cowdery (1909–53), one of the youngest women poets of the renaissance, made her career very much in the heart of the New York artistic scene. Born in Philadelphia, she came to New York, "frequented the cabarets of Harlem and Greenwich Village," and took on a conspicuously modernist persona: "A photograph of her published by *The Crisis* in 1927 as one of that year's prizewinners reveals a young woman of unusual beauty, style, and originality, with a bow tie, tailored jacket and short, slicked-down hair" (*Dreams*, 226). Like Angelina Weld Grimké, Cowdery loved women; unlike Grimké, she published lesbian love poetry (like "Farewell," about a lover's departure) during her lifetime.

Cowdery's poems speak with wit as well as passion. "A Brown Aesthete Speaks" (*Dreams*, 88–89) ironically traces the complicated dances of black and white culture in the 1920s. Her speaker goes from being "quite pleased with myself, / With my unkempt curls, unhealthy pores—myself" to learning about "Beauty" from Keats and Poe while "I fired your furnaces, / Served your parties, / Washed your dishes"; did I complain, she asks her white interlocutor, "when you required of me the sad songs of my fathers? / Or when your body lilted to the sway of new folk music?" Although it casts a sardonic light both on black ambitions to white European culture and white appropriations of black "primitive" culture, "A Brown Aesthete" is not nostalgic in the end for any supposedly pure, uncontaminated cultural identity. Alluding to Matthew Arnold's "Dover Beach," her speaker cries, "Oh friend, let's be kind to one another!"—for we are all creatures of cosmetics and artifice, without fixed natural identities, a modernist point that Cowdery's gender-crossing urban persona also made in life.

From Georgia Douglas Johnson's concern for black motherhood, to Mae V. Cowdery's urban black lesbian presence in the pages of *Crisis*: up close, the women writers of the Harlem Renaissance period defy easy generalizations about their writing and about women's place in early-twentieth-century African-American culture more broadly. Assessing their achievement fairly would require that we pay due attention to venturesome and unfamiliar figures like Mae Cowdery. It would also require us, however, to reconsider the criteria by which more conservative writers like Jessie Redmon Fauset have been found wanting, and to search out the historical relationships between such seemingly disparate women. An important "female support system," Maureen Honey argues, was "crucial" for these writers; when it "began to disintegrate toward the end of the decade" of the 1920s, its loss helped propel many of these writers into silence or isolation (*Dreams*, 31). Fittingly, it is a comparable network of women—writers like Toni Morrison and Alice Walker, critic and poet Gloria T. Hull, critics Deborah McDowell and Maureen Honey, among many others—that is pulling the women of the renaissance back into visibility again.

CHAPTER 11

Voices from the Margins: Autobiography, Political Fiction, and Political Poetry

Writers in the experimental modernist tradition often thought of themselves as reworking the relationship between art and life in ways unknown to nineteenth-century literature. This reworking, however, did not take one fixed form for all of experimental modernism; it was a diverse, lively project spanning many different kinds of literature, many different literary movements.

For novelists of consciousness like Dorothy Richardson and Virginia Woolf, this project took the form of trying to render a fluid reality perceived in the mind rather than a reality of fixed objects observed from the vantage point of a presumably neutral, also fixed, authority. Other novelists, seemingly more committed to the realism (and the possible poetry) of the object world, like Willa Cather, nevertheless decentered or found alternatives to nineteenth-century realism's favorite plot for women, the marriage plot. Radical experimentalists like Gertrude Stein and Mina Loy aspired to a language that would be a reality in itself rather than simply a picture, within agreed-upon conventions, of a reality already known.

The writers discussed in this chapter had other relationships to the great modernist project of reworking the boundaries between art and life.

Some of them were working-class or immigrant women whose realities may never have had expression in literature before. Most of them were reformers and political activists of one kind or another, committed to working on the world in literature, to be sure, but also in other ways.

We have already seen several instances of how the political commitments of modern women writers informed their work. To recall only a few examples, Virginia Woolf's feminist and pacifist essays share concerns with her novels; Edna St. Vincent Millay's late poetry encouraged the United States to enter World War II; Lady Gregory's plays fostered Irish nationalism; Susan Glaspell's chastised American political repression and xenophobia.

Most of these writers, however, approached politics from within a realm of writing securely identified as "literature." The writers I will look at in this chapter either wrote in genres, like autobiography, that are hard to characterize definitively as fact or fiction; or they blurred the boundaries between "literature" and other kinds of writing; or they openly challenged assessments of their work as "literature;" or they challenged standards of literary decorum that deny lyric poetry (especially by women) the right to address political topics.

Women activists and reformers who wrote their autobiographies described lives to which stereotypes of women's focus on romance were wholly inadequate. Early-twentieth-century autobiographers of working-class and immigrant experience, like those in Margaret Davies's Women's Co-operative Guild (Anzia Yezierska and Agnes Smedley among them), struggled to find form in writing for lives on the margins. Charlotte Perkins Gilman, also an important reformer-autobiographer, wrote short stories that amusingly refused to swaddle didactic intentions in layers of commentary, sentimentalism, or naturalistic incident along with utopian novels schematizing alternative societies. Josephine Herbst and Meridel Le Sueur moved back and forth between fiction and journalism, sometimes creatively combining the two.

Finally, Genevieve Taggard and Muriel Rukeyser wrote some of the early twentieth century's most successful political poetry. By establishing women's right to address political issues in poetry, they did as much as outrageous 1920s experimentalists like Edith Sitwell and Mina Loy to move twentieth-century women's poetry decisively away from the nineteenth-century stereotype of the sentimental domestic "poetess."

The late nineteenth and early twentieth centuries saw an upsurge of women's reform work and political work—in the area of women's rights, certainly, but also in education, antiwar activism, and projects aimed at relieving urban misery. In the early decades of the twentieth century, many of these women wrote their autobiographies. In England, Fabian socialist Beatrice Webb (1858–1943) published *My Apprenticeship* (1926), her account of how an upper-middle-class young woman came to investigate urban slums. Radical suffrage activist Emmeline Pankhurst (1858–1928) wrote *My Own Story* (1913) in the thick of women's struggle for the vote in England, explaining how a middle-class woman found it possible to contemplate committing acts of sabotage and going to jail for a cause. In the United States, Jane Addams (1860–1935) wrote of her *Twenty Years at Hull-House* (1912) and *The Second Twenty Years at Hull-House* (1930), explaining how a wealthy young woman had found herself impelled to found a settlement house in the slums of Chicago.

Women reformers who wrote their autobiographies faced the challenge of telling a woman's story not centered upon love and romance, and found different solutions. Beatrice Webb, for instance, wrote *My Apprenticeship* almost in the manner of an investigative report, embedding documents and official testimonies into her own narrative, breaking her task down to headings and subheadings—with only a few of them relating openly to personal life or feelings.

Webb announces at the beginning of *My Apprenticeship*, in fact, "I have neither the desire nor the intention of writing an autobiography" as traditionally understood. She hopes instead to "describe the craft of a social investigator as I have practiced it." As a sociologist, she recognizes that "the very subject-matter of my science is society; its main instrument is social intercourse; thus I can hardly leave out of the picture the experience I have gathered, not deliberately as a scientific worker, but casually as child, unmarried woman, wife and citizen."[1] She aims not at conveying the immediacy of her own feelings, but at understanding her own character as a product of its circumstances.

Webb is typical of many of the reformer-autobiographers in being a middle-class, even modestly wealthy woman, raised in a home that answered to upper-middle-class ideals of domesticity, assuming middle-class standards of human identity. Radical in many ways, these middle-class autobiographers still cannot speak for women who had to struggle harder for forms of identity that these autobiographers can take for granted.

The early twentieth century produced many important autobiographies and autobiographical novels written by women who were not born to the middle class. For working-class and immigrant women writers, the ability to write in one's native tongue, to have a small space of privacy in which to think and feel safe, even the right to call one's body one's own could not be taken for granted; they were hard-won.

In 1931 a volume appeared in England under an unusual set of auspices: *Life as We Have Known It*, a collection of autobiographical essays written by working-class women, edited by Margaret Llewelyn Davies, the noted socialist and founder of the Women's Co-operative Guild, prefaced with a long introductory letter by Virginia Woolf, one of England's foremost experimental modernists, and published by Virginia and Leonard Woolf's Hogarth Press. [2]

This conjunction of experimental modernism and working-class autobiography was unusual, but not altogether fortuitous, as Woolf's introductory letter suggests. Although Woolf herself was always uncomfortable and inefficient at organized political activity, she had been politically conscious and committed enough at one time to teach night classes for working women and men, and her husband, Leonard, was actively involved in socialist politics. [3] What she read in *Life as We Have Known It*, Woolf acknowledged, was alien to her in many ways. Whether it "is literature or not literature," she wrote, "I do not presume to say, but that it explains much and reveals much is certain. . . . These voices are beginning only now to emerge from silence into half articulate speech. These lives are still half hidden in profound obscurity" (xxxxi). As someone committed to extending the boundaries of "literature" in her own writing, as someone always fascinated by "lives of the obscure," Woolf had to recognize in the writings of working-class women an inchoate double of her own feminist modernism. [4]

The working-class lives in the Davies volume strike many themes common to other working-class women's autobiographies of the twentieth century, especially the matter of the interrelationships between money and sexuality, gender and class. Mrs. Layton, author of the longest memoir in the collection, recalls receiving (and rejecting) casual invitations to prostitution, invitations men took it for granted they could offer to women who were servants and out in public (26). Another author, Mrs. Scott, notes that her "first clear recollection is of the time when I was about three years of age, when we lived near a hollow where a little girl had been maltreated and killed by a gang of youths" (81): the sense of being unprotected in dangerously public spaces marks her sense of her own gender and class identity.

The autobiographies in *Life as We Have Known It* speak of empowerment, however, not just of victimization. Marriage for most of these narrators is not the secure harbor painted for middle-class women—not necessarily because husbands are brutal, but because they, too, are vulnerable to sickness, unemployment, and inadequate wages. Yet working-class social institutions like the mission hall (84) provide alternatives to the conservative Church of England; women's work, especially when professionalized, as in the case of midwifery, in which Mrs. Layton takes a certificate, can sometimes provide steady living; and the activities of the Women's Co-operative Guild itself foster women's self-respect and financial security as a group.

Taken together, the narratives in *Life as We Have Known It* challenge normatively middle-class standards of what constitutes a novelistic happy or sad ending and provide glimpses, both somber and sturdy, of lives and meanings constructed along different lines of meaning. And therein lies one kinship at least with the experimental modernism of Woolf and other, more privileged women writers.

Anzia Yezierska (1880?–1970) was born in Russian Poland; with her parents and siblings, she emigrated to the Jewish ghetto in New York's Lower East Side sometime in the last decade of the nineteenth century. Her autobiographical novel *Bread Givers* (first published in 1925) and her stories (many of them collected and still available in *The Open Cage*, 1979) recount her efforts to learn English and leave the ghetto, and her later struggles with the pains of assimilation into WASP American culture.

Bread Givers chronicles the rise and Americanization of Sara Smolinsky: her childhood of domestic and sweatshop work, her escape to college, her eventual middle-class success as a teacher, her happy engagement to the Gentile principal of the school at which she teaches. Unlike most of the working-class narratives of *Life as We Have Known It*, *Bread Givers* tries to conclude its own story of life on the margins with the pattern of a middle-class novelistic happy ending. The story of Sara's rise and engagement, however, is shadowed at every turn by her ambivalent conflict with her father and the culture he represents; and even at the novel's end, this conflict's resolution is far from clear.

A Talmudic scholar and holy man without fixed office in the community, Sara's father expects that his wife and daughters will support him in his all-important work: "Women had no brains for the study of God's Torah, but they could be the servants of men who studied the Torah."[5] He sees the women of his family as financial assets—bread givers—who owe it to him to take in boarders, bring home wages, and marry rich husbands to keep the houschold afloat. His contribution is the power of the word—reading and prayers for God, curses for enemies, and a story for his wife (who "licked up Father's every little word, like honey" [12]) when she is on the point of rebellion.

It is the power of the word, of course, that Yezierska herself and her heroine, Sara, eventually manage to win and turn into bread for themselves: Yezierska as a writer, Sara as a teacher. In order to attend night school and eventually college, Sara must fight not only her father's intransigent religious belief that "only through a man has a woman an existence" (137), but her father's very concrete reluctance to give up his stake in her as a financial asset he owns.

Sara's faith in the power of education and the word to secure upward mobility—a faith derived, as she herself acknowledges, from Horatio Alger–style stories in the Sunday papers (155)—links her at once to the dominant American culture and, ironically, back to the father she defies. Moreover, the father himself, Thomas Ferraro points out, is less disaffected from American life than his rhetoric claims: he uses his traditional authority to "manipulate [his] children's lives in the name of familial upward mobility," surely a dominant American value.[6]

These hidden resemblances come full circle at *Bread Givers*' end, when Sara asks her father (left uncared-for by the death of Sara's mother and the craven indifference of his second wife) to come live with her. He will consent, he says, only if she promises "to keep sacred all that is sacred to me"—to keep kosher and the sabbath, with all their domestic demands on women (295). Sara's husband-to-be gladly accepts the proposed arrangement, since he hopes to study Hebrew with the learned old man.

So once again, learning and the power of the word are to be passed from man to man, leaving women out. Even though she fulfills her individual ambitions and engages herself to a Gentile, Sara discovers what turns out to be true for the other, less dramatically assimilated Jewish women of her family: "reestablishing patriarchy produces in ethnic women the uncanny sensation of never having left their ghetto home" (Ferraro, 563).

Here the autobiographical element of *Bread Givers* ends, for Yezierska herself kept writing after college, left her first and second marriages, sold stories to magazines, and eventually went to Hollywood for a time as a screenwriter, fleeing family responsibilities.[7] She became celebrated in the 1920s as a voice of the other America, became obscure in the 1930s, and later wrote stories and another autobiographical novel, *Red Ribbon on a White Horse* (1950), eloquent about the difficulties of being celebrated as an "other" voice within a dominant culture. She could neither leave home completely nor return to it to recover her voice; what Yezierska had to write came from being between worlds, between homes, rather than in them.

Agnes Smedley (1892–1950) survived a childhood of brutal poverty in the American West to become an internationally known journalist and activist. Her interest in Asian movements of national liberation led her first into work on behalf of Indian nationalists fighting against British imperial rule, then into covering the Chinese Revolution from the viewpoint of the Red Army. Smedley published several volumes about her Chinese experience, but remains best known for her early autobiographical novel, *Daughter of Earth* (1929).[8]

Written in the aftermath of a severe nervous breakdown and a bout with psychoanalysis, *Daughter of Earth* combines an account of its first-person narrator's psychological and sexual development with her awakening political consciousness. Marie Rogers's first memory, she acknowledges, may be a dream: "My father was holding me close to his huge body in sleep" (8). Her early life centers around love and admiration for her father, combined with jealousy and fear of her stern, even abusive mother. Marie's alienation from her mother is compounded, early on, by her dim apprehension of her parents' sexual relationship, overheard in the tiny cabin the family shares. Regarding her mother as powerless and sullied, she turns to her father, even though he values sons over daughters (16–17).

It is not difficult to trace the influence of Smedley's own psychoanalysis upon her reconstruction of Marie's childhood, with its dual emphasis on the daughter's rivalrous love of the father and on what Freud called "the primal scene" of the child witnessing parental intercourse. The Freudian framework, however, does not become a straitjacket, for Smedley invests it with the specificity of the family's and Marie's sheer struggle to survive.

Marie's love and admiration for her father is eventually clouded by her growing awareness of his drinking and his failure to help provide for the family; her mother, her siblings, and Marie herself assume more and more of the burden. She observes that her aunt Helen can challenge the father's abusive dominance because she has work and money of her own. Marie's difficult relationship with her mother finally becomes an alliance when she defends her mother against her father, who is prepared to whip her with a rope (113–14). She remains determined not to live her mother's life, but realizes that handing over her destiny to a man like her father is not a way of escape; she resolves not to depend financially on men either in marriage or in less conventional relationships like those of her aunt Helen.

As Marie struggles to live out this resolve, Smedley points again and again to what recent feminist critics have described as the tangled interplay of gender and class. Sex in one way or another always goes with money: Marie is safe when doing prestigious work as a schoolteacher, but vulnerable to sexual assault when traveling as a sales representative for a magazine or working for male employers. Fathers and husbands prize virginity in daughters as passport to the supposed economic security of marriage; by working for money, Marie unintentionally puts herself into the vulnerable category of women who are rented, not bought once and for all.

In response to all these threats to her independence, Marie disowns sexuality entirely, concentrating instead on fighting her way to an education. She meets and marries a more privileged fellow student, but insists on retaining her financial equality and hopes that the marriage will remain a friendship. When she does become pregnant (twice), she finds an abortion with difficulty (one of the most scandalous parts of her story, to early-twentieth-century readers), and the marriage soon collapses.

Her husband and his sister, however, have introduced Marie to the world of socialist politics in the San Francisco Bay area. Dismayed by her friends' bent for idealizing the poor, Marie nevertheless finds socialism a way of giving her individual struggle a broader meaning. And when she meets Indian nationalists, she is doubly interested, attracted both to their political message and to the Indians as persons. Moving to New York, beginning her career as a journalist, and devoting herself to the Indian Independence movement, Marie finally comes to a place at which work and desire may intersect: "when knowledge and love become one, a force has been created that nothing can break" (265).

The intersection of work and desire, however, is anything but simple or happy. Many of the Indian men with whom Marie works are contemptuous of women; even the gentle Indian whom she marries cannot overcome his jealousy of her past.[9] Marie discovers what Smedley herself and many other leftist women of the early twentieth century would discover: that leftist and nationalist movements often lacked or were hostile to feminist concerns.

The entanglement of sex and politics in *Daughter of Earth* reaches a climax when Marie is sexually assaulted by an Indian friend (who later turns out to be a traitor to the nationalist movement), then arrested for sedition; the police threaten to reveal her sexual involvements with Indian men to the press. Marie goes to jail without cooperating, only to be released when World War I ends and spy hysteria abates. The episode, however, ends her marriage by discrediting her husband politically; and the novel ends with Marie despairing of both love and work.

Daughter of Earth begins by disclaiming any status as art: "What I have written," the narrator says, "is not a work of beauty, created that someone may spend an hour pleasantly. . . . It is the story of a life, written in desperation, in unhappiness" (7). Yet this defensive opening poses a dichotomy between beauty and truth, romance and knowledge, life and art, love and work, that the book itself painfully struggles to undo. Like her mother's "crazy-quilt," Smedley's life-art is an object of use, pieced together of worn materials, but something more as well: "the crazy-quilt held me for hours. It was an adventure" (8).

Toward the end of her long career, Charlotte Perkins Gilman (1860–1935), like many other turn-of-the-century reformers and writers, wrote her autobiography, *The Living of Charlotte Perkins Gilman* (1935). Gilman's reputation today rests less on her autobiography and nonfiction (although her 1898 *Women and Economics* is still read as a pioneering work of feminist theory) than on her short stories and utopian novels, many of which appeared in the *Forerunner*, a magazine Gilman wrote and produced herself from 1909 to 1916. Like later left-wing women writers of the 1920s, 1930s, and 1940s, Gilman believed that fiction could be a powerful force for social change.

"The Yellow Wallpaper" (1892), one of her earliest stories, is by far her most famous. Confined to an isolated bedroom for nervous illness, a young wife sees women in the room's patterned wallpaper and tears it down—to her husband's eventual shock—in an effort to free them. The story's ending is ambiguous, its atmosphere domestic gothic, its narrator, perhaps, unreliable. Yet Gilman's intentions, she later insisted, were simple: "It was not intended to drive people crazy, but to save people from being driven crazy, and it worked."[10]

Gilman's later stories tend to wear their intentions on their sleeves, far more so than "The Yellow Wallpaper." They cheerfully flout expectations that literature should be difficult or undidactic. The protagonists of "When I Was a Witch" and "If I Were a Man" (GR, 21–38) undergo exactly the transformations spelled out in the titles, with illuminating consequences. "Making a Change," "Turned," and "The Widow's Might" show how women manage to change unhappy lives, sometimes with the aid of other women (GR, 66–74, 87–106).

To see the problem, in these stories, is to have it solved. The appeal of the stories lies precisely in their optimism; they attempt to persuade readers of Gilman's own belief that feminist reforms (like shared child rearing and a single sexual standard) were in reach because they were basically in everyone's interest. In that very optimism, however, also lie the stories' limitations. As Ann J. Lane observes, stories like these "are splendid embodiments of [Gilman's] advice to those who feel trapped, for she offers a way out. But such a resolution necessitated creating problems that can be resolved by will, energy, and imagination, and so she avoided any situation which lacked that possibility."[11]

By locating their reforms in a clearly imaginary world, Gilman's utopian novels—chief among them Herland (written in 1915)—acknowledge the distance between life as it is and life as it might be. Herland examines men's resistance to a different sexual order by bringing three male explorers into a community composed entirely of women. Once brought in, they cannot leave until the community decides it is safe for them to do so (as usual in such fictions); meanwhile, therefore, Terry (the chauvinist), Jeff (the exponent of Southern chivalry), and Vandyck, the narrator (a sociologist, thus presumably self-conscious about his own social prejudices) learn about Herland—and eventually come to love three beautiful young Herlanders.

Much of Herland centers around the issues of sexuality provoked by the three men's courtships. Indeed, the novel virtually debates questions about women's and men's sexuality that were raging around 1915 (in the context of the new Freudian psychology and the beginnings of a sexual revolution): Do women have any independent sexual drive of their own? Is male sexuality naturally different from women's? If so, should we seek to change either men's or women's sexuality in order to create happier (hetero)sexual relationships?

Herland's answers to these vexing questions are teasingly equivocal. Before the men's arrival, the sexuality of the Herlanders seems to have been subsumed in childbearing (which occurs in the absence of men). A Herlander about to have a child experiences "a period of utter exaltation"; if she thinks it socially best not to have a child at this time, she can, through self-discipline, "voluntarily defer it."[12] Herlanders thus enjoy one of the great ideals of nineteenth-century feminists: "voluntary motherhood"—childbearing at the mother's will rather than as an unwanted consequence of male sexual demands.

Even in Herland, however, there are hints that motherhood does not completely subsume women's sexual interests. Musing on his own courtship of a Herlander, Vandyck claims that "There was no sex-feeling to appeal to, or practically none. Two thousand years' disuse had left very little of the instinct; also we must remember that those who had at times manifested it as atavistic exception were often, by that very fact, denied motherhood" (92).

Reading between Vandyck's lines, we learn that some Herlanders do seem to experience a sexual desire outside of maternity (and one seen as disqualifying them for maternity). Gilman cannot quite paint women as naturally asexual, even in the absence of men. (The possibility of lesbian sexuality, a newly charged social topic in 1915, haunts *Herland*; how do Herland's "atavistic exceptions" express their desire without men?) And the novel's outcome would seem to confirm Vandyck's belief in the women's natural, if "long-forgotten," (hetero)sexual feeling: each of the three explorers successfully courts his chosen Herlander.

Yet all is still not well. The couples misunderstand one another's expectations about sexuality, and ultimately Terry attempts to rape his wife. Herland being well-ordered, and Herlanders strong, he does not succeed; but the incident points up the lack of common ground between Terry's conception of men's "natural" sexual needs and the Herlander's conception of sex's "natural" purpose, reproduction. Vandyck finds his own male sexuality more malleable, the attractions of egalitarian friendship more compelling, than he would have expected. Even Vandyck, however, is not fully satisfied with the bargain so far. At the novel's end, as the couples are set to return to our world, it remains unclear what sexual balance will finally be struck between them.

Gilman's representation of female sexuality in *Herland* seems historically poised between nineteenth-century ideals of asexual, maternal womanhood and emerging twentieth-century ideals of women as equal companions to men in every realm, including the sexual. The question of female sexuality profoundly troubles *Herland*, and rules out the kinds of quick resolutions Gilman favored in her short stories. Yet *Herland*'s very contradictions on this subject make it fascinating reading; like most good utopias, it challenges readers to participate in an ongoing thought experiment about issues that are not settled.

✻   ✻   ✻

Josephine Herbst (1892–1969) was one of many American writers and radicals of the first half of the century who came from the Midwest. Like many of them, she left the Midwest as soon as she could, leaving her native Sioux City, Iowa, to earn a bachelor's degree in English at the University of California at Berkeley, then moving to New York City, then joining the great American expatriation to Europe—first to Berlin, where postwar hyperinflation made life very cheap for Americans with dollars (as Djuna Barnes and Agnes Smedley also discovered), then on to Paris. She returned to the United States in 1924, in time to be at her mother's deathbed in Sioux City. Afterward she settled into a house in Buck's County, Pennsylvania. Buck's County would be the home from which Herbst later traveled again to Europe, covering developments in the Spanish Civil War, and around the United States, where she wrote about labor struggles during the Depression.[13]

Both Herbst's early wanderings and her later journalism helped shape her major fictional achievement of the 1930s, the trilogy comprising *Pity Is Not Enough* (1933), *The Executioner Waits* (1934), and *Rope of Gold* (1939). All three volumes are loosely woven historical novels, or family sagas, told in what seem almost a set of related short stories rather than a single continuous narrative. (Story cycles—like Joyce's *Dubliners*, Katherine Mansfield's New Zealand stories, and Sherwood Anderson's *Winesburg, Ohio*—had already come by the 1920s to present a serious twentieth-century challenge to the traditionally unified novel.) Ranging from the Civil War up to the present, from Seattle to Buck's County to rural Iowa and Oregon, the trilogy chronicles the shifting fortunes of the Trexler-Wendel family.

The Executioner Waits pays special attention to two of the Wendel daughters, Victoria and Rosamund, tracing their personal lives against the historical background of the United States late in World War I. Rosamund marries a soldier and moves to Seattle after he is shipped off to France. Impatient with small-town life, Victoria joins her there; like many other young people during the wartime labor scarcity, they hope to find good work but soon find themselves caught up in a city divided by the great Seattle general strike.

Herbst's ear for her characters' dialogue (both internal and external) and her ability to evoke the vivid daily minutiae of social turmoil (Victoria and Rosamund's landlady, fearing the worst in the strike, fills up every last container in her boardinghouse with water) make *The Executioner Waits* gripping but not simple reading. The book requires its readers to stitch together a comprehensive picture of a nation from the juxtaposed stories of the members of a single family. Moreover, Herbst interleaves her chronicle of the years 1918–29 (the book ends in the first months of the Depression) with glimpses of the Depression-era struggles to follow. One such interlude, for instance, set on an "Iowa Farm, 1932," shows a group of farmers gathering to protest and, they hope, head off foreclosure on a fellow farmer's mortgage.[14]

Herbst died before she could see scenes like this one enacted again in Iowa, some fifty years after *The Executioner Waits*, but she probably would not have been surprised by them. Her innovative fictional technique of chronicle, juxtaposition, and interpolation demands, after all, that readers judge the present by the past and take responsibility for the future lying implicit in the present.

The life and work of the journalist, activist, and fiction writer Meridel Le Sueur (b. 1900) has centered upon her native Midwest. Born in Iowa, she spent her childhood in Texas, Oklahoma, and Kansas; moved around the country's great cities—Chicago, New York, San Francisco, Los Angeles—in her late teens and twenties, experimenting with acting and eking out a living; and in 1929 settled near her family in Minnesota, where she would observe and write about the strikes, breadlines, and suffering that made up the texture of everyday life in the Depression.

Le Sueur's first published story was "Persephone" (1927) an adaptation of the ancient fertility myth to a modern Midwestern setting. Mother-child relationships and themes of fertility figure in other stories Le Sueur wrote in the 1920s and 1930s; among the most successful of them is "Annunciation," the title work in her first collection of short stories, published in 1935. Narrated by a young pregnant woman, "Annunciation" contrasts the narrator's delight in her pregnancy with the Depression's surrounding despair. Unable to seek work herself any longer, the narrator waits day after day in a boardinghouse room while the child's father, Karl, goes out in search of work and food. If he finds work, he comes home, often drunk. If not, "he does not come back at night," and the narrator goes "out on the street walking to forget how hungry I am."[15] During the day, the narrator meditates upon the splendid pear tree outside her room's porch, linking its fertility to her own.

"Annunciation" hints that the narrator's pregnancy prompts both a nascent social consciousness, a heightened awareness of other people ("I have been sitting here and it seems as if the wooden houses around me had become husks that suddenly as I watched began to swarm with livening seed" [129]), and the impulse to write ("There is something I want to say, something I want to make clear for myself and others" [124]). Le Sueur would later make these connections between maternity and social consciousness explicit in her novel *The Girl* (not published until 1978, but written mostly in the 1930s and 1940s), where "the memory of maternity . . . is linked to history and class consciousness for women."[16]

As in the career of Josephine Herbst, Le Sueur's journalism and her fiction informed one another. She wrote many pieces in the 1930s that, like Dorothy Parker's "Soldiers of the Republic," hovered on the boundary between journalism and fiction without being in any way false to facts. First-person, participatory articles like "Women on the Breadlines" and "Women Are Hungry" (*Ripening*, 137–57) brought home women's neglected plight in the Depression and are still informative and moving today, given the tendency of our cultural memory to envision only men on the breadlines, only male breadwinners struggling to bring food to families.

Like many other left-wing writers of the 1930s, Le Sueur would become all but unknown to literary history after World War II and the onset of McCarthyism. Yet she continued to write and is still writing, amid a revival of interest in her work spurred by feminist criticism and the revival of historicism in literary studies.

Of all forms of literature, poetry is often thought to keep the greatest distance from everyday life; it is seldom seen as a particularly likely vehicle for social criticism or protest. Our resistance to thinking of poetry as political (I can speak, I suspect, for many readers trained in American schools up through the 1970s) is in part a legacy of the New Criticism's powerful interpretations of poetry. The New Criticism, which gained popularity among academic literary critics during the 1940s and 1950s, helped reinforce ideas about poets and poetry that had been cultural commonplaces to some extent before: that poetry stood apart from the conflicts of the world and made beautiful compensation for them, that it treated universal emotions or tensions of human life rather than particular historical struggles, that it unified through metaphoric language what could not be unified on the level of day-to-day existence.[17]

The New Criticism's rise in the 1940s and 1950s, especially in the United States, helped obscure an important body of poetry from the 1920s and 1930s that did not conform to New Critical prescriptions. Our "cultural memory," as Cary Nelson argues, actively repressed the political, activist, in some cases working-class poetry written by many American writers before and during World War II. Some women whom we tend to think of primarily as love-poets—like Edna St. Vincent Millay—also, as we have seen, wrote poetry about the Sacco and Vanzetti case, poverty, fascism, and war. Others, like Genevieve Taggard and Muriel Rukeyser, made politics in one form or another the consistent focus of their best work.

Genevieve Taggard (1894–1948) was born in rural Washington state but was raised in Hawaii by her missionary parents. When the family returned to Washington, Taggard was overwhelmed by the grimness of impoverished rural life in a harsh climate.[18] She escaped to the University of California at Berkeley in 1914, and there—in common with Agnes Smedley and Josephine Herbst—began to interest herself in radical politics. In the 1920s she edited the journals *Freeman* and the *Measure*, as well as a volume of radical verse collected from left-wing magazines. She did much of her writing in the 1930s from Vermont, where she had bought a farm; the tension between the countryside's beauty and the lives lived there energized some of her finest poems.

"Up State—Depression Summer" (CWU, 50–53) tells the fate of a farm and its family, "Yankee as cider." The cloud over the farm looms in summer ("June was sinister sweet. Can you eat wild flowers?") and seizes on the family's daughter: "The trouble veered / And found a body small, for spring infection, / White as the May, slim shoulders and naked ear / Open for poison." The lyric description of the girl echoes *Hamlet* (whose father dies of poison in the ear), only to fall into harsh colloquialism: "Suddenly the kid was sick." The parents go about their business, unable to afford medicine, while "the kid died as slowly as she could." Her death locks the parents in separate grief and foretells the poem's harshly compressed ending: "They sold the calf. That fall the bank took over."

"Up State—Depression Summer" makes its point without overt commentary by the narrator, but Taggard could also be effective in poems attempting a more direct prophetic voice, like her "Night Letter to Walt Whitman." Even her most didactic, direct poems seldom lack wit and surprise. "Feeding the Children" ends with a plain call to "Vote the strike," but begins with the sardonic observation that "Women are conservative. That is / They want life to go on . . ." (CWU, 54). Directed both at "apolitical" women themselves and at the conservative male authorities who bask in the cliché of women's conservatism, Taggard's poem encourages women to see activism as the clear extension of their own traditional roles.

As "Feeding the Children" suggests, Taggard both embraced her identity as a woman writer and sought to divorce it from stereotypical ideas of women and women poets particularly. She later wrote that many of her poems were "about the experiences of women," but that she had "refused to write out of a decorative impulse because I conceive it to be the dead-end of much feminine talent. A kind of literary needlework."[19] Taggard admired and wrote about a New England recluse, Emily Dickinson, who sometimes conceived of her own poetry as a kind of needlework, but she insisted on her own right as a woman to the public voice of a Whitman as well.[20]

Muriel Rukeyser (1913–80) won the Yale Younger Poets Award for her first collection of poems, *Theory of Flight* (1935). Like Genevieve Taggard, Rukeyser laid claim early on to a Whitman-sized, public voice. The first poem in *Theory of Flight*, "Poem out of Childhood," recalls Whitman's "Out of the Cradle Endlessly Rocking," with its account of the roots of the poet's vocation in childhood.[21]

Where Whitman in "Out of the Cradle" learned of love and death alone by the seashore, however, Rukeyser's recollections are insistently social, beginning with memories of seeing a syphilitic woman at a concert (3). "Not Sappho, Sacco. / Rebellion pioneered among our lives," she says, rejecting the Greek poetess of tradition for the executed anarchist, but not rejecting the past wholesale: "Organize the full results of that rich past / open the windows" (5).

The long title poem of *Theory of Flight*, critic Louise Kertesz points out, deserves comparison to Hart Crane's epic poem of America, *The Bridge*. Like *The Bridge*, "Theory of Flight" uses "a technological achievement, the airplane, to symbolize the successes and possibilities of American civilization" (Kertesz, 1). "The Gyroscope," the second section of "Theory of Flight," sees in technology an image of human "desire, and of its worth. . . . / Power electric-clean, gravitating outward at all points, / moving in savage fire," rather than limited to the private contact of two sexual human bodies (23). Rukeyser sets this technological hymn to desire, however, against a bitterly realistic picture of a mining town down on its luck (30–31). Drawing on experimental modernist techniques of collage and juxtaposition, Rukeyser breaks down the barriers between public and private forms of life, between lyricism and social realism.

Rukeyser's next volume, *U.S. 1* (named after the highway that runs down the east coast of the United States, from Maine to Florida) began with another long poem or sequence of poems, "The Book of the Dead." More realistic in its concerns but no less ambitious than "Theory of

Flight," "The Book of the Dead" assembles a collage of stock quotations, fictional testimony, letters, and doctors' reports to "reflect on and amplify the body of facts at its core: the cynical destruction of workers' lives to maximize profit in constructing a 1930s tunnel in West Virginia" (Nelson, 112). The poem questions the classic American myth of innocence taking to the open road, "fanatic cruel legend at our back and / speeding ahead the red and open west" (105), but ends by affirming it in a revised form, as "desire, field, beginning. Name and road, / communication to these many men, / as epiloque, seeds of unending love."

Muriel Rukeyser's contributions to American poetry, and especially to the modernist long poem or poetic sequence, have been neglected by critics for many years. Writing in 1951, fellow poet Louise Bogan rejected Rukeyser's ambitiously political poetry by calling it "a deflated Whitmanian rhetoric"; Rukeyser, in her opinion, was "the one woman poet of her generation to put on sibyl's robes, nowadays truly threadbare."[22]

In the 1950s heyday of post–World War II political quietism and conformism, Bogan may well have had her reasons to doubt the viability of prophetic political poetry—especially as written by women. In the aftermath of the 1960s, the rise of the second feminist movement, and the renewed American interest in historical literary studies, Rukeyser's work, along with that of other women discussed in this chapter, has begun to assume new importance. Rukeyser herself lived to see her work included in pioneering feminist anthologies of poetry (Kertesz, 2). She must have recognized in such feminist projects the fulfillment of her own imperative from the 1930s, demanding that we "Organize the full results of that rich past."

CHAPTER
12

Conclusion: Modernism
beyond the Ending

Endings, as Rachel Blau DuPlessis argues in her study of twentieth-century women writers, are difficult places. "Any resolution" to a story, DuPlessis finds, "can have traces of the conflicting materials that have been processed within it. It is where subtexts and repressed discourses can throw up one last flare of meaning; it is where the author may side-step and displace attention from the materials that a work has made available" (*Writing beyond the Ending*, 3). Where nineteenth-century writers most frequently contained the conflicts explored by their plots in endings of marriage or death, twentieth-century women writers, DuPlessis argues, often looked for ways of "writing beyond" those endings—although this is not a goal that can be achieved in any simple or final way.

What DuPlessis argues of fictional narratives applies to critical studies of literature as well. Like novels, critical histories of literature and literary movements have conventions that shape their beginnings, middles, and endings. Sometimes—as with a book in a critical series, like this one—these conventions are quite strict; but whether their conventions are specifically spelled out or informally understood, works of criticism, like novels, tend to highlight what does fit their conventions of conclusion, and to shift attention away from what does not. Thus endings come to seem realistic, natural, and inevitable in some respects, in criticism as in novels.

There are alternatives, in criticism as in novels. Remembering Virginia Woolf's *To the Lighthouse* and its doubled ending—with Cam, James, and their father arriving at the lighthouse on the one hand, and Lily Briscoe, alone, trying to finish her painting on the other—my conclusion will tell a double story about women's modernism and its endings. I hope this strategy will make it plain that critical endings are matters of human choice, desire, design, and belief, rather than natural facts; and, further, that it will suggest how and why many critics of early-twentieth-century women's writing today are revising their stories about the endings of women's modernism.

One important story about the end of modernism might begin this way: In 1945, after World War II finally ended, the world wanted nothing so much as to restore its sense of order, stability, and safety. In England and the United States particularly, men came back from the theaters of war looking for a job, a house, a wife, children—all the ordinary things denied them during the war years, and pinched for long years before that, during the Great Depression. Women who had joined the work force during the war left it, whether voluntarily or otherwise. Postwar propaganda reversed wartime messages, assuring women that their only natural place was in the home; employers followed up propaganda with dismissal notices to those women who did not want to vacate high-paying jobs for returning soldiers. Wartime assembly lines converted to peacetime production, especially in the United States, which had escaped large-scale bombing and devastation during the war. New suburbs mushroomed, providing housing for (it was always assumed) nuclear families and their new washing machines, toasters, and automobiles.

International politics realigned themselves in the new configurations of the Cold War. The Soviet Union, temporarily an ally during the fight to throw back Hitler, became the enemy when it annexed its small bordering countries, overrun on the Red Army's way to Berlin. Internally, England and especially the United States responded with vociferous repression of enemies of all kinds.

Many writers and intellectuals in England and the United States had already abandoned the Soviet Union, the Communist party, and socialist politics during the late 1930s and early 1940s—out of disillusionment with the Soviet Union's ambiguous role in the Spanish Civil War, or out of moral revulsion for what became known of Stalin's purges and executions at home. Government agents in England and the United States shadowed Communists, former Communists, and suspected Communist sympathizers. In the United States, Joseph McCarthy launched his notorious witch-hunt after Communists in government and public life. Many well-known writers—among them women like Lillian Hellman, Meridel Le Sueur, and Josephine Herbst—either were summoned to testify before congressional committees on their political affiliations, or were put under surveillance of some kind, or simply found themselves less and less able to publish and make a living.

It is less well known today that McCarthy also targeted homosexuals in public life, as did some local authorities ambitious of his distinction. McCarthy's vision of postwar American uniformity seamlessly embraced sexual as well as ideological conformity. The suburban house, capitalism's great answer to the Soviet Union, demanded that couples march into it two by two with their separate roles clearly defined. Like Cam and James's voyage to the lighthouse, the great postwar voyage home in the late 1940s and early 1950s was a trip that segregated women and men into two distinct forms of identity.

Literature retreated, at least in this version of modernism's end, from radical public purposes and large, ambitiously experimental forms. In American women's poetry, for example, Louise Bogan's tightly crafted lyrics of personal experience were better received than Muriel Rukeyser's oracular political poetry. The situation for many surviving left-wing modernist writers and critics is suggested by the 1950 suicide of F. O. Matthiessen, the critic and writer, who left a note saying that "as a Christian and a Socialist, believing in international peace, I find myself terribly oppressed by the present tensions."[1] He could have added that the times were hostile to his homosexuality as well as to his politics. Rukeyser wrote a moving elegy for Matthiessen in which she observed that both the world's violence and its hope were denied by the authorities "Who tried to guard us from suicide and life" (CP, 406).

The literary modernism of the years 1910–45 was fast receding into history during the postwar decade—meaning not that it was being forgotten, but that it was being ordered, reordered, cataloged, and explained. Literary critics call this process "canonization": the struggle to arrive at a sense of a period's great authors and at final versions of their great texts, to assemble anthologies of great writers, to incorporate them into textbooks. Whatever its merits or practical necessity, canonization always changes what it touches. Arriving at a canon of a modernist writer's work might mean, for example, taking a poem out of the little magazine in which it first appeared, surrounded perhaps by artwork, essays, and topical journalism; footnoting the poem's mythological or literary references; and finally placing the poem in an anthology that might well omit the date and place of its original publication. Is this now the same modernist poem?

When modernism began to be canonized in the 1940s, 1950s, and 1960s, modernism changed. As Sandra Gilbert and Susan Gubar have argued (in *No Man's Land*), along with Cary Nelson (in *Repression and Recovery*) and other recent critics, modernism tended to be shorn of its historical and political contexts, or seen only as a retreat from those contexts into a purely formal world of artistic freedom and experimentation.

As the modernist canon contracted into recognizable shape during the postwar years, it included fewer and fewer women and African-American writers, and made less and less connection with the broader social movements of its time. The politics of several of the writers considered most central to the canon, in fact, came to be seen as matters for hushed apology: William Butler Yeats was a fascist sympathizer in his later years, and Ezra Pound had actually broadcast fascist propaganda during the war. Moreover, in the absence of organized feminist movements after World War II, issues of gender and sexuality were often not seen as matters of genuine political or intellectual consequence; as a result, what women modernists (and men as well, for that matter) had had to say about these burning social issues became invisible or trivialized.

Movements within the theory of literary criticism helped shape not only what was included in the evolving modernist canon, but how what was included might be read and interpreted. By focusing upon the literary work as a self-contained and unchanging aesthetic object, the New Criticism of the 1940s and 1950s did its best to sever the modernist achievements of writers like Yeats and Pound from particular social conflicts, seeing them instead as resolutions of timelessly universal human tensions, without actionable consequences in any world apart from the literary work. Like the united front of the suburban house, which rested upon the supposedly balanced dualism of husband and wife, the canonical modernist poem in the eye of the New Criticism depended upon a balanced dualism of opposing forces for its controlled, dynamic unity.

This is one possible story of modernism's ending, but like all endings, it excludes some things that do not fit. Not everyone was happy to go back to the suburban house after World War II; for black Americans particularly, the years following the war were the cradle of a new civil rights movement, as the return of black soldiers once more underscored the contradiction between black Americans' commitment to their country and their country's commitment to them. In the literary world, not every writer was happy to write to New Critical criteria, or to accept her or his exclusion from the evolving modernist canon; not every critic forgot about women writers, or chastised writers who continued to work in ambitious or politicized forms. Moreover, this story is now being actively rewritten by feminist scholars who owe their existence to the very real cracks in the postwar happy ending.

Postwar uniformity was partly illusory, and in any case could not completely preclude questions about women and women's roles. Simone de Beauvoir's pioneering postwar feminist work, *The Second Sex*, was translated into English in 1952. Her appropriation of existentialist philosophy to a critical analysis of woman's situation as the "other" of male-dominated culture (the defective mirror of man, who unlike her can claim to be the universal human being) gave a voice to women's discontent with their service roles in the nuclear household, and would provide philosophical underpinnings for a renascent feminist movement in the 1960s—the movement that, in turn, helped impel feminist literary criticism into the academy.

Feminist literary criticism has evolved through certain stages, each with its own particular implications for the way we look at literary modernism. The first stage, inaugurated by de Beauvoir in *The Second Sex* and developed at length in Kate Millett's *Sexual Politics* (1970), looked at images of women in literature authored by men—including influential male modernist writers like D. H. Lawrence and James Joyce. Feminist critics argued that these characters did not represent a universal truth about women, but rather men's projections of what they desired or feared in women.[2]

Feminist literary criticism's next project was to find and reevaluate the work of women writers who had been taken seriously in their own time, but whose work had since been relegated to the margins of the canon or left out entirely. Feminist critics advertised the fact, for instance, that H. D. had written long poems about war and civilization, not just short poems about flowers and trees. Organizations like the Virago Press in London began reissuing some of the many, many novels published by British women earlier in the century. Shared concerns among women writers emerged into visibility as more women were read, and read next to one another rather than as the one woman in a group of male writers. Women's writing, feminist critics began to argue, constituted a "women's literary tradition," a meaningful grouping with its own history. Like Lily Briscoe at the end of *To the Lighthouse*, feminist critics stood in front of a blank canvas and struggled to bring to life a picture of the missing foremother, or foremothers, of literary history: women as they represented themselves, not as they were represented by men's fears and desires.[3]

The best new work on women and modernism tends to combine the aims of earlier feminist criticism. Like Gilbert and Gubar in *No Man's Land*, it sees early-twentieth-century writers of both sexes as engaged in struggles over images of women—and of men. It seeks to recover and appreciate women writers in their particular historical contexts and to understand better the relationships among them, contexts and relationships illuminated in works like Shari Benstock's *Women of the Left Bank*. While studying women writers as a group, however, it remembers that not all women of the early twentieth century wrote alike. Charlotte Nekola and Paula Rabinowitz's *Writing Red* and Cary Nelson's *Repression and Recovery* remind us that the identities of modern women writers were not shaped by gender alone, but by different race, class, political, and artistic allegiances.[4]

Most impressively of all, black feminist critics have assembled a large and growing body of work on the modernist renaissance of black women's writing and its relationship to the efflorescence of black women's writing later on in the century. If readers and critics of women's modernism hope to "organize the full results of that rich past" (to borrow Muriel Rukeyser's words a last time), they will read beyond the ending of this book and into the rich history of black women and twentieth-century literature.

Chronology

1900	*Die Traumdeutung (The Interpretation of Dreams)*, by Sigmund Freud.
1901	Queen Victoria of England dies; Edward VII succeeds to the throne.
1902	Carrie Chapman Catt, American feminist, organizes the International Suffrage Alliance. Lady Augusta Gregory, in collaboration with William Butler Yeats, founds the Irish National Theatre in Dublin.
1902–1904	Pauline Hopkins edits the *Colored American Magazine*.
1903	National Women's Trade Union League founded in the United States. Emmeline Pankhurst and her daughters found the radical suffrage organization, the Women's Social and Political Union, in Manchester, England. *The Souls of Black Folk*, by W. E. B. Du Bois, argues that "the problem of the twentieth century is the problem of the color-line."
1905	*The House of Mirth*, by Edith Wharton.
1907	Cubist exhibition in Paris. *Sonnets to Duse*, by Sara Teasdale.
1909	National Association for the Advancement of Colored People (NAACP) founded in New York City. *Three Lives*, by Gertrude Stein. Premiere of *Chains*, by Elizabeth Baker.
1909–1912	Years of labor unrest in Great Britain and the United States, including major strikes by working women.
1910	Death of Edward VII; George V succeeds to the throne. Post-Impressionist exhibition in London introduces Cézanne and other modern painters to England.
1911	The Triangle fire in New York City kills 146 women workers in a garment sweatshop, leading to a Senate investigation of working conditions for women and children. *Ethan Frome*, by Edith Wharton.

1913   Paris opening of Stravinsky's *Le Sacre du printemps (The Rite of Spring)*, choreographed by Nijinsky; near-riot in audience. Armory exhibition brings modernist painting to New York and other American cities; also publicizes Gertrude Stein, who lends her paintings to the show and whose work critics link to cubism. *O, Pioneers!* by Willa Cather.

1913–1914   Years of peak activity in campaign for women's suffrage in England; demonstrations, vandalism, and civil disobedience lead to imprisonment of more than 1,000 suffragettes.

1914   World War I begins, drawing many English women into work as nurses, and in war production, ambulance corps, and war relief efforts. Crisis in Ireland and England over Irish Home Rule; Irish nationalists favor, Protestants in Northern Ireland oppose establishing Irish parliament. *Tender Buttons*, by Gertrude Stein.

1915   Women's Peace Party organized in Washington, D.C., calling for the abolition of war. First class of young women graduates from Daytona School for Girls (later Bethune-Cookman College), founded by Mary McLeod Bethune, noted black educator. Margaret Sanger and Emma Goldman are jailed in the United States for distributing information on contraceptives. *The Voyage Out*, by Virginia Woolf. *Pointed Roofs* (part 1 of *Pilgrimage*), by Dorothy Richardson. *The Song of the Lark*, by Willa Cather.

1916   Jane Addams founds the Women's International League for Peace and Freedom in Zurich. *Sea Garden*, by H. D.

1916–1921   Edith Sitwell edits *Wheels*.

1917   Russian Revolution brings Bolsheviks to power. The United States enters the war. Worst race riot in American history, in East St. Louis, Illinois, burns six thousand black inhabitants out of their homes. *Renascence and Other Poems*, by Edna St. Vincent Millay.

1918   Truce on the battlefields. England grants the vote to women over thirty. *The Return of the Soldier*, by Rebecca West. *My Ántonia*, by Willa Cather.

1918–1919   American and Allied troops intervene unsuccessfully in Russian civil war; Western governments fear spread of Communist revolution. Deadly influenza epidemic in Europe and the United States.

1919   Treaty of Versailles formally ends the war; total military casualties come to some seven million dead. In the United States, "red raids" on Communists, Socialists, and labor activists lead to deportation of 249, including Emma Goldman. Race riots break out in Washington, D.C., Chicago, and other cities. Walter Gropius founds the Bauhaus, modernist school of architecture and art. *Mary Olivier: A Life*, by May Sinclair.

1919–1926   Jessie Redmon Fauset serves as literary editor of the *Crisis*, magazine of the NAACP.

1920   League of Nations founded. Oxford University grants degrees to women for the first time. The Nineteenth Amendment is ratified; American women gain the right to vote. *The Age of Innocence*, by Edith Wharton. *A Few Figs from Thistles*, by Edna St. Vincent Millay.

1921   Marie Stopes opens England's first birth control clinic, in London. *Poems*, by Marianne Moore. *Nets to Catch the Wind*, by Elinor Wylie. *Bee Time Vine*, by Gertrude Stein. *The Verge*, by Susan Glaspell, opens in production by the Provincetown Players.

1922   Mussolini and the Fascist party come to power in Italy.

1923   Equal Rights Amendment introduced for the first time to the U.S. Congress. Yale University awards Edith Wharton the honorary degree of Doctor of Letters. *A Lost Lady*, by Willa Cather. *Lunar Baedeker & Time-tables*, by Mina Loy. First performance of *Facade*, by Edith Sitwell, with music by William Walton.

1924   *Mrs. Dalloway*, by Virginia Woolf. *There Is Confusion*, by Jessie Redmon Fauset. *Observations*, by Marianne Moore, wins the Dial Award.

1925   *Barren Ground*, by Ellen Glasgow. *Bread Givers*, by Anzia Yezierska. "Einige psychische Fogen des anatomischen Geschlechts-unterschieds" ("Some Psychical Consequences of the Anatomical Distinction between the Sexes"), by Sigmund Freud.

1925–1929   Marianne Moore edits the *Dial*.

1926   British Imperial Conference redefines British Empire as the British Commonwealth of Nations, granting more rights of self-government to some former colonies. "Seven College Conference" (soon known as the Seven Sisters) is organized, incorporating the seven major women's liberal arts colleges in the United States. First and only issue of *Fire!!* appears in November, with contributions from Zora Neale Hurston and Gwendolyn Bennett.

1927   Sacco and Vanzetti executed in United States. *To the Lighthouse*, by Virginia Woolf. *Death Comes for the Archbishop*, by Willa Cather. *Plumes*, by Georgia Douglas Johnson, awarded first place in *Opportunity* playwriting competition. *Fool's Errand*, by Eulalie Spence, wins the Samuel French prize in the David Belasco Little Theatre Tournament. *Caroling Dusk*, anthology edited by Countee Cullen, includes work by several women poets of the Harlem Renaissance.

1928   British government extends suffrage to women between 21 and 30 years of age, equalizing men's and women's voting rights. *The Well of Loneliness*, by Radclyffe Hall; three months later seized and tried for obscenity in Britain.

1929   England's first Labour Prime Minister, Ramsay Macdonald, forms a government. *A Room of One's Own*, by Virginia Woolf. *Plum Bun*, by Jessie Redmon Fauset. *Daughter of Earth*, by Agnes Smedley.

1929–1939   U.S. stock market crashes in October 1929. Economic depression spreads worldwide, sponsoring fascism on the European continent and constricting women's economic opportunities. Conditions are worst in the United States and Germany, already ravaged by postwar inflation and heavily dependent on American capital. In Germany, Nazism tells women that their proper place is in the home; in the United States, widespread unemployment fosters disapproval of women taking more desirable and better-paying "men's work."

1930   Association of Southern Women for the Prevention of Lynching founded in Atlanta. *After Leaving Mr. Mackenzie*, by Jean Rhys. *Flowering Judas*, by Katherine Anne Porter.

1931   Scottsboro Case, in which eight black men are sentenced to death for raping a white woman, raises outcry against "legalized lynching." *All Passion Spent*, by Vita Sackville-West.

1932   Franklin D. Roosevelt elected to U.S. presidency, promising activist approach to alleviating the country's economic misery.

1933   Adolf Hitler comes to power in Germany; many Jews, writers, and intellectuals flee to western Europe and the United States. Frances Perkins is named secretary of labor, becoming the first woman to hold a post in the U.S. Cabinet. *The Autobiography of Alice B. Toklas*, by Gertrude Stein.

1934   Beginning of the Moscow show trials, purging Stalin's political enemies in the Soviet Union. *The Children's Hour*, by Lillian Hellman.

1935   National Council of Negro Women founded in New York; Mary McLeod Bethune selected as first president. *Selected*

	Poems, by Marianne Moore. *Mules and Men*, by Zora Neale Hurston. *A House and Its Head*, by Ivy Compton-Burnett. *Theory of Flight*, by Muriel Rukeyser, wins the Yale Younger Poets award. "The White Horses of Vienna," by Kay Boyle, wins the O. Henry prize.
1936	Anticontraceptive provisions of the Comstock law are struck down in the United States. Death of George V; Edward VIII takes the throne, only to abdicate, a few months later, in order to marry Wallis Simpson, an American divorcée. George VI then succeeds to the throne. *Nightwood*, by Djuna Barnes. *The Pangolin, and Other Verse*, by Marianne Moore. *Gaudy Night*, by Dorothy Sayers.
1936–1939	Spanish Civil War.
1937	*Their Eyes Were Watching God*, by Zora Neale Hurston.
1938	Germany annexes Austria and part of Czechoslovakia. *Three Guineas*, by Virginia Woolf. *Pilgrimage* (4 vols.), by Dorothy Richardson. *The Death of the Heart*, by Elizabeth Bowen.
1939	Germany and Russia attack Poland; England and France enter World War II. *Pale Horse, Pale Rider*, by Katherine Anne Porter. *The Little Foxes*, by Lillian Hellman.
1940	Battle of Britain; Royal Air Force eventually turns back the German bombers.
1940–1945	Recruited both by government propaganda and the prospect of higher pay, women again enter nontraditional jobs in the English, and after 1941, the American labor forces, replacing men gone to war. Still larger numbers of women go into traditional women's work—clerical and service jobs—during the war. Some state day-care provision for women with children.
1941	Japan attacks Pearl Harbor; the United States declares war on Japan and Germany. Virginia Woolf commits suicide; *Between the Acts* is posthumously published. *What Are Years*, by Marianne Moore. *Watch on the Rhine*, by Lillian Hellman.
1942	Hitler decrees the "Final Solution," calling for the extermination of European Jews. *The Murder of Lidice*, by Edna St. Vincent Millay.
1944	D-day, 22 June: Allies invade occupied Europe. *The Walls Do Not Fall* (part one of *Trilogy*) by H. D. *Nevertheless*, by Marianne Moore. *The Ballad and the Source*, by Rosamund Lehmann.
1945	Germany surrenders in May; the United States drops atomic

bombs on Hiroshima and Nagasaki in August, ending the war with Japan. United Nations founded in San Francisco. *Tribute to the Angels* (part two of *Trilogy*) by H. D.

1946   Death of Gertrude Stein. *The Flowering of the Rod* (part three of *Trilogy*) by H. D.

Notes and References

Chapter One

1. Paula Giddings, *When and Where I Enter: The Impact of Black Women on Race and Sex in America* (New York: William Morrow, 1984), 205; hereafter cited in text.
2. Carroll Smith-Rosenberg, "The New Woman as Androgyne: Social Disorder and Gender Crisis, 1870–1936," in *Disorderly Conduct: Visions of Gender in Victorian America* (New York: Oxford University Press, 1985), 245; hereafter cited in text.
3. Susan J. Leonardi, *Dangerous by Degrees: Women at Oxford and the Somerville College Novelists* (New Brunswick and London: Rutgers University Press, 1989), 33.
4. Julie A. Matthaei, *An Economic History of Women in America: Women's Work, the Sexual Division of Labor, and the Development of Capitalism* (New York: Schocken Books, 1982), 205; hereafter cited in text.
5. For information on the promises and actual performance of labor-saving technologies for women, see Susan Strasser's *Never Done: A History of American Housework* (New York: Pantheon, 1982).
6. The statistics are complex and not always consistent, but do show, for example, that women made up 47 percent of all American undergraduates in 1920, only 31 percent in 1950; 6 percent of all American physicians were women in 1910, 4.6 percent in 1940. See Nancy F. Cott, *The Grounding of Modern Feminism* (New York and London: Yale University Press, 1987), 219; hereafter cited in text.
7. John D'Emilio and Estelle Freedman, *Intimate Matters: A History of Sexuality in America* (New York: Harper & Row, 1988), 223; hereafter cited in text.
8. Bonnie S. Anderson and Judith P. Zinsser, *A History of Their Own: Women in Europe from Prehistory to the Present*, vol. 2 (New York: Harper & Row, 1988), 285; hereafter cited in text.
9. See Rosalind Petchesky, *Abortion and Woman's Choice: The State, Sexuality, and Reproductive Freedom* (Boston: Northeastern University Press, 1985), 1–66, for a survey of women's efforts at reproductive control; hereafter cited in text.
10. Carroll Smith-Rosenberg: "The Female World of Love and Ritual: Relations between Women in Nineteenth-Century America," in *Disorderly Conduct*, 53–76.
11. Cited in Gerda Lerner, ed., *Black Women in White America* (New York: Vintage Books, 1973), 291.

12. Barbara Omolade, "Hearts of Darkness," in *Powers of Desire: The Politics of Sexuality*, Ann Snitow, Christine Stansell, and Sharon Thompson, eds. (New York: Monthly Review Press, 1983), 362.

13. Margaret Randolph Higonnet, Jane Jenson, Sonya Michel, and Margaret Collins Weitz, eds., Introduction to *Behind the Lines: Gender and the Two World Wars* (New Haven and London: Yale University Press, 1987), 4; hereafter cited in text as *BL*.

14. Margaret Higonnet and Patrice Higonnet, "The Double Helix," in *BL*, 41.

15. M. H. Abrams, "Modernism," in *A Glossary of Literary Terms* (New York: Holt, Rinehart and Winston, 1988), 109.

16. Andreas Huyssen makes this argument in *After the Great Divide: Modernism, Mass Culture, Postmodernism* (Bloomington: Indiana University Press, 1986), 44–62.

17. Cited in Sandra M. Gilbert and Susan Gubar, *No Man's Land: The Place of the Woman Writer in the Twentieth Century*, vol. 1, *The War of the Words* (New Haven and London: Yale University Press, 1988), 22.

18. Virginia Woolf, "Professions for Women," in *The Death of the Moth and Other Essays* (New York: Harcourt, Brace, 1942), 236–37.

19. Josephine Donovan finds such an ambivalent relationship between the two different generations of American women novelists she studies in *After the Fall: The Demeter-Persephone Myth in Wharton, Cather, and Glasgow* (University Park and London: Pennsylvania State University Press, 1989). See chapter 6 of the present volume.

20. Virginia Woolf, *A Room of One's Own* (New York: Harcourt Brace Jovanovich, 1929), 79.

21. Gilbert and Gubar attempt to treat issues of literary form in their chapter on "Sexual Linguistics," 227–70. What they deal with in this chapter, however, is less literary form as such than a literary theme that they call "linguistic fantasy"—women's and men's "fantasies" or myths of having a particular, powerful relationship to language. Literary form, however, is not simply reducible to a fantasy, because it does not exist sheerly on the level of psychology; it is the way different literary works are actually constructed.

22. Toril Moi, *Sexual/Textual Politics: Feminist Literary Theory* (New York and London: Methuen, 1985), 9.

23. Cary Nelson, *Repression and Recovery: Modern American Poetry and the Politics of Cultural Memory, 1910–1945* (Madison and London: University of Wisconsin Press, 1989); hereafter cited in text.

Chapter Two

1. See Ezra Pound, *Literary Essays*, ed. T. S. Eliot (Norfolk, Conn.: New Directions, 1954), 3–4; and T. E. Hulme, "Romanticism and Classicism," in *Twentieth Century Literary Criticism: A Reader*, ed. David Lodge (London: Longman, 1972), 93.

2. Louis L. Martz, Introduction to H. D., *Collected Poems: 1912–1944* (New York: New Directions, 1983), xiii.

3. Susan Stanford Friedman, *Psyche Reborn: The Emergence of H. D.* (Bloomington: Indiana University Press, 1981), 4; hereafter cited in text.

4. Rachel Blau DuPlessis, *Writing beyond the Ending: Narrative Strategies of Twentieth-Century Women Writers* (Bloomington: Indiana University Press, 1985), 67.
5. See Friedman, chapter 5, for an extended account of how H. D. reacted to Freud's theories about women.
6. Gillian Hanscombe and Virginia L. Smyers, *Writing for Their Lives: The Modernist Women 1910–1940* (Boston: Northeastern University Press, 1987), 70.
7. See Hanscombe and Smyers, *Writing for Their Lives*, 129–30.
8. Marianne Moore, *The Complete Poems of Marianne Moore* (New York: Macmillan, 1981); all further citations hereafter taken from this edition.
9. T. S. Eliot, cited by Helen Vendler in "Marianne Moore," reprinted in *Marianne Moore: Modern Critical Views*, ed. Harold Bloom (New York and New Haven: Chelsea House, 1987), 79.
10. See Patricia C. Willis, *Marianne Moore: Vision into Verse* (Philadelphia: Rosenbach Museum & Library, 1987), 61.
11. Marie Borroff traces Moore's fascination with "promotional prose"—the prose of advertisement and feature journalism—in *Language and the Poet: Verbal Artistry in Frost, Stevens, and Moore* (Chicago: University of Chicago Press, 1979).
12. Margot Holley, *The Poetry of Marianne Moore: A Study in Voice and Value* (Cambridge and New York: Cambridge University Press, 1987), 113, 115.

Chapter Three

1. See Barbara Ehrenreich and Deidre English, *For Her Own Good: 150 Years of the Experts' Advice to Women* (New York: Doubleday, 1978), for an account of how early-twentieth-century child-rearing literature authored by men came to view mothers as responsible for their children's ills.
2. Alice Meynell, *The Poems of Alice Meynell* (London: Hollis and Carter, 1947), 31; hereafter cited in text as *Poems*.
3. On Meynell's participation in the suffrage movement, see June Badeni, *The Slender Tree: A Life of Alice Meynell* (Padstow, Cornwall: Tabb House, 1981), 210.
4. See Judith Skeels, "Alice Meynell," in *British Women Writers: A Critical Reference Guide*, ed. Janet Todd (New York: Continuum, 1989) for one such reading.
5. See Penelope Fitzgerald, *Charlotte Mew and Her Friends* (London: Collins, 1984), 31; hereafter cited in text.
6. James Smith, "Charlotte Mew," in Todd, ed., *British Women Writers*, 463.
7. Charlotte Mew, *Collected Poems* (London: Duckworth, 1953), 31; hereafter cited in text as *Poems*.
8. Mina Loy, "Aphorisms on Futurism," in *The Last Lunar Baedeker*, ed. Roger Conover (Highlands, N.C.: Jargon Society, 1982); hereafter cited in text as *Baedeker*.
9. Mina Loy, letter to Mabel Dodge, cited in Hanscombe and Smyers, *Writing for Their Lives*, 116; hereafter cited in text.
10. On the history of *Wheels*, see Victoria Glendinning, *Edith Sitwell: A Unicorn among Lions* (New York: Alfred A. Knopf, 1981), 56–61; hereafter cited in text.
11. Edith Sitwell, *The Canticle of the Rose: Poems 1917–1949* (New York: Vanguard

Press, 1949), xi–xii. All citations of Sitwell's poetry are taken from this collection, hereafter cited in text as *CR*.

12. See G. A. Cevasco, *The Sitwells: Edith, Osbert, and Sacheverell* (Boston: Twayne, 1987), 26–28.

13. William York Tindall, *Forces in Modern British Literature* (New York: Knopf, 1947), 122.

14. Jose Garcia Villa, ed., *A Celebration for Edith Sitwell*, Direction number 7 (Norfolk, Conn.: New Directions, 1948).

15. Carol B. Schoen, *Sara Teasdale* (Boston: Twayne, 1987), 19; hereafter cited in text.

16. Sara Teasdale, *The Collected Poems of Sara Teasdale* (New York: Macmillan, 1957), 35; hereafter cited in text as *CP*.

17. Sara Teasdale, ed., *The Answering Voice: One Hundred Love Lyrics by Women* (1917; revised, with more recent poems added, New York: Macmillan, 1928).

18. See Judith Farr, *The Life and Art of Elinor Wylie* (Baton Rouge: Louisiana State University Press, 1983), 17, 30; hereafter cited in text.

19. For a discussion of how women writers have explored the problem of the female body as art object, see Susan Gubar, "'The Blank Page' and the Issues of Female Creativity," in *The New Feminist Criticism: Essays on Women, Literature, and Theory*, ed. Elaine Showalter (New York: Pantheon, 1985), 292–313.

20. Elinor Wylie, *Collected Poems* (New York: Alfred A. Knopf, 1954), 41; hereafter cited in text as *CP*.

21. Edna St. Vincent Millay, *Collected Lyrics* (New York: Harper & Brothers, 1943), 118–24; hereafter cited in text as *CL*.

22. Anne Cheney's *Millay in Greenwich Village* (University, Ala.: University of Alabama Press, 1975) is a useful source on these years in Millay's life.

23. Norman A. Brittin, *Edna St. Vincent Millay* (New York: Twayne, 1967), 138.

24. Edna St. Vincent Millay, *Conversation at Midnight* (New York: Harper & Brothers, 1937), 36; hereafter cited in text as *Conversation*.

25. On Bogan's early publications, see Elizabeth Frank, *Louise Bogan: A Portrait* (New York: Alfred A. Knopf, 1985), 40ff; hereafter cited in text.

26. Louise Bogan, "Medusa," in *The Blue Estuaries: Poems 1923–1968* (New York: Farrar, Straus and Giroux, 1969), 4; hereafter cited in text as *BE*.

27. Louise Bogan, "Marianne Moore," in *Selected Criticism: Poetry and Prose* (New York: Noonday Press, 1955), 155; hereafter cited in text as *SC*.

28. Maria K. Mootry and Gary Smith, eds., *A Life Distilled: Gwendolyn Brooks, Her Poetry and Fiction* (Urbana and Chicago: University of Illinois Press, 1987), 55; hereafter cited as *A Life*.

29. Gwendolyn Brooks, *Report from Part One* (Detroit: Broadside Press, 1972), 56; hereafter cited in text as *Report*.

30. Gwendolyn Brooks, *A Street in Bronzeville* (New York: Harper & Brothers, 1945), 11; hereafter cited in text as *Bronzeville*.

31. Hortense J. Spillers, "Gwendolyn the Terrible: Propositions on Eleven Poems," in Mootry and Smith, *A Life*, 225.

32. Houston A. Baker, Jr., "The Achievement of Gwendolyn Brooks," in Mootry and Smith, *A Life*, 25.

33. Spillers, in Mootry and Smith, *A Life*, 226.

Chapter Four

1. Virginia Woolf, "Modern Fiction," in *The Common Reader*, 1st ser. (New York: Harcourt, Brace & World, 1925), 151; hereafter cited in text as *CR*.

2. Dorothy Richardson, foreword to *Pilgrimage*, (London: Virago, 1979), 1:11.

3. See Rachel Blau DuPlessis, *Writing beyond the Ending*, 1–19, for an excellent discussion of the ideological dominance of the marriage/death narrative in the novel.

4. The most readily available complete editions of *Pilgrimage* today are probably the four-volume editions by the Popular Library (New York, 1976) and Virago (London, 1979). Volume 1 includes *Pointed Roofs* (originally published in 1915), *Backwater* (1916), *Honeycomb* (1917); volume 2, *The Tunnel* (February 1919), *Interim* (December 1919); volume 3, *Deadlock* (1921), *Revolving Lights* (1923), *The Trap* (1925); and volume 4, *Oberland* (1927), *Dawn's Left Hand* (1931), *Clear Horizon* (1935), *Dimple Hill* (1938), and *March Moonlight* (1967). All citations hereafter are from the Virago edition, by volume and page number.

5. May Sinclair, "The Novels of Dorothy Richardson," in the *Little Review* (April 1918); cited in Hanscombe and Smyers, *Writing for Their Lives*, 187.

6. Gloria G. Fromm, *Dorothy Richardson: A Biography* (Urbana and Chicago: University of Illinois Press, 1977), 128; hereafter cited in text.

7. See Fromm, 173–74, for a brief account of Richardson's knowledge of and attitude toward psychoanalysis.

8. See Quentin Bell, *Virginia Woolf: A Biography* (New York: Harcourt Brace Jovanovich, 1974), chapters 3–4, esp. pp. 62–54.

9. Louise De Salvo, *Virginia Woolf: The Impact of Childhood Sexual Abuse on Her Life and Work* (Boston: Beacon Press, 1989).

10. Bell notes such timing, and Phyllis Rose's *Woman of Letters: A Life of Virginia Woolf* (New York: Oxford University Press, 1978) generally agrees.

11. Berenice A. Carroll, "'To Crush Him in our Own Country': The Political Thought of Virginia Woolf," *Feminist Studies* 4 (1978): 116–17.

12. Virginia Woolf, *The Voyage Out* (1915; reprint, New York: Harcourt Brace Jovanovich, 1968), 326–27, 329, 350–51.

13. Virginia Woolf, *Night and Day* (1919; reprint, New York: Harcourt Brace Jovanovich, 1973), 506.

14. E. M. Forster, *Selected Letters of E. M. Forster*, ed. Mary Lago and P. N. Furbank (Cambridge: Harvard University Press, 1985), 2:32.

15. See Joan Bennett, *Virginia Woolf: Her Art as a Novelist*, 2d ed. (Cambridge: Cambridge University Press, 1964), 95–96; and J. K. Johnstone, *The Bloomsbury Group: A Study of E. M. Forster, Lytton Strachey, Virginia Woolf, and Their Circle* (London: Secker and Warburg, 1954), 332–34.

16. Virginia Woolf, 26 January 1920, *A Writer's Diary*, ed. Leonard Woolf (New York: Harcourt, Brace and Company, 1954), 22.

17. Rachel Bowlby, *Virginia Woolf: Feminist Destinations* (Oxford and New York: Basil Blackwell, 1988), 101; hereafter cited in text.

18. Alex Zwerdling, *Virginia Woolf and the Real World* (Berkeley, Los Angeles, and London: University of California Press, 1986), 64; hereafter cited in text.

19. Virginia Woolf, *Jacob's Room* (1922; reprint, New York: Harcourt Brace Jovanovich, 1978), 151; hereafter cited in text as *JR*.

20. Virginia Woolf, *Mrs. Dalloway* (1925; reprint, New York: Harcourt Brace Jovano-vich, 1964), 280, 283; hereafter cited in text as *MD*.
21. Emily Jensen, "Clarissa Dalloway's Respectable Suicide," in *Virginia Woolf: A Feminist Slant*, ed. Jane Marcus (Lincoln and London: University of Nebraska Press, 1983), 178.
22. Virginia Woolf, *To the Lighthouse* (1927; reprint, New York: Harcourt Brace Jovan-ovich, 1964), 53–57; hereafter cited in text as *TTL*.
23. Cam and James's voyage to sexual difference strongly recalls Freud's account of how girls and boys come to their separate gender identities. For an extended discussion of the novel's relationship to Freudian thought, see Bowlby, *Virginia Woolf*, 64–79.
24. Virginia Woolf, *A Room of One's Own* (1929; reprint, Harcourt Brace Jovanovich, 1963), 109; hereafter cited in text as *Room*.
25. As Woolf first designed it, *The Years* (originally entitled *The Pargiters*) was to have factual essay-chapters interspersed with chapters of narrative. She shortly abandoned this plan; some of the essay material, however, found its way into *Three Guineas* (1938), Woolf's prose polemic on women, society, and war.
26. Claire Sprague, Introduction to *Virginia Woolf: A Collection of Critical Essays* (Englewood Cliffs, N.J.: Prentice-Hall, 1971), 2.
27. E. M. Forster, from *Two Cheers for Democracy*, reprinted in Sprague, 23.

Chapter Five

1. Douglas Hewitt, *English Fiction of the Early Modern Period 1890–1940* (London and New York: Longman, 1988), 110–28, 196–97; hereafter cited in text.
2. May Sinclair, *The Three Sisters* (1914; reprint, New York: Dial Press, 1985), 3; here-after cited in text.
3. Jean Radford, Introduction to Sinclair, *The Three Sisters*, ix–x.
4. May Sinclair, *Mary Olivier: A Life* (1919; reprint, New York: Dial Press, 1980), 34; hereafter cited in text.
5. On May Sinclair's use of the Freudian distinction between sublimation and repres-sion, see Sydney Janet Kaplan's *Feminine Consciousness in the Modern British Novel* (Urbana: University of Illinois Press, 1975), 68. In the technical vocabulary of psy-choanalysis, sublimation is the process of turning sexual energy toward nonsexual ends, "higher" aims, that are approved by the conscious self; in repression, by con-trast, sexual energy remains unconscious but finds indirect expression in neurotic symptoms.
6. Radclyffe Hall, *The Well of Loneliness* (New York: Blue Ribbon Books, 1928), 5; hereafter cited in text.
7. See Bell, *Virginia Woolf*, 2:138–39.
8. Cited in Blake Nevius, *Ivy Compton-Burnett*, Columbia Essays on Modern Writers, no. 47 (New York: Columbia University Press, 1970), 20.
9. Nevius, *Ivy Compton-Burnett*, 21; hereafter cited in text.
10. Nancy R. Harrison, *Jean Rhys and the Novel as Women's Text* (Chapel Hill: Uni-versity of North Carolina Press, 1988), 61; hereafter cited in text.
11. Albert Alvarez's description of Rhys as "absolutely nonintellectual," however, neglects the novelist's intellectual work on her own terms of selection, composition, and point

of view. See Alvarez, "The Best Living English Novelist," *New York Times Book Review*, 17 March 1974, p. 7. Harrison argues that Alvarez's words, intended as a compliment, are obliquely sexist (62–63).

12. Jean Rhys, *After Leaving Mr. Mackenzie* (New York: Harper & Row, 1931), 49; hereafter cited in text.

13. Rebecca West, *The Return of the Soldier* (1918), reprinted in *Rebecca West: A Celebration*, ed. Samuel Hynes (New York: Viking Press, 1977), 66; hereafter cited in text.

14. Samuel Hynes, "Introduction: In Communion with Reality," in *Rebecca West: A Celebration*, xi.

15. Rebecca West, *Harriet Hume: A London Fantasy* (1928; reprint, New York: Dial Press, 1980), 93; hereafter cited in text.

16. In one telling incident, Arnold takes pleasure, while following Harriet, in comparing her to a woman he is about to steal from another man (103–4). The source of his pleasure is male rivalry; only rarely can he directly enjoy the beautiful for itself.

17. West published her own study of the novelist, *Henry James*, in 1916. Isabelle's name and predicament recall James's Isabel Archer, in *The Portrait of a Lady*. See Motley F. Deakin, *Rebecca West* (Boston: Twayne, 1980), 149.

18. Rebecca West, *The Thinking Reed* (New York: Viking Press, 1936), 386; hereafter cited in text.

19. Sackville-West's own memoir of her affair with Violet Keppel, along with a biographical essay by her son Nigel, may be found in Nigel Nicolson, *Portrait of a Marriage* (New York: Atheneum, 1973). She fictionalized their relationship in her novel *Challenge*, which was posthumously published after being suppressed in her lifetime (New York: Avon, 1975).

20. Vita Sackville-West, *All Passion Spent* (1931; reprint, New York: Dial Press, 1984), 148–49; hereafter cited in text.

21. Victoria Glendinning, Introduction to Sackville-West, *All Passion Spent*, xii.

22. Romanticism typically values the poet's spirit, or the state of artistic inspiration itself, over actual (and necessarily limited) artistic works.

23. Mona Van Duyn, "Pattern and Pilgrimage: A Reading of *The Death of the Heart*," in *Elizabeth Bowen: Modern Critical Views*, ed. Harold Bloom (New York: Chelsea House, 1987), 13.

24. Elizabeth Bowen, *To the North* (1932; reprint, Harmondsworth: Penguin, 1986), 13; hereafter cited in text.

25. See Smith-Rosenberg, "The Female World of Love and Ritual"; Nancy F. Cott, *The Bonds of Womanhood: "Woman's Sphere" in New England, 1780–1835* (New Haven: Yale University Press, 1977); and the Introduction, above.

26. Elizabeth Bowen, *The Death of the Heart* (1938; reprint, Harmondsworth: Penguin, 1989), 38–39; hereafter cited in text.

27. See Harriet S. Chessman's "Women and Language in the Fiction of Elizabeth Bowen," in Bloom, *Elizabeth Bowen*, 123–38, for a discussion of Portia and Anna as author figures.

28. Rosamund Lehmann, "The Future of the Novel?" in *Britain Today*, 122 (June 1946), 10–11.

29. Sydney Janet Kaplan notes other similarities between Mrs. Ramsay and Sybil Jardine; see *Feminine Consciousness*, 128.

30. Rosamund Lehmann, *The Ballad and the Source* (1944; reprint, London: Virago Press, 1982), 100; hereafter cited in text.
31. For a reading of *The Ballad and the Source* as a dark rewriting of the Demeter-Persephone myth, see Sydney Janet Kaplan, "Rosamund Lehmann's *The Ballad and the Source*: A Confrontation with 'The Great Mother,'" *Twentieth Century Literature* 27, no. 2 (Summer 1981):127–45.

Chapter Six

1. Richard Chase's *The American Novel and Its Tradition* (1957; reprint, New York: Gordian Press, 1978), 1–28, is the classic statement of this view of American fiction.
2. See Deborah E. McDowell, "'The Changing Same': Generational Connections and Black Women Novelists," in *Reading Black, Reading Feminist: A Critical Anthology*, ed. Henry Louis Gates, Jr., (New York: Meridian, 1990), 91–99, for a discussion of how earlier black women novelists adapted the traditions of the domestic or sentimental novel.
3. See Nina Baym's classic essay, "Melodramas of Beset Manhood: How Theories of American Fiction Exclude Women Authors," reprinted in *The New Feminist Criticism: Essays on Women, Literature and Theory*, ed. Elaine Showalter (New York: Pantheon, 1985), 63–80, for an analysis of the masculinity of the American critical tradition.
4. Josephine Donovan's *New England Local Color Literature: A Women's Tradition* (New York: Ungar, 1983), is the major feminist study of Jewett, Freeman, and their tradition of women's realism.
5. In *After the Fall: The Demeter-Persephone Myth in Wharton, Cather, and Glasgow* (University Park and London: Pennsylvania State University Press, 1989), Josephine Donovan reads the younger novelists' qualified revolt against the earlier women local colorists as a "fall," a choice of male values against those of women's traditional nineteenth-century sphere. While Donovan's analysis is interesting and important, she surely overidealizes and mystifies the ideology and practice of women's "separate sphere" in declaring it a female-dominated Eden.
6. R. W. B. Lewis, *Edith Wharton: A Biography* (New York: Harper & Row, 1975), 35; hereafter cited in text.
7. Edith Wharton, *The House of Mirth* (1905; reprint, New York: Scribner's, 1969); hereafter cited in text.
8. Wai-chee Dimock, "Debasing Exchange: Edith Wharton's *The House of Mirth*," *PMLA* 100, no. 5 (October 1985):787; hereafter cited in text. Dimock cites Wharton's judgment on Seldon from a letter to Sara Norton, 26 October 1906.
9. Dimock sees Lily's gesture as self-defeating, and Seldon's regret as self-serving; she argues that the end of *The House of Mirth* forecloses any genuine possibility for change from within Lily's milieu. From a psychoanalytic perspective, Cynthia Griffin Wolff judges Lily's suicide as a regressive retreat from adulthood, in *A Feast of Words: The Triumph of Edith Wharton* (New York: Oxford University Press, 1977), 131. Some feminist critics have argued, however, that Lily's sympathy for the working-class mother who befriends her, and her bond with the infant (which she recalls as she sinks into death), prefigure a "new world of female solidarity," a cross-class

alternative to Lily's former life of competition among women for rich men. See Elaine Showalter, "The Death of the Lady (Novelist): Wharton's *House of Mirth,*" in *Modern Critical Views: Edith Wharton* ed. Harold Bloom (New York: Chelsea House, 1986), 152–53.

10. Candace Waid points out that "Wharton places two of her own unfinished works on the desk of Ralph Marvell," in her introduction to *The Custom of the Country* (1913; reprint, New York: New American Library/Penguin, 1989), ix.

11. Judith Fryer, *Felicitous Space: The Imaginative Structures of Edith Wharton and Willa Cather* (Chapel Hill and London: University of North Carolina Press, 1986), 103; hereafter cited in text.

12. Thorstein Veblen, *The Theory of the Leisure Class* (New York: Macmillan, 1899).

13. Edith Wharton, *A Backward Glance* (New York: Appleton-Century, 1934), 293–94.

14. Edith Wharton, *Ethan Frome* (New York: Scribner's, 1911), 3; hereafter cited in text.

15. Cynthia Griffin Wolff discusses the importance of the narrator in *A Feast of Words,* 161–84; it seems to me, however, that little in the narrator's characterization or in Wharton's own comments on the novel justifies Wolff's extreme emphasis on the narrator's neurotic unreliability.

16. Edith Wharton, *Summer* (1917; reprint, New York: Harper & Row, 1979), 29; hereafter cited in text.

17. See Carol Wershoven's survey of the critical controversy in "The Divided Conflict of Edith Wharton's *Summer,*" in *Colby Library Quarterly* 21, no. 1 (March 1985):5–10. Wershoven's effort to minimize the incestuous nature of lawyer Royall's desire, however, seems strained. From a slightly different, and Freudian, perspective, Cynthia Griffin Wolff also minimizes the problem of the father figure's incestuous desire (see her introduction to *Summer*); her reading bears out one feminist critique of Freudian thought, that psychoanalysis (along with the family structure it describes) tacitly connives at father-daughter incest.

18. Edith Wharton, *The Age of Innocence* (1920; reprint, New York: Scribner's, 1980), 335.

19. See Judith Fryer's *Felicitous Space,* 120–25, for a critical reading of Archer's tastes in the novel.

20. Ellen Glasgow, *The Woman Within* (New York: Harcourt, Brace and Company, 1954), 77–104.

21. Marjorie R. Kaufman, "Ellen Glasgow," in *Notable American Women,* Edward T. James, Janet Wilson James, and Paul S. Boyer, eds. (Cambridge: Belknap Press of Harvard University, 1971), 2:46.

22. See Glasgow's preface to *Barren Ground* (1925; reprint, San Diego and New York: Harcourt Brace Jovanovich, 1985), vii.

23. Ellen Glasgow, *Virginia* (1913; reprint, New York: Penguin, 1989), 4; hereafter cited in text.

24. Ellen Glasgow, *A Certain Measure* (New York: Harcourt, Brace and Co., 1943), 79.

25. Ellen Glasgow, *Barren Ground* (1925; reprint, San Diego and New York: Harcourt Brace Jovanovich, 1985), 12; hereafter cited in text as *BG*.

26. See Josephine Donovan, *After the Fall,* chapter 5, and Linda W. Wagner, *Ellen Glasgow: Beyond Convention* (Austin: University of Texas Press, 1982), for feminist readings; and M. Thomas Inge, ed., *Ellen Glasgow: Centennial Essays* (Charlottesville: University Press of Virginia, 1976), for a survey of Glasgow's critical reputations.

27. Zora Neale Hurston, *Dust Tracks on a Road: An Autobiography* (1942; 2d ed., Urbana and Chicago: University of Illinois Press, 1984), 156.
28. Zora Neale Hurston, *Mules and Men* (1935; reprint, Urbana and Chicago: University of Illinois Press, 1978), 3; hereafter cited in text.
29. Zora Neale Hurston, *Their Eyes Were Watching God* (1937; reprint, Urbana and Chicago: University of Illinois, 1978), 9; hereafter cited in text as *Eyes*.
30. Molly Hite observes that "Janie's discovery and use of her narrating voice emerges as the major action" of *Their Eyes Were Watching God.* See "Romance, Marginality, and Matrilineage: *The Color Purple* and *Their Eyes Were Watching God*," in *Reading Black, Reading Feminist,* ed. Gates, 433.
31. Marjorie Pryse, "Zora Neale Hurston, Alice Walker, and the 'Ancient Power' of Black Women," in *Conjuring: Black Women, Fiction, and Literary Tradition,* ed. Marjorie Pryse and Hortense J. Spillers (Bloomington: Indiana University Press, 1985), 15.
32. Blyden Jackson, Introduction to Zora Neale Hurston, *Moses, Man of the Mountain* (1939; reprint, Urbana and Chicago: University of Illinois Press, 1984), xv–xvi.
33. Francoise Lionnet, "Autoethnography: The An-Archic Style of *Dust Tracks on a Road,*" in *Reading Black, Reading Feminist,* ed. Gates, 395. Lionnet's essay offers a helpful response to those critics who have complained of Hurston's irony and untrustworthiness in her autobiography.
34. Willa Cather, "The Novel Demeuble," in *Willa Cather on Writing,* ed. Stephen Tennant (New York: Knopf, 1949), 42–43; hereafter cited in text as *ND.*
35. On Cather's relationship to romantic literature and thought, see Susan J. Rosowski, *The Voyage Perilous: Willa Cather's Romanticism* (Lincoln and London: University of Nebraska Press, 1986).
36. See Judith Fryer, *Felicitous Space,* 210–14, for an excellent discussion of the novel's relationship to contemporary reactions to the Brooklyn Bridge.
37. Willa Cather, *O Pioneers!* (1913; reprint, New York: Penguin, 1989), 70–75; hereafter cited in text as *OP.*
38. See Blanche Gelfant's introduction to *O Pioneers!* for a discussion of Cather's literary models in the novel.
39. Willa Cather, *The Song of the Lark* (1915; reprint, Boston: Houghton Mifflin, 1983), 251; hereafter cited in text.
40. Willa Cather, *My Ántonia* (Boston: Houghton Mifflin, 1918); hereafter cited in text.
41. Blanche Gelfant, "The Forgotten Reaping-Hook: Sex in *My Ántonia,*" in *Willa Cather: Modern Critical Views,* ed. Harold Bloom (New York: Chelsea House, 1985), 121. Other critics have linked Jim Burden's sexual remoteness with Cather's lesbianism.
42. Willa Cather, *A Lost Lady* (1923; reprint, New York: Random House, 1972), 171.
43. Willa Cather, *Death Comes for the Archbishop* (1927; reprint, New York: Random House, 1971); hereafter cited in text.
44. Cited in Rosowski, *The Voyage Perilous,* 160.
45. Alfred Kazin was among the first critics to label both Cather and Glasgow elegists, in *On Native Grounds: An Interpretation of Modern American Prose Literature* (New York: Reynal & Hitchcock, 1942), 247–64.
46. Mary Austin, *Earth Horizon* (Boston: Houghton Mifflin, 1932); hereafter cited in text as *EH.*

47. Esther Lanigan Stineman, *Mary Austin: Song of a Maverick* (New Haven and London: Yale University Press, 1989), 40.

Chapter Seven

1. Shari Benstock explores the different Parisian ambiences sought out by Wharton, Stein, Barnes, and other writers in *Women of the Left Bank: Paris, 1900–1940* (Austin: University of Texas Press, 1987).
2. For an excellent collection of essays on women's twentieth-century experimental writing, and on the historical relationship between avant-gardes and ideas of the feminine, see Ellen G. Friedman and Miriam Fuchs, eds., *Breaking the Sequence: Women's Experimental Fiction* (Princeton, N.J.: Princeton University Press, 1989).
3. Gertrude Stein, *Three Lives* (1909; reprint, New York: Random House, 1936); hereafter cited in text.
4. Gertrude Stein, *The Autobiography of Alice B. Toklas* (New York: Random House, 1961), 54.
5. Richard Kostelanetz, Introduction to *The Yale Gertrude Stein* (New Haven: Yale University Press, 1980), xxi.
6. Marjorie Perloff, *The Poetics of Indeterminacy: Rimbaud to Cage* (Princeton, N.J.: Princeton University Press, 1981), 75.
7. For an excellent introduction to the debate over whether to read Stein for the autonomy of her signifiers or for her covert signifieds, see Harriet Chessman, *The Public Is Invited to Dance: Representation, the Body, and Dialogue in Gertrude Stein* (Stanford: Stanford University Press, 1989), 1–15; hereafter cited in text.
8. Marianne DeKoven, *A Different Language: Gertrude Stein's Experimental Writing* (Madison: University of Wisconsin Press, 1983), 42; hereafter cited in text.
9. On Stein's "continuous present," see DeKoven, *Different Language*, 32–45, and Chessman, *Public*, 48. Stein herself used the term in her essay "Composition as Explanation" (1926), in *What Are Masterpieces?* (1940; reprint, New York: Pitman, 1970), 23–38.
10. Michael J. Hoffman, looking at *Three Lives* along with *The Making of Americans*, written immediately afterward, finds it clear that "Stein believes in both racial and national types" (*Gertrude Stein* [Boston: Twayne, 1976], 30). Harriet Chessman comments on "the racism evident in the descriptions of characters in 'Melanctha,'" and ascribes it to "Stein's interest in achieving an authoritative narrative voice" (*Public*, 211–12n2). Wendy Steiner explores Stein's fascination with typing character, and her interest in overtly sexist and anti-Semitic turn-of-the-century pseudoscience, in *Exact Resemblance to Exact Resemblance: The Literary Portraiture of Gertrude Stein* (New Haven and London: Yale University Press, 1978), 37ff.
11. Cited in *Selected Writings of Gertrude Stein*, ed. Carl Van Vechten (New York: Random House, 1946), 298; hereafter cited in text as *SW*.
12. The issue of racism in *Three Lives* is closely related to the problem of the narrator's authority and the narrator's relationship to Stein herself. DeKoven argues that the narrator is deliberately "obtuse," that "we are able simultaneously to chart the limits of the narrator's perception and to see beyond them" (*Different Language*, 28), although she does not press the question of the narrator's racism.

13. Jayne L. Walker, *The Making of a Modernist: Gertrude Stein from "Three Lives" to "Tender Buttons"* (Amherst: University of Massachusetts Press, 1984), 30. Walker offers another valuable discussion of the narrator in *Three Lives*.

14. DeKoven borrows the phrase "lively words" from Stein's *Lectures in America* (DeKoven, *Different Language*, 46).

15. Gertrude Stein, *Lectures in America* (1935; reprint, Boston: Beacon Press, 1985), 188; hereafter cited in text as *LIA*.

16. For detailed discussions of Stein's literary portraiture and its philosophical underpinnings, see Wendy Steiner's *Exact Resemblance to Exact Resemblance* and her introduction to *Lectures in America*.

17. Pamela Hadas, "Spreading the Difference: One Way to Read Gertrude Stein's *Tender Buttons*," *Twentieth Century Literature* 24, no. 1 (Spring 1978): 57–75.

18. Elizabeth Fifer examines Stein's erotic code in "'Is Flesh Advisable?': The Interior Theater of Gertrude Stein," *Signs* 4, no. 3 (Spring 1979):472–83.

19. James R. Mellow, *Charmed Circle: Gertrude Stein and Company* (New York: Praeger, 1974), 370; hereafter cited in text.

20. *The Mother of Us All* was performed in 1947 at Columbia University and published in *Last Operas and Plays* (New York: Rinehart, 1949). On the opera's staging, see Chessman, *Public*, 232n1 and 233n6; see also Chessman's excellent reading of Stein's text itself, 199–202.

21. *The Book of Repulsive Women* was published by Barnes's friend Guido Bruno as vol. 2, no. 6, of *Bruno's Chap Books* (November 1915).

22. *A Book* was also published through a friend of Barnes's, Horace Liveright (New York: Boni and Liveright, 1923).

23. Djuna Barnes, *Ryder* (New York: Liveright, 1928).

24. On Barnes's response to the censorship and the fate of the censored manuscript passages, see Andrew Field, *Djuna: The Formidable Miss Barnes* (Austin: University of Texas Press, 1985), 127.

25. Djuna Barnes, *Ladies Almanack* (1928; reprint, New York: Harper & Row, 1972); hereafter cited in text.

26. Djuna Barnes, *Nightwood* (1936; reprint, New York: New Directions, 1961); hereafter cited in text.

27. Donna Gerstenberger, "The Radical Narrative of Djuna Barnes's *Nightwood*," in *Breaking the Sequence*, ed. Friedman and Fuchs, 130.

Chapter Eight

1. Joseph M. Flora, Introduction to *The English Short Story 1880–1945: A Critical History* (Boston: Twayne, 1985), xiv; hereafter cited as Flora.

2. See Flora, *English Short Story*, xv, and Philip Stevick, Introduction to *The American Short Story 1900–1945: A Critical History* (Boston: Twayne, 1984), 8; hereafter cited in text.

3. Andreas Huyssen, "Mass Culture as Woman: Modernism's Other," in *The Great Di-*

vide: Modernism, Mass Culture, Postmodernism (Bloomington: Indiana University Press, 1986), 44–62.

4. Katherine Mansfield, "The Tiredness of Rosabel," in *The Short Stories of Katherine Mansfield* ed. John Middleton Murray (New York: Alfred A. Knopf, 1965), 3; hereafter cited in text as *SKM*.

5. Katherine Mansfield, quoted in Rhoda B. Nathan, *Katherine Mansfield* (New York: Continuum, 1988), 51; hereafter cited in text.

6. On Porter's reception, see Jane Krause DeMouy, *Katherine Anne Porter's Women: The Eye of Her Fiction* (Austin: University of Texas Press, 1983), 4; hereafter cited in text.

7. Robert Penn Warren, "Irony with a Center," in *Katherine Anne Porter: Modern Critical Views*, ed. Harold Bloom (New York: Chelsea House, 1986).

8. Katherine Anne Porter, "Flowering Judas," in *The Collected Stories of Katherine Anne Porter* (New York: Harcourt, Brace & World, 1965), 95; hereafter cited in text as *CS*.

9. Dorothy Parker, "Testament," in *The Portable Dorothy Parker* (New York: Penguin, 1973), 47–51; hereafter cited in text as *DP*.

10. For an account of Parker's actions during the demonstrations, and of her subsequent political activism, see Marion Meade, *Dorothy Parker: What Fresh Hell Is This?* (New York: Penguin, 1989), 178ff; hereafter cited in text.

11. See Kay Boyle and Robert MacAlmon, *Being Geniuses Together 1920–1930*, rev. ed. (Garden City, N.Y.: Doubleday, 1968), and Sandra Whipple Spanier, *Kay Boyle: Artist and Activist* (New York: Paragon, 1988), 6–10; hereafter cited in text.

12. Edmund Wilson, "Kay Boyle and the *Saturday Evening Post*," in *Classics and Commercials: A Literary Chronicle of the Forties* (New York: Random House, 1962), 128–32.

13. Kay Boyle, *Fifty Stories* (Garden City, N.Y.: Doubleday, 1980); hereafter cited in text as *FS*.

14. The judge was Clifton Fadiman; see Spanier, *Kay Boyle*, 120.

15. Mary Lavin, *Tales from Bective Bridge* (Boston: Little, Brown, 1942), 97; hereafter cited in text as *Tales*.

16. Kathleen Gregory Klein, *The Woman Detective: Gender and Genre* (Urbana and Chicago: University of Illinois Press, 1988), 8; hereafter cited in text.

17. Not until recently have women writers really entered "hard-boiled" fiction in large (or successful) numbers; Sara Paretsky, in the United States, is at the head of this expanding group.

18. Robert Barnard, *A Talent to Deceive: An Appreciation of Agatha Christie* (New York: Dodd, Mead & Co., 1980), 26; hereafter cited in text.

19. Agatha Christie, *The Moving Finger* (1942; reprint, New York: Berkley, 1984).

20. Gillian Gill finds Christie a much more radically feminist writer than I do, in *Agatha Christie* (New York: Macmillan, 1990).

21. Dorothy Sayers, *Strong Poison* (1930; reprint, New York: Harper & Row, 1987), 3–17.

22. Dorothy Sayers, *Gaudy Night* (1936; reprint, New York: Harper & Row, 1986); hereafter cited in text as *GN*.

23. Dorothy Sayers, *Busman's Honeymoon* (New York: Avon, 1968), 36.

24. Susan J. Leonardi, *Dangerous by Degrees: Women at Oxford and the Somerville College Novelists* (New Brunswick, N.J.: Rutgers University Press, 1989), 87–88.

Chapter Nine

1. For useful historical surveys of the period, see T. W. Craik, ed., *The Revels History of Drama in English*, vols. 7 and 8 (London: Methuen, 1977–78).

2. For a list of women involved with alternative theater groups, see Helen Krich Chinoy and Linda Walsh Jenkins, eds., *Women in American Theatre: Careers, Images, Movements* (New York: Crown, 1981), 4–5.

3. Lady Augusta Gregory, *Seven Short Plays* (St. Clair Shores, Mich.: Scholarly Press, 1970), 58; hereafter cited in text.

4. Elizabeth Baker, *Chains* (London: Sidgwick & Jackson, 1911), 13; hereafter cited in text.

5. Kenneth Richards, "Some Alternative Theatres," in *The Revels History of Drama in English*, vol. 7, ed. T. W. Craik (London: Methuen, 1978), 112.

6. Elizabeth Baker, *The Price of Thomas Scott* (London: Sidgwick & Jackson, 1913), 33.

7. Walter J. Meserve's "Rachel Crothers," in *Notable American Women: The Modern Period*, Barbara Sicherman and Carol Hurd Green, eds. (Cambridge: Belknap Press of Harvard University, 1980) 174–75, points to this division in Crothers's work.

8. Rachel Crothers, *Let Us Be Gay* (New York: Samuel French, 1929), 165.

9. Rachel Crothers, *Susan and God* (New York: Random House, 1938), 129; hereafter cited in text.

10. Lois Gottlieb, "Looking to Women: Rachel Crothers and the Feminist Heroine," in *Women in American Theatre*, ed. Chinoy and Jenkins, 143.

11. Susan Glaspell, *Trifles*, in *Plays* (Boston: Small, Maynard & Co., 1920), 1–30; hereafter cited in text as *Plays*.

12. Arthur E. Waterman, *Susan Glaspell*, (Boston: Twayne, 1966), 74; hereafter cited in text.

13. Susan Glaspell, *The Verge*, in *Three Plays* (London: Ernest Benn, 1924); hereafter cited in text.

14. Shirley Graham, *His Day Is Marching On: A Memoir of W. E. B. Du Bois* (Philadelphia: J. B. Lippincott, 1971), 17.

15. Kathy A. Perkins, *Black Female Playwrights: An Anthology of Plays before 1950* (Bloomington: Indiana University Press, 1989), 209.

16. Shirley Graham, *I Gotta Home*, in *Black Female Playwrights*, ed. Perkins, 231; hereafter cited in text.

17. For Graham's own recollections of the trial and events leading up to it, see *His Day Is Marching On*, 92–173.

18. Carl Rollyson, *Lillian Hellman: Her Legend and Her Legacy* (New York: St. Martin's Press, 1988), 39; hereafter cited in text.

19. Lillian Hellman, *The Children's Hour*, in *Four Plays* (New York: Random House, 1942), 78; hereafter cited in text.

20. On the way typical melodrama conveys a partial and mystified form of social knowledge, see Martha Vicinus, "'Helpless and Unfriended': Nineteenth-Century Domestic Melodrama," *New Literary History* 13 (1981):127–44.

Chapter Ten

1. David Levering Lewis, *When Harlem Was in Vogue* (New York: Alfred A. Knopf, 1981), 27; hereafter cited in text.

2. Cited in Abby Arthur Johnson and Ronald Maberry Johnson, *Propaganda and Aesthetics: The Literary Politics of Afro-American Magazines in the Twentieth Century* (Amherst: University of Massachusetts Press, 1979), 6.

3. Jean Wagner, *Black Poets of the United States: From Paul Laurence Dunbar to Langston Hughes*, trans. Kenneth Douglas (Urbana and Chicago: University of Illinois Press, 1973), 163.

4. For an introduction to the debate, see Johnson and Johnson, *Propaganda*, 1–66, and Wagner, *Black Poets*, 170–72.

5. Wallace Thurman, "Negro Artists and the Negro," *New Republic* 52 (31 August 1927):37.

6. On the publication of and reactions to *Fire!!*, see Johnson and Johnson, *Propaganda*, 77–84, and Lewis, *Harlem*, 193–97.

7. Gloria T. Hull, *Color, Sex, and Poetry* (Bloomington and Indianapolis: Indiana University Press, 1987), 7–11; hereafter cited in text.

8. Arthur P. Davis and Michael W. Peplow, *The New Negro Renaissance: An Anthology* (New York: Holt, Rinehart and Winston, 1975), 70–71.

9. Claude MacKay, cited in Deborah McDowell, "Introduction: Regulating Midwives," in Jessie Redmon Fauset, *Plum Bun: A Novel without A Moral* (1928; reprint, Boston: Beacon Press, 1990), xxx.

10. Deborah E. McDowell, "The Neglected Dimension of Jessie Redmon Fauset," in *Conjuring*, ed. Pryse and Spillers, 88; and McDowell, "Introduction: Regulating Midwives," xix.

11. Jessie Redmon Fauset, *There Is Confusion* (1924; reprint, Boston: Northeastern University Press, 1989).

12. See Thadious M. Davis, Introduction to *There Is Confusion*, xxiii–xxiv, for an account of the dinner.

13. McDowell, "Introduction: Regulating Midwives," xv.

14. Jessie Redmon Fauset, *Plum Bun*, 112; hereafter cited in text.

15. McDowell, "Introduction: Regulating Midwives," xix.

16. Perkins, *Black Female Playwrights*, 5; hereafter cited in text as Perkins.

17. Georgia Douglas Johnson, *Plumes*, in *Black Female Playwrights*, ed. Perkins, 26; hereafter cited in text.

18. Marita Bonner, *The Purple Flower*, in *Black Female Playwrights*, ed. Perkins, 196; hereafter cited in text.

19. Eulalie Spence, *A Fool's Errand*, in *Black Female Playwrights*, ed. Perkins, 131.

20. Eulalie Spence, *Undertow*, in *Black Female Playwrights*, ed. Perkins, 113; hereafter cited in text.

21. Maureen Honey, ed., *Shadowed Dreams: Women's Poetry of the Harlem Renaissance* (New Brunswick and London: Rutgers University Press, 1989); hereafter cited in text as *Dreams*.

22. See Gloria T. Hull's biographical essay on Dunbar-Nelson in *Color, Sex, and Poetry*, 33–104.

23. On Grimké's ancestry and biography, see Hull, *Color, Sex, and Poetry*, 106–52.

Chapter Eleven

1. Beatrice Webb, *My Apprenticeship* (1926; reprint, Cambridge: Cambridge University Press, 1979), 1.
2. *Life as We Have Known It*, by Co-operative working women, ed. Margaret Llewelyn Davies, with an introductory letter by Virginia Woolf (1931; reprint, London: Virago, 1977); hereafter cited in text.
3. On Virginia and Leonard Woolf's relationship to Margaret Llewelyn Davies, see Bell, *Virginia Woolf*, 2:35–36.
4. See Virginia Woolf, "Lives of the Obscure," in *The Common Reader*, 109–36.
5. Anzia Yezierska, *Bread Givers* (1925; reprint, New York: Persea Books, 175), 11; hereafter cited in text.
6. Thomas J. Ferraro, "'Working Ourselves Up' in America: Anzia Yezierska's *Bread Givers*," *South Atlantic Quarterly* 89, no. 3 (Summer 1990):562; hereafter cited in text.
7. Most conspicuously, Yezierska left her daughter in the care of her in-laws; see Louise Levitas Henriksen's biography of her mother, *Anzia Yezierska: A Writer's Life* (New Brunswick, N.J.: Rutgers University Press, 1988).
8. Agnes Smedley, *Daughter of Earth* (1929; reprint, Old Westbury, N.Y.: Feminist Press, 1973); hereafter cited in text. The novel was published in serial form in a German magazine, the *Frankfurter Zeitung*, before appearing as a book in the United States.
9. Here *Daughters of Earth* departs from Smedley's actual life in two important respects: Smedley actually spent these years working in Berlin, not New York, and the Indian activist she lived with for several years was legally married to someone else. See Janice R. MacKinnon and Stephen R. MacKinnon, *Agnes Smedley: The Life and Times of an American Radical* (Berkeley: University of California Press, 1988), for an account of how Smedley revised her own life in her autobiographical novel.
10. Charlotte Perkins Gilman, "Why I Wrote 'The Yellow Wallpaper'" (1913), in *The Charlotte Perkins Gilman Reader: "The Yellow Wallpaper" and Other Fiction*, ed. Ann J. Lane (New York: Pantheon, 1980), 20; hereafter cited in text as GR.
11. Ann J. Lane, *To Herland and Beyond: The Life and Work of Charlotte Perkins Gilman* (New York: Pantheon, 1990), 291.
12. Charlotte Perkins Gilman, *Herland* (New York: Pantheon, 1979), 70; hereafter cited in text.
13. See Elinor Langer, *Josephine Herbst* (Boston: Little, Brown, 1984) for the best available account of Herbst's life.
14. Josephine Herbst, *The Executioner Waits* (New York: Harcourt, Brace and Company, 1934), 134–35.
15. Meridel Le Sueur, "Annunciation," in *Ripening: Selected Work*, ed. Elaine Hedges (New York: Feminist Press, 1990), 130; hereafter cited in text.
16. Paula Rabinowitz, "Maternity as History: Gender and the Transformation of Genre in Meridel Le Sueur's *The Girl*," *Contemporary Literature* 29, no. 4 (Winter 1988): 545.
17. For an influential discussion of the New Critical legacy, see Frank Lentricchia, *After the New Criticism* (Chicago: University of Chicago Press, 1980).
18. See Genevieve Taggard's autobiographical "Preface: Hawaii, Washington, Vermont"

in *Calling Western Union* (New York: Harper & Brothers, 1936), for an account of her early life; hereafter cited in text as *CWU*.

19. From the dust jacket to Taggard's *Collected Poems, 1918–1938* (New York: Harper & Brothers, 1938); cited in Nelson, *Repression and Recovery*, 182.

20. Genevieve Taggard's *The Life and Mind of Emily Dickinson* (New York: Knopf, 1930) was one of the first scholarly studies of Dickinson.

21. All quotations from Muriel Rukeyser's poetry are taken from *The Collected Poems of Muriel Rukeyser* (New York: MacGraw Hill, 1978).

22. Louise Bogan, cited in Louise Kertesz, *The Poetic Vision of Muriel Rukeyser* (Baton Rouge: Louisiana State University Press), 43; hereafter cited in text.

Chapter Twelve

1. Cited in Kertesz, *The Poetic Vision of Muriel Rukeyser*, 271.

2. Many articles have been written by now about the various stages of feminist criticism. Most agree on the first two stages set out here. See Elaine Showalter, "Toward a Feminist Poetics" and "Feminist Criticism in the Wilderness," in *The New Feminist Criticism*, ed. Showalter.

3. Showalter's highly influential "Feminist Criticism in the Wilderness" (first published in 1981) called on feminist critics to move from reading images of women as authored by men toward what she called "gynocriticism," or the reading of women's own writing. Sandra Gilbert and Susan Gubar's *The Madwoman in the Attic: The Woman Writer and the Nineteenth-Century Literary Imagination* (New Haven: Yale University Press, 1979) envisioned feminist criticism's project as the recovery of a great "mother of us all," the composite figure of a women's literary tradition.

4. Charlotte Nekola and Paula Rabinowits, eds., *Writing Red: An Anthology of American Women Writers, 1930–1940* (New York: Feminist Press, 1987); includes valuable introductory essays on the period and the writers anthologized.

Selected Bibliography

Primary Sources

Austin, Mary. *Earth Horizon*. Boston: Houghton Mifflin, 1932.

Baker, Elizabeth. *Chains*. London: Sidgwick & Jackson, 1911.

————. *The Price of Thomas Scott*. London: Sidgwick & Jackson, 1913.

Barnes, Djuna. *Ladies Almanack*. 1928. Reprint. New York: Harper & Row, 1972.

————. *Nightwood*. 1936. Reprint. New York: New Directions, 1961.

Bogan, Louise. *The Blue Estuaries: Poems 1923–1968*. New York: Farrar, Straus and Giroux, 1969.

————. *Selected Criticism: Poetry and Prose*. New York: Noonday Press, 1955.

Bonner, Marita. *The Purple Flower*. 1928. Reprinted in *Black Female Playwrights: An Anthology of Plays before 1950*, edited by Kathy A. Perkins. Bloomington and Indianapolis: Indiana University Press, 1989.

Bowen, Elizabeth. *To the North*. 1932. Reprint. Harmondsworth: Penguin, 1986.

————. *The Death of the Heart*. 1938. Reprint. Harmondsworth: Penguin, 1989.

Boyle, Kay. *Fifty Stories*. Garden City, N.Y.: Doubleday, 1980.

———— and Robert McAlmon. *Being Geniuses Together*. Garden City, N.Y.: Doubleday, 1968.

Brooks, Gwendolyn. *A Street in Bronzeville*. New York: Harper & Brothers, 1945.

————. *Report from Part One*. Detroit: Broadside Press, 1972.

Cather, Willa. *O Pioneers!* 1913. Reprint. New York: Penguin, 1989.

————. *The Song of the Lark*. 1915. Reprint. Boston: Houghton Mifflin, 1983.

————. *My Ántonia*. Boston: Houghton Mifflin, 1918.

————. *A Lost Lady*. 1923. Reprint. New York: Random House, 1972.

————. *Death Comes for the Archbishop*. 1927. Reprint. New York: Random House, 1971.

————. *Willa Cather on Writing*. Edited by Stephen Tennant. New York: Alfred A. Knopf, 1949.

Christie, Agatha. *The Moving Finger*. 1942. Reprint. New York: Berkley, 1984.

Compton-Burnett, Ivy. *A House and Its Head*. London: William Heinemann, 1935.

Crothers, Rachel. *Let Us Be Gay*. New York: Samuel French, 1929.

————. *Susan and God*. New York: Random House, 1938.

DAVIES, MARGARET LLEWELYN, ed. *Life as We Have Known It*. 1931. Reprint. London: Virago, 1977.

DOOLITTLE, HILDA [H. D.]. *Collected Poems: 1912–1944*. Edited by Louis L. Martz. New York: New Directions, 1983.

FAUSET, JESSIE REDMON. *Plum Bun*. 1928. Reprint. Boston: Beacon Press, 1990.

———. *There Is Confusion*. 1924. Reprint. Boston: Northeastern University Press, 1989.

GILMAN, CHARLOTTE PERKINS. *The Charlotte Perkins Gilman Reader: "The Yellow Wallpaper" and Other Fiction*. Edited by Ann J. Lane. New York: Pantheon, 1980.

———. *Herland*. 1915. Reprint. New York: Pantheon, 1979.

GLASGOW, ELLEN. *Virginia*. 1913. Reprint. New York: Penguin, 1989.

———. *Barren Ground*. 1925. Reprint. San Diego and New York: Harcourt Brace Jovanovich, 1985.

———. *The Woman Within*. New York: Harcourt, Brace and Company, 1954.

GLASPELL, SUSAN. *Plays*. Boston: Small, Maynard, 1920.

———. *Three Plays*. London: Ernest Benn, 1924.

GRAHAM, SHIRLEY. *I Gotta Home*. 1939. Reprinted in *Black Female Playwrights: An Anthology of Plays before 1950*, edited by Kathy A. Perkins. Bloomington and Indianapolis: Indiana University Press, 1989.

———. *It's Morning*. 1940. Reprinted in *Black Female Playwrights*.

———. *His Day Is Marching On: A Memoir of W. E. B. Du Bois*. Philadelphia: J. B. Lippincott, 1971.

GREGORY, LADY AUGUSTA. *Seven Short Plays*. St. Clair Shores, Mich.: Scholarly Press, 1970.

HALL, RADCLYFFE. *The Well of Loneliness*. New York: Blue Ribbon Books, 1928.

HELLMAN, LILLIAN. *Four Plays*. New York: Random House, 1942.

HERBST, JOSEPHINE. *The Executioner Waits*. New York: Harcourt, Brace and Company, 1934.

HONEY, MAUREEN, ed. *Shadowed Dreams: Women's Poetry of the Harlem Renaissance*. New Brunswick and London: Rutgers University Press, 1989.

HURSTON, ZORA NEALE. *Mules and Men*. 1935. Reprint. Urbana and Chicago: University of Illinois Press, 1978.

———. *Their Eyes Were Watching God*. 1937. Reprint. Urbana and Chicago: University of Illinois Press, 1978.

———. *Moses, Man of the Mountain*. 1939. Reprint. Urbana and Chicago: University of Illinois Press, 1984.

———. *Dust Tracks on a Road: An Autobiography*. (1942.) 2d ed. Urbana and Chicago: University of Illinois Press, 1984.

JOHNSON, GEORGIA DOUGLAS. *Plumes*. 1927. Reprinted in *Black Female Playwrights: An Anthology of Plays before 1950*, edited by Kathy A. Perkins. Bloomington and Indianapolis: Indiana University Press, 1989.

LAVIN, MARY. *Tales from Bective Bridge*. Boston: Little, Brown, 1942.

LEHMANN, ROSAMUND. *The Ballad and the Source*. 1944. Reprint. London: Virago Press, 1982.

LE SUEUR, MERIDEL. *Ripening: Selected Work*. Edited by Elaine Hedges. New York: Feminist Press, 1990.

LOWELL, AMY. *Complete Poetical Works*. Boston: Houghton Mifflin, 1955.

LOY, MINA. *The Last Lunar Baedeker*. Highlands, N.C.: Jargon Society, 1982.

MANSFIELD, KATHERINE. *The Short Stories of Katherine Mansfield*. Edited by John Middleton Murray. New York: Alfred A. Knopf, 1965.

MEW, CHARLOTTE. *Collected Poems*. London: Duckworth, 1953.

MEYNELL, ALICE. *The Poems of Alice Meynell*. London: Hollis and Carter, 1947.

MILLAY, EDNA ST. VINCENT. *Conversation at Midnight*. New York: Harper & Brothers, 1937.

———. *Collected Lyrics*. New York: Harper & Brothers, 1943.

MOORE, MARIANNE. *The Complete Poems of Marianne Moore*. New York: Macmillan, 1981.

NEKOLA, CHARLOTTE, and PAULA RABINOWITZ, eds. *Writing Red: An Anthology of American Women Writers, 1930–1940*. New York: Feminist Press, 1987.

PARKER, DOROTHY. *The Portable Dorothy Parker*. New York: Penguin, 1973.

PORTER, KATHERINE ANNE. *The Collected Stories of Katherine Anne Porter*. New York: Harcourt, Brace & World, 1965.

RHYS, JEAN. *After Leaving Mr. Mackenzie*. New York: Harper & Row, 1931.

RICHARDSON, DOROTHY. *Pilgrimage*. 4 vols. London: Virago, 1979.

RUKEYSER, MURIEL. *The Collected Poems of Muriel Rukeyser*. New York: MacGraw Hill, 1978.

SACKVILLE-WEST, VITA. *All Passion Spent*. 1931. Reprint. New York: Dial Press, 1984.

———. *Family History*. 1932. Reprint. New York: Penguin, 1987.

SAYERS, DOROTHY. *Strong Poison*. 1930. Reprint. New York: Harper & Row, 1987.

———. *Gaudy Night*. 1936. Reprint. New York: Harper & Row, 1986.

SINCLAIR, MAY. *The Three Sisters*. 1914. Reprint. New York: Dial Press, 1985.

———. *Mary Olivier: A Life*. 1919. Reprint. New York: Dial Press, 1980.

SITWELL, EDITH. *The Canticle of the Rose: Poems 1917–1949*. New York: Vanguard Press, 1949.

SMEDLEY, AGNES. *Daughter of Earth*. 1929. Reprint. Old Westbury, N.Y.: Feminist Press, 1973.

SPENCE, EULALIE. *Fool's Errand*. 1927. Reprinted in *Black Female Playwrights: An Anthology of Plays before 1950*, edited by Kathy A. Perkins. Bloomington and Indianapolis: Indiana University Press, 1989.

———. *Undertow*. 1929. Reprinted in *Black Female Playwrights*.

STEIN, GERTRUDE. *Three Lives*. 1909. Reprint. New York: Random House, 1936.

———. *The Autobiography of Alice B. Toklas*. 1933. Reprint. New York: Random House, 1961.

———. *Lectures in America*. 1935. Reprint. Boston: Beacon Press, 1985.

———. *Selected Writings of Gertrude Stein*. Edited by Carl Van Vechten. New York: Random House, 1946.

———. *The Yale Gertrude Stein*. Edited by Richard Kostelanetz. New Haven: Yale University Press, 1980.

TAGGARD, GENEVIEVE. *Calling Western Union*. New York: Harper & Brothers, 1936.

———. *Collected Poems, 1918–1938*. New York: Harper & Brothers, 1938.

TEASDALE, SARA. *The Collected Poems of Sara Teasdale*. New York: Macmillan, 1928.

WEBB, BEATRICE. *My Apprenticeship*. 1926. Reprint. Cambridge: Cambridge University Press, 1979.

WEST, REBECCA. *Harriet Hume: A London Fantasy*. 1928. Reprint. New York: Dial Press, 1980.

———. *The Thinking Reed*. New York: Viking, 1936.

———. *Rebecca West: A Celebration*. New York: Viking Press, 1977.

WHARTON, EDITH. *The House of Mirth*. 1905. Reprint. New York: Scribner's, 1969.

———. *Ethan Frome*. New York: Scribner's, 1911.

———. *The Custom of the Country*. 1913. Reprint. New York: New American Library/ Penguin, 1989.

———. *Summer*. 1917. Reprint. New York: Harper & Row, 1979.

———. *The Age of Innocence*. 1920. Reprint. New York: Scribner's, 1980.

———. *A Backward Glance*. New York: Appleton-Century, 1934.

WOOLF, VIRGINIA. *The Voyage Out*. 1915. Reprint. New York: Harcourt Brace Jovanovich, 1968.

———. *Jacob's Room*. 1922. Reprint. New York: Harcourt Brace Jovanovich, 1978.

———. *Mrs. Dalloway*. 1925. Reprint. New York: Harcourt Brace Jovanovich, 1964.

———. *The Common Reader*. 1st ser. 1925. Reprint. New York: Harcourt, Brace & World, 1956.

———. *To the Lighthouse*. 1927. Reprint. New York: Harcourt Brace Jovanovich, 1964.

———. *Orlando: A Biography*. 1928. Reprint. New York: Harcourt Brace Jovanovich, 1973.

———. *A Room of One's Own*. 1929. Reprint. New York: Harcourt Brace Jovanovich, 1963.

———. *The Waves*. 1931. Reprint. New York: Harcourt, Brace & World, 1959.

———. *The Years*. 1937. Reprint. New York: Harcourt Brace Jovanovich, 1965.

———. *Three Guineas*. New York: Harcourt, Brace, 1938.

———. *Between the Acts*. 1941. Reprint. Harcourt Brace Jovanovich, 1969.

WYLIE, ELINOR. *Collected Poems*. New York: Alfred A. Knopf, 1954.

YEZIERSKA, ANZIA. *Bread Givers*. 1925. Reprint. New York: Persea Books, 1975.

Secondary Sources

Reference Works

BLAIN, VIRGINIA, ISOBEL GRUNDY, and PATRICIA CLEMENTS, eds. *The Feminist Companion to Literature in English*. New Haven: Yale University Press, 1990. Includes British, American, and Commonwealth writers; gives references to recent critical works.

JAMES, EDWARD T., JANET WILSON JAMES, and PAUL S. BOYER, eds. *Notable American Women*. 3 vols. Cambridge: Belknap Press of Harvard University, 1971. Detailed entries by respected scholars; now somewhat dated.

TODD, JANET, ed. *British Women Writers: A Critical Reference Guide*. New York: Continuum, 1989. Recent, fairly detailed essays with critical references.

Studies of Historical and Social Issues

ANDERSON, BONNIE S., and JUDITH P. ZINSSER. *A History of Their Own: Women in Europe from Prehistory to the Present*, vol. 2. New York: Harper & Row, 1988. Comprehensive history of women in modern Europe, including England.

COTT, NANCY F. *The Grounding of Modern Feminism.* New York and London: Yale University Press, 1987. Examines transition from the nineteenth-century "woman movement" to twentieth-century feminism.

D'EMILIO, JOHN, and ESTELLE FREEDMAN. *Intimate Matters: A History of Sexuality in America.* New York: Harper & Row, 1988. Fine introduction to the new social history of sexuality and gender.

GIDDINGS, PAULA. *When and Where I Enter: The Impact of Black Women on Race and Sex in America.* New York: William Morrow, 1984. Surveys black women's history from the aftermath of the Civil War through the 1960s.

HIGONNET, MARGARET, JANE JENSON, SONYA MICHEL, and MARGARET COLLINS WEITZ, eds. *Behind the Lines: Gender and the Two World Wars.* New Haven and London: Yale University Press, 1987. Essays on twentieth-century war's gendering of women and men.

LEVERING, DAVID LEWIS. *When Harlem Was in Vogue.* New York: Alfred A. Knopf, 1981. Comprehensive historical and cultural survey of the Harlem Renaissance, although not particularly attentive to issues of gender.

General Studies of Literary Issues in the Period, 1900–1945

BENSTOCK, SHARI. *Women of the Left Bank: Paris, 1900–1940.* Austin: University of Texas Press, 1987. Explores the Parisian milieu and the work of writers like Stein, Barnes, and Wharton.

CHINOY, HELEN KRICH, and LINDA WALSH JENKINS, eds. *Women in American Theatre: Careers, Images, Movements.* New York: Crown, 1981. Essays on playwrights, theaters, and actresses.

CRAIK, T. W., ed. *The Revels History of Drama in English.* 8 vols. London: Methuen, 1977–78. Valuable essays on theatrical institutions as well as particular playwrights.

DuPLESSIS, RACHEL BLAU. *Writing beyond the Ending: Narrative Strategies of Twentieth-Century Women Writers.* Bloomington: Indiana University Press, 1985. Examines modernist women's revisions of traditional endings; chapters on Woolf, H. D., and other writers.

FLORA, JOSEPH M., ed. *The English Short Story, 1880–1945: A Critical History.* Boston: Twayne, 1985. Includes an important chapter on Woolf and Mansfield, by Joanne Trautmann Banks.

FRIEDMAN, ELLEN G., and MIRIAM FUCHS, eds. *Breaking the Sequence: Women's Experimental Fiction.* Princeton, N.J.: Princeton University Press, 1989. Includes material on Woolf, Richardson, Stein, and Barnes, among others.

GILBERT, SANDRA M., and SUSAN GUBAR. *No Man's Land: The Place of the Woman Writer in the Twentieth Century.* Vol. 1. *The War of the Words.* New Haven and London: Yale University Press, 1988. Sees modernists of both genders as engaged in struggles over the emergence of women into public life and changing definitions of masculinity and femininity.

HANSCOMBE, GILLIAN, and VIRGINIA L. SMYERS. *Writing for Their Lives: The Modernist Women 1910–1940.* Boston: Northeastern University Press, 1987. Brief biographical and critical studies of H. D., Dorothy Richardson, Amy Lowell, Djuna Barnes; chapters on issues of publication for modernist women.

HUYSSEN, ANDREAS. *After the Great Divide: Modernism, Mass Culture, Postmodernism.*

Bloomington: Indiana University Press, 1986. Theoretical essays on modernism and postmodernism, including modernism's contradictory self-gendering.

JOHNSON, ABBY ARTHUR, and RONALD MABERRY JOHNSON. *Propaganda and Aesthetics: The Literary Politics of Afro-American Magazines in the Twentieth Century.* Amherst: University of Massachusetts Press, 1979. Excellent survey of an important area of modern African-American culture.

KAPLAN, SYDNEY JANET. *Feminine Consciousness in the Modern British Novel.* Urbana: University of Illinois Press, 1975. Chapters on Sinclair, Richardson, Lehmann, and other writers.

NELSON, CARY. *Repression and Recovery: Modern American Poetry and the Politics of Cultural Memory, 1910–1945.* Madison and London: University of Wisconsin Press, 1989. Argues that standard literary histories of modernism have repressed a large body of political poetry important to American modernism.

STEVICK, PHILIP, ed. *The American Short Story, 1900–1945: A Critical History.* Boston: Twayne, 1984. Historical survey of the field.

Critical Studies of Individual Writers or Small Groups of Writers

BOWLBY, RACHEL. *Virginia Woolf: Feminist Destinations.* Oxford and New York: Basil Blackwell, 1988. Poststructuralist, feminist approach to Woolf's writing.

CHENEY, ANNE. *Millay in Greenwich Village.* University, Ala.: University of Alabama Press, 1975. Useful introduction to the Village modernist scene.

CHESSMAN, HARRIET. *The Public Is Invited to Dance: Representation, the Body, and Dialogue in Gertrude Stein.* Stanford: Stanford University Press, 1989. Draws on poststructuralist and psychoanalytic theories of women's relationship to language.

DEKOVEN, MARIANNE. *A Different Language: Gertrude Stein's Experimental Writing.* Explores the evolution of Stein's experimental styles.

DEMOUY, JANE KRAUSE. *Katherine Anne Porter's Women: The Eye of Her Fiction.* Austin: University of Texas Press, 1983. Close mythical and psychoanalytic study of Porter's women characters.

DONOVAN, JOSEPHINE. *After the Fall: The Demeter-Persephone Myth in Wharton, Cather, and Glasgow.* University Park and London: Pennsylvania State University Press, 1989. Examines the three novelists' use of the mother-daughter myth as an index of their alienation from nineteenth-century women's culture.

FARR, JUDITH. *The Life and Art of Elinor Wylie.* Baton Rouge: Louisiana State University Press, 1983. Illuminates Wylie's attitudes toward women as art objects in her poetry.

FIELD, ANDREW. *Djuna: The Formidable Miss Barnes.* Austin: University of Texas Press, 1985. Lively, detailed appreciation of Barnes's life and works, drawing on personal interviews.

FITZGERALD, PENELOPE. *Charlotte Mew and Her Friends.* London: Collins, 1984. Account of Mew's life in the historical context of her relationships with other important modernists.

FRANK, ELIZABETH. *Louise Bogan: A Portrait.* New York: Alfred A. Knopf, 1985. Examines Bogan's career and ambivalent relationships with other women writers.

FRIEDMAN, SUSAN STANFORD. *Psyche Reborn: The Emergence of H. D.* Bloomington: Indiana University Press, 1981. Looks at H. D.'s engagement with myth and psychoanalysis in the period leading up to *Trilogy*.

FRYER, JUDITH. *Felicitous Space: The Imaginative Structures of Edith Wharton and Willa Cather.* Chapel Hill: University of North Carolina Press, 1986. Examines the novelists' work in the historical context of ideas about homes, decoration, building, and landscape.

GATES, HENRY LOUIS, JR., ed. *Reading Black, Reading Feminist: A Critical Anthology.* New York: Meridian, 1990. Contains several important essays referring to Zora Neale Hurston's work.

GLENDINNING, VICTORIA. *Elizabeth Bowen: Portrait of a Writer.* New York: Alfred A. Knopf, 1978.

———. *Edith Sitwell: A Unicorn among Lions.* New York: Alfred A. Knopf, 1981. Both sympathetic and well-written biographies, although not incorporating much critical discussion of the work.

HARRISON, NANCY R. *Jean Rhys and the Novel as Women's Text.* Chapel Hill: University of North Carolina Press, 1988. Looks at gendered forms of speech in Rhys's novels.

HOLLEY, MARGOT. *The Poetry of Marianne Moore: A Study in Voice and Value.* Cambridge and New York: Cambridge University Press, 1987. Close reading of poems in the context of philosophical and biographical issues.

HULL, GLORIA T. *Color, Sex, and Poetry: Three Women Writers of the Harlem Renaissance.* Bloomington and Indianapolis: Indiana University Press, 1987. Pioneering biographical and critical essays on Alice Dunbar-Nelson, Angelina Weld Grimké, and Georgia Douglas Johnson.

KERTESZ, LOUISE. *The Poetic Vision of Muriel Rukeyser.* Baton Rouge and London: Louisiana State University Press, 1980. Excellent close reading of Rukeyser's poetry, and analysis of the literary politics of her reputation.

LANE, ANNE J. *To Herland and Beyond: The Life and Work of Charlotte Perkins Gilman.* New York: Pantheon, 1990. Sets Gilman's fiction in biographical and historical contexts.

LEONARDI, SUSAN J. *Dangerous by Degrees: Women at Oxford and the Somerville College Novelists.* New Brunswick and London: Rutgers University Press, 1989. Chapters on conditions in the Oxford women's colleges and on several novelists, including Dorothy Sayers.

LEWIS, R. W. B. *Edith Wharton: A Biography.* New York: Harper & Row, 1975. The standard biography of Wharton.

MACKINNON, JANICE R., and STEPHEN R. MACKINNON. *Agnes Smedley: The Life and Times of an American Radical.* Berkeley and Los Angeles: University of California Press, 1988. First authoritative biography and study of Smedley's autobiographical works.

MARCUS, JANE, ed. *Virginia Woolf: A Feminist Slant.* Lincoln and London: University of Nebraska Press, 1983. Collection of recent feminist essays.

MEADE, MARION. *Dorothy Parker: What Fresh Hell Is This?* New York: Penguin, 1987. Biography of Parker's life and work, with information on her publishing history and political involvements.

MELLOW, JAMES R. *Charmed Circle: Gertrude Stein and Company.* New York: Praeger, 1974. Details Stein's involvement in Parisian circles of modernist art and literature.

MOOTRY, MARIA K., and GARY SMITH, eds. *A Life Distilled: Gwendolyn Brooks, Her Poetry and Fiction.* Urbana and Chicago: University of Illinois Press, 1987. Essays on the scope of Brooks's career.

NATHAN, RHODA B. *Katherine Mansfield*. New York: Continuum, 1988. Useful introductory study, dividing Mansfield's stories into several thematic groups.

PRYSE, MARJORIE, and HORTENSE J. SPILLERS, eds. *Conjuring: Black Women, Fiction, and Literary Tradition*. Bloomington: Indiana University Press, 1985. Contains important essays on Zora Neale Hurston, Pauline Hopkins, and Jessie Redmon Fauset, among others.

ROLLYSON, CARL. *Lillian Hellman: Her Legend and Her Legacy*. New York: St. Martin's Press, 1988. Authoritative biography of Hellman's theatrical career and involvement in political controversy.

ROSE, PHYLLIS. *Woman of Letters: A Life of Virginia Woolf*. New York: Oxford University Press, 1978. Counters Woolf's image as frail, disembodied, and detached, emphasizing her productivity in many kinds of literary activity.

ROSOWSKI, SUSAN J. *The Voyage Perilous: Willa Cather's Romanticism*. Lincoln and London: University of Nebraska Press, 1986. Examines in detail Cather's relationship to romantic ideas of nature and the imagination.

SPANIER, SANDRA WHIPPLE. *Kay Boyle: Artist and Activist*. New York: Paragon, 1988. Looks at the life and work of a writer deeply involved in many modernist publishing and political ventures.

STINEMAN, ESTHER LANIGAN. *Mary Austin: Song of a Maverick*. New Haven and London: Yale University Press, 1989. Feminist reading of Austin's life and work, including her relationships with other important modernists of the American West.

VILLA, JOSÉ GARCÍA, ed. *A Celebration for Edith Sitwell. Direction*, no. 7. Norfolk, Conn.: New Directions, 1948. Appreciative essays by critics and fellow modernist writers, including W. B. Yeats and Gertrude Stein.

WAGNER, LINDA. *Ellen Glasgow: Beyond Convention*. Austin: University of Texas Press, 1982. Feminist discussion of Glasgow's rebellion against the strictures of Southern womanhood.

WATERMAN, ARTHUR E. *Susan Glaspell*. Twayne's United States Authors Series, no. 101. Boston: Twayne, 1966. Study of the plays in the context of Glaspell's involvement with the Provincetown players.

WOOLF, CYNTHIA GRIFFIN. *A Feast of Words: The Triumph of Edith Wharton*. New York: Oxford University Press, 1977. Close psychoanalytic study of Wharton's life and work.

ZWERDLING, ALEX. *Virginia Woolf and the Real World*. Berkeley, Los Angeles, and London: University of California Press, 1986. Argues that Woolf's writings engage, rather than flee, the social and material world.

Index

About the Author

Mary Loeffelholz is assistant professor of English at Northeastern University in Boston, where she teaches nineteenth- and early-twentieth-century literature, literary theory, and feminist theory. She is the author of *Dickinson and the Boundaries of Feminist Theory* (University of Illinois Press, 1991) and a contributor to *The Feminist Companion to Literature in English* (Yale University Press, 1990). Her articles on Emily Dickinson, John Milton, nineteenth-century women writers, and nineteenth-century women's political rhetoric have appeared in the journals *Genders* and *Legacy* as well as in several edited collections of essays.

About the Editor

Kinley E. Roby is Professor of English at Northeastern University. He is the 20th-Century Field Editor of the Twayne English Authors Series, Series Editor of Twayne's Critical History of British Drama, and General Editor of Twayne's Women and Literature Series. He has written books on Arnold Bennett, Edward VII, and Joyce Cary and edited a collection of essays on T. S. Eliot. He makes his home in Sudbury, Massachusetts.